STARTING & RUNNING

a Coffee Shop

LINDA FORMICHELLI and MELISSA VILLANUEVA

ALPHA

Publisher: Mike Sanders
Development Editor: Christy Wagner
Art Director: William Thomas
Cover Designer: Jessica Lee
Book Designer/Compositor: Ayanna Lacey
Proofreader: Lisa Starnes
Indexer: Celia McCoy

First American Edition, 2019
Published in the United States by DK Publishing
6081 E. 82nd Street, Indianapolis, Indiana 46250

ISBN: 9781465483799
Library of Congress Catalog Card Number: 2019936933

Note: This publication contains the opinions and ideas of its author(s). It is intended to
provide helpful and informative material on the subject matter covered. It is sold with
the understanding that the author(s) and publisher are not engaged in rendering
professional services in the book. If the reader requires personal assistance or advice, a
competent professional should be consulted. The author(s) and publisher specifically
disclaim any responsibility for any liability, loss, or risk, personal or otherwise, which is
incurred as a consequence, directly or indirectly, of the use and application of any of the
contents of this book.

Trademarks: All terms mentioned in this book that are known to be or are suspected of
being trademarks or service marks have been appropriately capitalized. Alpha Books,
DK, and Penguin Random House LLC cannot attest to the accuracy of this information.
Use of a term in this book should not be regarded as affecting the validity of any
trademark or service mark.

DK books are available at special discounts when purchased in bulk for sales
promotions, premiums, fund-raising, or educational use. For details, contact: DK
Publishing Special Markets, 1450 Broadway, Suite 801, New York, NY 10018 or
SpecialSales@dk.com.

Printed and bound in USA.

Reprinted from *Idiot's Guides: Starting and Running a Coffee Bar.*

Contents

Part 4   **Deciding Which Products to Sell**   *137*

Appendixes

Introduction

Coffee fuels the American economy. Think about it. In addition to its obvious economical value, coffee fuels the economy in a much more meaningful way—getting people out of bed in the morning and pushing them to work. Every morning, timers click on coffee pots and a new batch of beans begins to brew. Commuters line up in coffee shop drive-thrus to get a to-go cup of their favorite pick-me-up. The green Starbucks siren pops up all over, in towns big and small, beckoning to coffee lovers.

We'd love to see coffee shops in every town from coast to coast, serving coffee aficionados cup after cup. But the truth is, many people still rely on convenience stores and small restaurants for their coffee—establishments that typically brew a pot and then leave it sitting on the burner for an hour or two. Why do so many settle for coffee that's more of an afterthought when they could savor the freshest, most delicious brew?

This book is for those who want to man the pumps themselves, who want to provide their fellow coffee-loving citizens a tasty brew made exactly how they want it, when they want it. Now's your chance to build a better coffee shop, one that treats its guests well and provides a good living for its owner—you!

All you need to get started is determination and energy. Getting the first is up to you, and as for the second … would you like a refill?

How This Book Is Organized

To help you go from the daily grind to grinding daily, this book is divided into five parts:

Part 1, Bean Business Basics, gives you an inside look at running a coffee shop and explains what kind of person can hold this type of business together. Sitcoms make serving drinks look like a lot of fun—and sure, it can be—but that fun comes thanks to hard work and perseverance.

Part 2, Getting Started, helps you lay the foundation of your coffee shop business, including writing a business plan, hiring expert help, building a brand identity, and finding the perfect location. Build your business smartly, and you increase its chances of surviving and thriving.

Part 3, Setting Up Shop, offers advice on how to choose a theme for your shop (if you want one) and design your space, both inside and out, to appeal to customers and provide them with the goods they want. You can't do it alone, though, so we also explain how to hire employees and train them to become the best baristas you can imagine.

Part 4, Deciding Which Products to Sell, covers the world of coffee beverages: hot and cold, plain and flavored, skinny and full fat. Beyond coffee and espresso, you have a hundred other drinks to choose from, not to mention food. We go over your choices and offer suggestions on what your customers should see when they walk through your door.

Part 5, Running a Successful Coffee Shop, helps you track inventory and sales, deal with difficult customers, and keep your store spic and span. We also look at ways to promote your business and even plan for the day when you can open store number two.

The book concludes with three appendixes that offer a glossary of coffee shop terms; an assortment of handy forms and checklists you can copy or alter as needed; and a helpful list of industry resources, suppliers, associations, and further resources.

Counter *Talk*	Throughout the book, we've included these fun Counter Talk sidebars. They offer helpful advice and insights Melissa has learned on the front lines of the coffee business.

Acknowledgments

From Linda Formichelli: A big thanks to Melissa Villanueva for, you know, writing the book together with me; my agent, Marilyn Allen; my husband, W. Eric Martin, and son, Traver Martin, for their unwavering support; and Christy Wagner and Brandon Buechley at Alpha Books for making every sentence and every page more on-point and helpful for our readers.

From Melissa Villanueva: A big thank you to Linda for putting my everyday experience into words in a fun and thoughtful way. Thank you to my husband, Angelo, who has always pushed me to dream and has been right there beside me to make my dreams come true. Thank you to our families, who believed in us when we were just two crazy kids who wanted to go into business with their 6-month significant other. Thank you to Caren Joan Public Relations for connecting us to Linda. Lastly, thank you to our Brewpoint Coffee team, who gives me the ability to work *on* our business rather than *in* our business. I recognize that not everyone gets the opportunity to make their coffee shop dreams come true. I am truly grateful for it, and I look forward to being a part of new coffee shop dreams thanks to this wonderful book.

Bean Business Basics

Coffee, java, joe—whatever you call it, you know you want to sell it! That's a good decision, because the coffee industry is booming. In Part 1, we talk about this growing section of the food service industry and help you discover whether the life of a coffee shop owner is for you as you shadow coauthor Melissa Villanueva, owner of three cafés and a wholesale roastery, on a typical day at one of her Brewpoint coffee shops.

Not sure you're ready to take on this challenge? We also explain how to get the skills you need by landing a job at a coffee shop for some hands-on training.

Why Coffee?

Coffee is big business both in the United States and around the world, and when you look closely at how coffee is made and served, it's easy to see why.

In the morning, coffee provides the *oomph* that gets people going. At work, it's the social lubricant that brings people together over breaks and snacks. After dinner, it's the relaxant that caps off a fine meal. Late at night, it's the preferred pick-me-up for truckers and college students. In short, coffee is a little bit of everything to everybody.

The appeal of coffee has made it one of the top five commodity imports in the United States, according to Commodity.com. Furthermore, the United States currently imports more than $6.3 billion of coffee each year, notes World's Top Exports (worldstopexports.com). Coffee sales comprise a multibillion-dollar business, and coffee-related business opportunities continue to grow in the United States, with new coffee shops opening each day in towns across the country.

But what do you really know about coffee? Let's take a closer look at the coffee bean's background and see how this modest drink became the fuel that fires the modern economy.

What Is Coffee, Anyway?

When the smell of freshly brewed coffee hits your nose in the morning, you probably think of it as something essential to your environment, like oxygen or water. Some people can't start their day without orange juice; others need their coffee. You may not realize it, but coffee has as much in common with orange juice as it does with the water with which it's produced. Coffee is actually derived from a fruit; coffee beans are the seeds of the red and purple fruit that grow on coffee trees.

In the wild, coffee trees can grow more than 35 feet tall, but to make it easier to harvest the beans, trees on plantations are kept to between 6 and 15 feet tall. Coffee trees don't produce any fruit until they're 3 to 5 years old, but once they start, they produce fruit for up to 60 years.

The white flowers on the coffee tree give way to red berries that resemble cherries during the growth process. The berry has a thin layer of flesh, and inside this pulp lie two seeds coated with a thin film that resembles parchment. These seeds, measuring only 8 to 11 millimeters long and taking 9 months to ripen, are the essence of coffee.

A Brief History of Coffee

So how did we get from the seeds to the brew? Who ever thought of skinning the fruit of the coffee tree, roasting the seeds, grinding them, and steeping the grounds in water? Seems kind of random, doesn't it?

The true origin of coffee is lost in time, but many legends have evolved around the substance, all starting with the fruit from which coffee begins.

Thank the Sheep

The most well-known story of coffee's origin, dating anywhere from 600 to 800 C.E., involves a sheep (or goat) herder named Kaldi who noticed something strange with his flock after moving the animals to a new pasture in the Ethiopian region of Caffa.

After eating the red berries from a certain plant in this new field, Kaldi's sheep became restless and excited, not even sleeping at night. Kaldi, curious about this development, tasted the berries himself and found that he was invigorated and more awake than usual.

A monk from a local monastery passed by and scolded Kaldi for "partaking of the devil's fruit." Kaldi managed to convince the monk that the berries had no ill effect, so the monk tested them himself, crushing the berries to powder and pouring hot water over the powder to make a drink.

Before long, word of this fabulous new drink spread throughout the monastery, and all the monks were using the berries to help them stay awake through their long hours of prayer. Word of the beans' power continued to spread, from monastery to monastery and then beyond. Thus the legend of coffee was born, with devout Muslims believing that the plant was a gift to reward the faithful.

Mocha Soup

Another legend, dating from about the same time period, involves an Arab who was banished, along with his followers, to the desert to die of starvation. Desperate to survive, the man and his friends boiled the fruit from an unknown plant to make soup.

The broth provided enough sustenance to save the exiles, and residents of the closest town, Mocha, took the survival of the banished men to be a testament to their religious faith. To honor the soup that aided their successful trip out of the desert, the plant and the beverage made from it were both named *mocha*.

Beans Break Out

Although the identity of the person who took the first sip of coffee remains unknown, the coffee plant spread from Ethiopia to the Arabian Peninsula and Turkey as users discovered its wondrous properties.

As the coffee plant entered new lands, users found new ways to consume it. The Galla tribe in Ethiopia, for example, used the beans as a type of energy bar, wrapping them in animal fat to provide them sustenance while they raided nearby areas. Others made wine from the pulp of the berries.

Turkey is believed to be the first country where coffee was roasted, brewed, and drunk, with the process starting sometime between 1000 and 1200 C.E. Turks often added spices like cinnamon, cloves, cardamom, and anise to the brew, which they called *qahwa,* a word that literally means "that which prevents sleep."

In 1475, the world's first coffee shop, Kiv Han, opened in Constantinople. Within a few years, the city was home to hundreds of coffee shops where people listened to music, played chess, talked with travelers and storytellers, and of course drank coffee. Coffee shops in Turkey came to be known as "Schools of the Wise" because patrons could learn much inside their walls. Coffee was considered so important that in the fifteenth century, Turkish law allowed a woman to divorce her husband if he failed to provide her with her daily quota of coffee.

Despite the wide acceptance of coffee, not everyone was pleased with the availability of the brew. In 1511, for example, Khair Beg, the governor of Mecca, banned coffee from the city because he feared it might fuel opposition to his rule. When the sultan heard of this decree, he ordered the governor be put to death.

Out of the Desert

The growth of coffee across the Arabian lands took many hundreds of years because traders jealously guarded their plants. Coffee beans couldn't be taken to other lands unless they had first been boiled in water or dried in the sun to kill any potential germ of growth within the seed.

Eventually, though, live seeds or plant cuttings made their way to non-Arabian lands, including India and Italy. Acceptance of the drink wasn't a foregone conclusion, though. Some Christians, unknowingly repeating the claims of earlier generations, dubbed coffee the "devil's drink." To their surprise, Pope Clement VIII, instead of banning coffee, baptized it. He claimed the drink was so delicious "it would be a pity to let the infidels have exclusive use of it."

Coffee came to Vienna, Austria, in 1683, after war ended between the city and invading Turks. A Polish army officer, Franz Georg Kolschitzky, who had previously served in Turkey, knew about the drink so when the Turkish army left behind stocks of coffee in their retreat, Kolschitzky claimed them for himself. He opened the first coffee house in Vienna, and his habit of filtering out the grounds and adding milk and sweetener established the tradition of Viennese coffee.

Coffee houses quickly sprang up in major cities across Europe, and these locations furthered the Turkish idea of gathering with your neighbors and seeing what everyone knows. In England, for instance, coffee houses earned the nickname "penny universities" because for the price of a penny, you could purchase a cup of coffee and learn incredible things from those around you. Fun fact: the practice of tipping waiters and waitresses apparently started in these English coffee houses. Customers who wanted good service and seating placed money in a tin labeled "To Insure Proper Service"; the first letters of each word in the phrase spelled "TIPS."

Not everyone in England agreed that coffee was a smart idea, however. In 1674, London saw the founding of The Women's Petition Against Coffee, which complained that husbands spent too much time enjoying themselves in coffee houses and not enough time at home. Part of their petition protested against "the grand inconveniences accruing to their sex from the excessive use of the drying and enfeebling liquor."

What about espresso? Although espresso is widely considered an Italian treat, the first espresso machine was actually invented by a Frenchman in 1822. Louis Bernard Rabaut's creation forced hot water through the coffee grounds instead of merely having the water drip through. Now we use his invention to create the fanciful espresso drinks so many of us crave.

Coming to the Americas

Coffee is believed to have been a part of American culture since Captain John Smith brought the plant across the ocean in 1607 while helping found the Jamestown colony in Virginia.

Despite this early introduction, coffee remained second in popularity behind tea. This finally changed in 1773 when Boston, Massachusetts, residents threw boxes of tea into Boston Harbor to protest the taxes placed on the tea by King George. People switched from tea to coffee to show their patriotic support for the Boston Tea Party.

Although the American colonists enjoyed drinking coffee, the growth of coffee as a business in the Americas resulted primarily from the efforts of a French naval officer, Gabriel Mathieu de Clieu. While in Paris on leave around 1720, de Clieu asked for clippings from the coffee tree in King Louis XIV's Royal Botanical Garden to bring back to the Caribbean island of Martinique, where de Clieu served.

De Clieu's request was turned down, but he raided the garden and stole a seedling from the greenhouse. The return trip to Martinique was harsh for both de Clieu and his prized possession. A jealous passenger stole a branch from the seedling; the ship was attacked and almost captured by pirates; and water grew scarce onboard, forcing de Clieu to use part of his own water ration to keep the plant alive. De Clieu finally made it back to Martinique, where he planted the tree on his estate and raised it under armed guard. By 1777, that one seedling had yielded an estimated 18 million trees.

Coffee came to Brazil in an equally roundabout way. As the Arabs had done centuries before, French and Dutch traders did everything they could in the seventeenth and eighteenth centuries to protect their monopoly of the coffee market. Brazil's emperor thwarted these efforts thanks to one Lieutenant Colonel Francisco de Melo Palheta.

In 1727, Palheta visited the colony of French Guiana to mediate a border dispute between the French and the Dutch. In addition to solving this crisis, Palheta began an affair with the governor's wife, who later presented him with live coffee seeds and cuttings from a plant as a farewell gift. These shoots are responsible for the enormous Brazilian plantations that enabled coffee to become an affordable drink for the general public.

By 1800, coffee had spread throughout the tropical belts of the Americas and on to Asia to become one of the most important commercial crops in the world.

The Booming Business of Coffee

As with many industries, the growth of coffee sales has resulted from a combination of smart business owners, lucky accidents, and chance.

Decaffeinated coffee, for instance, was invented in 1903 thanks to a ruined batch of coffee beans. German coffee importer Ludwig Roselius gave the beans to researchers, who used them to perfect the caffeine-removal process while leaving the flavor largely intact. Roselius marketed the creation under the brand name Sanka, a contraction of the phrase "sans [without] caffeine."

George Constant Washington, an English chemist, is responsible for the first mass-produced instant coffee. He got the idea while waiting for his wife to join him for coffee and watching a fine powder form on the spout of their silver coffee pot. After experimenting with different ways to create instant coffee, his finished product, Red E Coffee, hit the market in 1906.

Instant coffee took off in the United States during World War II, when American soldiers found Maxwell House instant coffee in their ration kits. As with cigarettes, the introduction of coffee to this market created a wealth of new users after they returned home.

In the 1920s, prohibition in the United States halted the (legal) sales of alcohol, and as a result, coffee sales boomed. Market forces also led to the creation of freeze-dried coffee. In the late 1930s, Brazil was choking on a surplus of coffee and asked food manufacturer Nestlé to create a product that could make use of the surplus. The result was Nescafé, which was first introduced in Switzerland in 1938.

Today, an estimated 15 different varieties of coffee trees are grown worldwide, with 1 acre of growth providing 15,000 pounds of coffee beans. Even with production on such a massive scale, prices for coffee have fluctuated wildly over the years. In 1989, for example, the coffee-growing nations of the world failed to reach a new agreement on exporting quotas, and as a result, the market was flooded and coffee prices plunged. Within a decade, though, prices had shot up in response to wide-scale crop failures, most notably in Brazil.

> **Counter** *Talk*   There's no shortage of ways to find and open a coffee shop. Melissa found her first one on craigslist.

What's in a Name?

Coffee shops, coffee bars, coffeehouses, and cafés all sell coffee, but technically they're different types of establishments. Let's break down the differences.

Coffee shops sell coffee and sometimes espresso but usually not espresso-based beverages. They also sell meals instead of just pastries and snacks. You're welcome to chill out in coffee shops over bottomless cups of coffee because it means you'll likely buy more food. Coffee shops are the same thing as diners.

Coffee bars are all about the coffee and espresso, with a focus on high-quality, handcrafted drinks. At a coffee bar, you drink and go; in fact, they often offer limited seating or no seating at all. You might find a coffee bar in the lobby of a hotel, for example.

Coffeehouses sell coffee and snacks, but what sets them apart from the rest are their hangout-friendly atmospheres. You might find music and other events at a coffeehouse that invite you to linger, plus comfy chairs and sofas to settle into.

Cafés are a mashup. You'll find all kinds of coffee drinks available, you can nosh on snacks or more substantial foods like sandwiches and quiche, you're welcome to hang out there with your laptop or a friend, and they sometimes offer live music and other events.

You, as a coffee shop owner, need to know the difference among these types of establishments, but most everyone else uses these terms interchangeably, just as we will in this book, and everyone knows what they mean. If anyone ever says to you, "Uh, I think you mean coffee *bar*" in a snooty tone, we encourage you to find another companion for your coffee dates.

Counter *Talk*   Even though coffee shop owners know the terminology, they don't always worry about it. When Melissa was researching how to start her business, she thought of it as a coffee *shop,* even though the only food it would serve was pastries.

Now you have a handle on the history of coffee, how robust the market is, and the difference among various types of coffee establishments. Are you ready to claim your piece of the pie? Next we look at what you need to know to succeed.

Why You?

Maybe it's your dream to tell your current employer to "Take this job and shove it"; sally forth on your own; and say good-bye to morning commutes, annoying coworkers, and getting up at 6 A.M.

Don't burn that bridge just yet. It takes a certain kind of personality, and heaping piles of commitment and motivation, to make it as a business owner. What's more, successful coffee shops often *open* by 6 A.M. to catch morning rush-hour commuters, which means you'll need to get up even earlier than usual!

Do you have the chops? Read on to discover the personality of a successful business owner, the pros and cons of going solo, and how to get coffee shop experience if you've spent your entire life on the customer side of the counter.

Do You Have What It Takes?

You need more than a free-flying spirit and the ability to fill a cup without spilling to make it as a coffee shop owner. Take the following quiz to see if you have what it takes.

Are You a Self-Starter?

❑ Yes   ❑ No

Unless you're financed to the hilt, as a small business owner, you usually start off doing every task in the business on your own, from marketing to sweeping the floors and everything in between. You need the motivation to rise early in the morning, phone people you don't want to talk to, and tackle even the most unpleasant jobs, all without a boss threatening to dock your pay if you mess up.

Are You a "People Person"?

❑ Yes   ❑ No

You'd think that if you were going solo, you'd be, well, solo. But in reality, you'll be dealing with all sorts of people—accountants, lawyers, and employees, not to mention (hopefully) hundreds upon hundreds of customers, many of whom haven't had their morning coffee yet.

Can you communicate and get along with a wide variety of people? Do you look forward to parties because you can meet new people, or do you hide in the closet and have someone tell you when it's over? Your personality will be a big selling point for many customers. The more of yourself you put into each transaction, the more likely they are to become repeat customers.

Are You Good at Making Decisions?

❑ Yes   ❑ No

If you take a half hour every morning deciding whether to wear the red shirt or the blue, you're in trouble. As a business owner, you'll be making decisions galore, from what color your business cards should be to how much to charge for an espresso.

In addition to decisions with long-term effects, you'll face a hundred daily situations that call for instant judgment, such as when a customer complains or a reporter calls to asks about the health benefits of caffeine. (Think it won't happen to you? Check out Chapter 23 for the scoop on dealing with the press.)

Are You a Goal-Setter?

❏ Yes ❏ No

Goals keep you motivated and provide direction for your activities, both daily and over the longer term. Sharing goals with employees helps them understand what you expect of them, in addition to making you more accountable for your own actions. After all, if you're not working toward these goals, why should they?

If you don't set goals, such as boosting flavored coffee sales by 30 percent or increasing the number of daily transactions by 50 percent, you leave your business floating on the whims of the economy at large. When the economy soars, your business will prosper, but when the economy tanks, your business will soon follow.

If the last goal you set was a New Year's resolution … and you broke it … think about how you can become a goal-setter—and more importantly, a goal-meeter.

Do You Have Money in the Bank?

❏ Yes ❏ No

Few businesses are profitable when they first open. You spend a lot of money setting up shop, and it takes time to gain a foothold in the community, build a regular customer base, and turn a profit.

This growth process is completely normal, and you need a stash of green stuff to pay for groceries and rent until your business starts earning. Most experts suggest having at least 6 months' worth of living expenses in the bank before taking the leap.

You also probably need to live the frugal lifestyle while your business gets up to speed. Can you cut costs and rein in your spending, or will you be continually whipping out the credit card?

Are You a Problem-Solver?

❏ Yes ❏ No

When confronted with a problem, do you jump to the task, or do you avoid the issue and cry to others for help? A business owner must be able to identify problems, from flagging sales to a choking customer, take aggressive action, and take responsibility for the results of his or her actions.

Of course, jumping into action is only half of being a problem-solver. Your first solution may not tame the trouble after all, so you must be ready to reevaluate the situation and try something new.

Are You a Great Communicator?

❑ **Yes**   ❑ **No**

As a business owner, you need to communicate with customers, employees, and suppliers on a daily basis—and by "communicate," we mean more than gossiping about your neighbors or recapping the latest episode of your favorite reality show.

You must express your needs and desires through both words and actions, while at the same time listening to and understanding what others are saying. Do you blame others for not grasping what you're trying to say, or do you search for new ways to present ideas so everyone understands?

Are You Good at Selling?

❑ **Yes**   ❑ **No**

Your business will sell coffee, tea, other drinks, and maybe food, too, but you, as an individual, must sell far more than the products on your menu. You also must sell a business plan to your lenders, sell the concept for your business to the public, and sell yourself as an expert to the press.

You need to be able to communicate your sales message concisely without sounding like a huckster. When you have a political discussion, can you convince someone from a different party to see things your way while avoiding an argument? Can you persuade your group of friends to see the movie you think they'll like better when they have their hearts set on another film? If so, you're a natural salesperson.

Are You Good at Organization?

❑ **Yes**   ❑ **No**

Do you know where your 2016 tax documents are? If so, can you find a particular receipt in those documents within 5 minutes?

This task might seem pointless, but as a small business owner, you need to track all sorts of papers and documents, as well as how much money you have coming in, whom you owe money to, how many pastries you sell on an average Saturday morning, and which employees can work when and for how long. Being able to create and maintain efficient filing and tracking systems is essential to your success as a businessperson.

Counter *Talk*   When Melissa took this quiz, she answered "No" to being a goal-setter, having money in the bank, and being organized. However, because her partner and husband, Angelo, was or had those things, it balanced out.

Are You a Leader?

❏ Yes ❏ No

If your business is successful (and we think it will be!), you'll probably want to hire employees. Can you inspire them to do everything from making correct change to cleaning toilets? Can you handle being the boss everyone will want to tell to "Take this job and shove it"?

Sometimes being a leader means making unpopular decisions—and sticking to them despite the fallout. At the same time, leading requires you to learn from your mistakes when a decision turns out to be wrong. You might be great at leading, but that doesn't mean you're always right!

Do You Have Your Family's Support?

❏ Yes ❏ No

Aside from you, the members of your family will be the ones most affected by your business. You'll probably be unavailable for long stretches of time as you work on developing the business, and you'll need privacy when you're creating a marketing plan or organizing a new menu. If your family isn't on board with this new venture, you need to think of a way to bring them on fast.

Do You Know Why You Want to Own a Coffee Shop?

❏ Yes ❏ No

Have you defined exactly why you want to do this? Understanding why you want to get into this business will help you push through the hard times. When a customer is yelling at you, the balance sheet doesn't look good, or your shipment of coffee stirrers is late, you can just keep your eye on the prize—whether that's being your own boss, interacting with your local community, or creating an environmentally friendly business.

How did you do? If you answered "No" to any of these questions, think long and hard about whether you can answer "Yes" before you say good-bye to the comfort and regularity of a 9-to-5 job—or how you might collaborate with someone whose strengths balance out your weaknesses.

The Pros and Cons of Being Your Own Boss

Perhaps, after working your way through our quiz, you're still persuading family members that now is the time for a coffee shop in your town. Or maybe you're still setting daily challenges for yourself to develop organizational skills.

These obstacles might seem unsettling, but you can look at them in a positive light: you care enough about following this path to change your ways and convince others to join you in your quest to open a coffee shop. You want to make this happen!

To ensure you know what you're getting into, in this section, we present the ups and downs of owning a business. Use this information to add to the mental picture you have of yourself as a business owner and help determine if you're ready to take the plunge.

The Drawbacks to DIY

First let's look at the negatives of owning your own business. Some of these are more serious than others, and only you can decide which ones might affect your decision to open your own coffee shop.

You have to be nice—to everyone. If a customer rubs you the wrong way, you have to grit your teeth, smile, and play nice. Sure, you have to do the same as an employee, but your employer will usually shield you from customers who are truly abusive. As a business owner, though, you're the one who has to deal with jerky customers and live with the fallout that results from their dissatisfaction. When they demand to see the manager, that's *you!*

Although you do have to put up with pain-in-the butt customers and suppliers, you don't have to tolerate behavior that violates your values. Your version of "being nice to everyone" can include asking a rude customer to leave or stepping back from a partnership because of a misalignment in values, as long as you communicate in a kind and thoughtful way.

Also, you won't have anyone to share locker-room chitchat with. If you open a small or mobile coffee bar and hire no employees, you'll have no one to complain to about that annoying customer or to bounce ideas off of while developing a new marketing plan. Are you used to working by yourself, or does the thought of being all by your lonesome make you lonely?

One alternative to talking to yourself is to find a business mentor, which we discuss in Chapter 4. Although not a substitute for the daily give-and-take of fellow employees, mentors can offer camaraderie, not to mention solid advice about running a business.

You'll also have to shop for and purchase your own equipment and supplies. When you're an employee, all those sticky notes, paper clips, staples, and pens are provided courtesy of your employer. When you're on your own, you have to schlep out to the office store yourself (or shop online) and cough up the dough to buy all those supplies—not to mention the printer, computer, and other pricey equipment. Fortunately, you can deduct business supplies from your taxes, but that doesn't make it hurt any less when you have to shell out $50 for a new ink cartridge for your printer.

This is a big one: no more company health insurance plan. Employees often take health insurance for granted, but small business owners don't. Finding an affordable health insurance plan for an individual can be painful. Your local Chamber of Commerce might offer coverage, but the cost is likely to be far higher than anything you've paid as an employee. You can also look for coverage offered under the Affordable Care Act through HealthCare.gov.

Don't forget higher taxes. Not only do you pay more for insurance, but Uncle Sam takes a larger chunk of your money as well. When you're an employee, your employer pays half of your Social Security taxes. When you go solo, you have to pony up for the entire tax bill on your own.

In addition to paying more taxes, you don't have the luxury of an employer who's responsible for deducting taxes from your regular paycheck. You have to do the taxes yourself or hire an accountant.

When you say good-bye to regular working hours, you also say good-bye to that steady biweekly paycheck. If your business doesn't make money, neither do you, and as with any business, the coffee trade will be crushingly busy during parts of the year and deadly slow during others. Like the fabled grasshopper, you must put aside money during the feast days to prepare for the inevitable famine.

Finally, owning a coffee shop means it's *all* on you. Often the biggest surprise for new business owners is the sheer number of operational details they overlook in a 9-to-5 job. Who empties the trash? Who empties the dumpster that holds the trash? Who changes the lightbulbs? Who buys the lightbulbs? Who answers sales calls? Now that you're in charge, responsibility for every detail, large or small, falls on you.

The Benefits of Business

A black cloud of anxiety might have formed over your head while you read the preceding list of liabilities associated with running your own business. But don't despair! For most people, the benefits of running a business far outweigh the negatives. There's still a lot you can look forward to when you're calling all the shots.

First up, you have (almost) unlimited income potential. As an employee, you make what your employer gives you for as many hours as she schedules. As a business owner, you set your own hours and set your own prices. If you can charge $10 for an espresso in your market and stay open 16 hours a day, that's nobody's business but your own.

Another nice bonus: your income goes into your own pockets. This ties in nicely with the previous perk. When you work for someone else, the fruits of your hard labor are delivered to your employers, who then pay you a fraction of that income. The health of the company is more important than the well-being of any individual worker, but that's probably small comfort to you.

When you're the top banana, you decide how much of the profit is rolled over into future expansion and how much is added to your personal bankroll. You can't keep all the money the business brings in—employees want to get paid, and banks tend to be fussy about being repaid for loans, for example—but the distribution of funds is largely up to you.

You also can set your own schedule. As an employee, you work according to someone else's schedule, but when you work for yourself, your schedule is your own. Want to open your business from 8 A.M. until 2 P.M. so you can walk your kid to and from school? Go for it. Want to be open from

6 P.M. to midnight to cater to studying students? As long as you can keep paying the bills, feel free to set the hours as you wish. (For more on setting business hours, see Chapter 7.)

If you love a challenge, you'll find that going it alone can be exciting. Every day is a new learning experience as you figure out how to bring in more customers, price your offerings, and deal with your employees. What could be more exciting than the opportunity to create your own success?

Speaking of success, you get all the credit for your success. If your business succeeds, it's thanks to your hard work, commitment, and rugged good looks—and everyone else knows it. You're not slaving away in a cubicle while some corporate bigwig takes credit for your good deeds.

To help you reach that success, you can choose your coworkers. When you worked for an employer, you had to deal with them all—the show-off, the whiner, the one who was always a half hour late. Well, guess what? Now that you own your own business, you can choose employees who fit with your personality and with that of your business, and you don't have to take any guff from anyone. You're the boss!

Finally, all your business equipment and supplies are deductible. When you buy an ink cartridge, laptop, coffee beans, or anything else for your business, you can deduct the cost from your income for tax purposes. It can still be a pain to provide your own business supplies, but at the end of the year when you're sweating over your taxes, you'll be pleasantly surprised to find that you owe less than you thought because of those deductions. Talk to your accountant for more information.

> **Counter** *Talk*   Something Melissa wishes she knew when she was starting out: some coffee distribution companies offer free equipment as long as you buy product through them. This would have easily saved her $5,000 to $10,000 in the beginning.

Are You Experienced?

So you want to open a coffee shop, but your experience in the coffee trade is limited to making a fresh brew when that annoying coworker drinks the last cup and leaves the pot empty. What's more, you've never run your own business, and you don't know a purchase order from a nondairy creamer.

What can you do to rack up some experience? Get a job at a coffee shop! No, we haven't lost our minds. Rather than borrow lots of money from the bank and lose it because you don't know what you're doing, take the time to work for someone who does and learn the trade while earning some start-up funds.

If you already have a job you can't afford to leave just yet, work part-time in the evenings or on the weekends … or even before work, because many coffee shops open long before the sun rises.

While working at a coffee bar, you'll learn how to do all these things:

* Deal with throngs of customers

* Brew a great cup of java

* Make specialty drinks such as espresso and chai

* Take money and make change

* Deal with other employees (while simultaneously watching how the employer works with her crew)

* Clean and maintain a coffee shop

* Design a coffee shop layout that works

* Order and restock supplies

* Open and close the shop

* Multitask, multitask, multitask!

If you're a good worker and the owner comes to trust you, she may even let you try your hand at marketing, dealing with suppliers, or other tasks a business owner must know to succeed.

Learning the ins and outs of the coffee trade this way also helps you understand the job from an employee's point of view, which should make you a better, more sympathetic manager in the future. You'll know which tasks take a long time to master and which ones your employees can handle without oversight.

Applying for a Coffee Shop Job

Job search sites and online classified ads are a good place to start when looking for a coffee shop job, don't rely on them exclusively. Visit coffee shops in person. Even if you're only picking up an application to fill out later, dress like a pro. You never know—the owner might want to talk to you right then!

Fill out the application neatly, in ink, either at home or right in the shop. For online applications, follow the instructions to a T. If the application asks for related experience, think about how your current or past jobs qualify you for the coffee shop position you desire. If, for example, you were a customer service manager, you know how to deal with customers. If you worked in marketing, you can communicate effectively. If you worked in retail, you have experience selling, merchandising, and taking payments.

To make an even better impression, turn in a résumé with your application. A résumé is a one- or two-page synopsis of your work experience, skills, and education laid out in an easy-to-read format. Whole books and websites are dedicated to the subject of writing résumés, so check out those resources for more advice.

Finally, include a cover letter with your application and résumé. In it, briefly explain why you want to work for that coffee shop specifically. What makes it seem like the place for you? Why *that* coffee shop and not the one down the street? This shows the owner you're not indiscriminately blanketing the neighborhood with applications, but rather you chose their shop for a reason.

Acing Your Interview

So the owner was impressed by your nicely completed application and your slick résumé and would like to interview you. Congratulations! Your foot is in the door. Here are a few tips to get you through the interview with style:

* Think ahead about the questions the shop owner may ask, such as your greatest strengths and weaknesses, why you want to work there, and so on. Rehearse your answers at home beforehand in front of a mirror.

* Recruit a friend or family member to role-play as the interviewer so you can get practice and feedback. They'll tell you whether you sound natural and confident or whether you need more practice time in the hot seat.

* Research the coffee shop ahead of time, and bring a list of questions with you to your interview to show your interest.

* On the day of your interview, arrive a few minutes early.

* Don't wear a suit if you're not applying for a management position, but do dress professionally.

* Tell the owner up front that you want to gain experience so you can open your own coffee shop.

The owner might be taken aback at first by your confession of wanting to open your own shop, but she'll likely be flattered you chose her shop to work in and be intrigued by the prospect of training you. Explain where and when you plan to open your shop so she'll know you won't be with her for years, and so she can view you as an apprentice rather than a competitor. (This assumes, of course, you don't plan to open a competing coffee shop right across the street!)

Getting a job when you're looking to fly solo might seem counterintuitive, but if you have no experience in the coffee industry, you should definitely consider the idea. After you land a job in a coffee shop, keep your eyes and ears open and soak in as much information as you can. Someday soon you'll be running your own shop!

Ready to find out what your day will look like when you work at a coffee shop—and when you *own* one? In the next chapter, we take you through a day in the life of a coffee shop owner.

A Day in the Life: Melissa Villanueva

You've read the previous two chapters and decided that nothing could suit your personality and entrepreneurial skills better than owning and running a coffee shop. Or maybe you skipped right to this page to see what daily life will be like when you open a shop of your own.

However you arrived here, we're eager to start your tour through a typical day as a coffee shop owner. Your tour guide is Melissa Villanueva, owner-operator of three coffee shops in the Chicago, Illinois, area. Melissa currently employs general managers to run the shops for her, but when she first started out, she and her husband opened the shop, closed it, and did everything else in between.

On this tour you learn everything that goes into running a coffee shop, from signing in to closing shop. Let's get started!

The Workday Begins

Our first shop, which is near a train station, was open from 8 A.M. until 4 P.M. because that's all Angelo and I could physically handle on our own. After hours, we'd work to improve the shop—for example, by installing a TV, hanging artwork, or putting in new furniture. But as soon as we brought on employees, we started opening at 6 A.M. on weekdays to supply caffeine to the business-people taking the train into Chicago. That meant we were there at the crack of dawn—5:30 A.M.

Our second café that's not near a station train opens at 7 A.M., and our third one inside a library opens at 9 A.M., when the library does. See how your location affects your hours? Your own hours of operation will depend on the customer base you serve. If you're located in a bedroom community, for example, you might open as early as 5 A.M. to service commuters before they head to work. For a coffee bar in a college town, your hours might change with the semesters. (For more on setting hours of operation, see Chapter 7.)

The skills you need: You wouldn't think showing up for work takes any special skills, but it does—namely punctuality and the willpower to wake up every morning, rain or shine, and go to work. Some days you'll feel like pulling the blankets over your head and going back to sleep, but as the owner of a business, you don't have this luxury—unless you don't mind customers migrating to your competition, that is.

Counter *Talk*   Be consistent with your hours. When Melissa bought a turnkey coffee shop, the one that had been in that space previously was known for not being open when it was supposed to be. The owners were a couple with no employees, and if they didn't feel like waking up early that day, the store would remain closed. People would show up during open hours to find the place dark. Not exactly the best customer experience.

Where to get them: The importance of being punctual has probably been pounded into you with every job you've ever had or any class you've taken from kindergarten on. Business owners, however, must keep in mind that opening a shop late loses not only current sales but also future business because customers will lose faith in late risers.

Before you even open your coffee shop, exercise your willpower by not allowing yourself to make excuses and put off what needs to be done. When the trash needs emptying, empty it. When the lawn needs mowing, don't push it off to the weekend. When the alarm clock rings, start moving immediately. Customers are counting on you for their morning java jolt!

Each day we use an SOP (that's standard operating procedures) list to stay organized. The SOP includes things like opening tasks, closing tasks, café checks, and shift changes. In the morning we …

* Put on our aprons.

* Sign in to our iPads.

* Count the cash drawer.

* Check the calendar to see if any events or catering orders are coming up so we can make a game plan.

* Turn on the music.

* Get the first batch of coffee ready.

* When the pastries are delivered, double-check and sign the invoice.

* Put out the pastries. (We call pastries that are past their on-sale date "crew food," and our staff enjoys chowing down on them.)

* Dial in the espresso, or calibrate the machine to create perfect shots. We do this every couple hours, and it takes about 15 minutes each time.

* Put out the sanitizing bucket.

* Check iced coffee levels.

* Brew iced teas.

* Stock the customer coffee prep station with creamers, sugar, napkins, and so on.

All this happens before a single customer walks in the door.

The skills you need: A clear head in the mornings—there's a lot going on!—math skills, the know-how to make a good cup of java, and the patience to do the same tasks every morning without getting bored. You also need self-motivated employees who'll work without prodding. You have enough on your own plate without having to watch theirs as well.

Where to get them: We explain how to train and motivate employees in Chapter 12 and break down how to prepare the perfect pot and track brew times in Chapters 14 and 15. As for not getting bored, make a game of your tasks each morning: How quickly can you do X? Can you do Y and Z at the same time and have everything come out right?

Yes, We're Open!

When it's time to open, we flip over the "Closed" sign to "Open," open the doors for business, and put the sidewalk sign outside. We greet the customers and start serving pastries and drinks. The first sales of the day! We do about 250 transactions in a day, and the first half of those are before noon.

As customers filter in, we take and fill orders and run the registers, chatting with customers the whole time. We clean as we go, wiping up drips and cleaning the steaming nozzle on the espresso machine. We wash dishes and replenish supplies so we never run out of, say, coffee cups while 20 people are waiting impatiently for their drinks. Keeping ahead of the game when it comes to cleaning and restocking also makes cleanup easier at closing time.

If there's a catering order that day, the calendar will note what time the customer is coming, whether the order is paid for or not, and who's picking it up. The shift manager is responsible for filling orders of 60 cups or less, and if it's more than that, the general manager or I will step in. A catering order takes about an hour to prep. We can do the coffee, tea, and hot chocolate in house, and we add the pastries to our usual pastry order 48 hours ahead of time.

Our original location has a meeting space for up to 12 people. If someone is renting it, we'll have the general manager step in to focus just on the meeting room. They may take food and drink orders there and bring them to the bar, and the customer will pay the tab at the end—that way we don't have 12 people waiting in line.

Counter *Talk*   Water flow is a big deal when you're handling large catering or meeting orders. When you have a lot of brewing to do, sometimes the water flow can't keep up. The brewer has two sides, but the barista can use only one side at a time and has to wait a minute between batches. Just something to think about if you're planning to offer catering or events.

The skills you need: Multitasking. You're serving customers, running the register, cleaning, and restocking all at once. Your brain is juggling orders, names, and change, and you can't afford to drop anything. Brewpoint locations have only one manager and two baristas on the clock, so multitasking is key to ensuring the bar and register are running smoothly while the catering orders are being prepped.

Where to get them: If you've never worked in a coffee shop (or other food-service establishment) to learn what it's like in a real-life, non-*Friends* situation, we suggest getting some hands-on experience. (See Chapter 2 for information on how to get a job in a coffee shop.) You'll learn how to balance your time so you can keep customers moving on one side of the counter while you clean and stock the other side.

Navigating the Waves of Customers

When we catch a break from taking orders, we travel around the seating area, clearing away empty cups customers left behind and wiping down tables. Because we put a high priority on engaging with customers and each other and encourage a culture of laughing and building relationships, we may be chatting while we work. Talking as we go is part of our job!

Speaking of engaging with customers, we may have to step in when a customer starts hassling a barista over, say, the lack of foam on her drink. She distinctly asked for extra foam, and look— hardly any at all! We don't bother asking for the employee's side of the story right then; we apologize to the customer and make her a new drink. We'll talk with the employee later to find out his side of the story, but we keep talk like this away from the customer's ears.

We emphasize to our employees that they have to be kind, but they don't have to take abuse. If I just can't make the customer happy, I tell them (nicely) that they might be happier getting their coffee elsewhere.

The skills you need: Being able to interact with customers in a polite and friendly manner and make them feel welcome is essential—as is keeping a level head when customers are less than happy.

Where to get them: We talk about all things customer related in Chapter 21.

Behind the Scenes

Customers see the obvious parts of our job, but they can't catch all the details we handle to keep the coffee shop running. We check the pastry case to see what's selling and send an order to the pastry shop for the next day's delivery. Along the same lines, we track stock levels on bottled drinks, stirrers, lids, soap, trash bags—you name it, we track it. We email suppliers throughout the day as we run low on things, and all day long the manager receives deliveries in the back, counts the cartons to match the totals listed on the invoice, and puts everything away.

Counter *Talk*	Keeping enough milk in the shop was one of the biggest challenges Melissa experienced at the beginning. They went through 15 to 20 gallons per day but didn't have enough refrigerator space to hold it all, so Melissa or Angelo would run to the supermarket to stock up whenever the shop ran low. What a waste of time and energy! Eventually she found a distributor who delivers every day.

We use a digital payment system I check occasionally to see an hour-by-hour record of sales. Every location has a back office with a desk, so I may check it there, or, if I'm on the road, I'll take a look through the payment system's mobile app.

What, it's afternoon already? Break time! Here in Illinois, if an employee works 7½ hours he's entitled to a 20-minute paid break, but our in-house policy is to offer a 30-minute unpaid break for 6½ hours of work. We owners can tough out the day and skip these breaks if need be, but employees probably aren't as eager to work all day without stopping.

The skills you need: An ability to see into the future—by which we mean you need to know how many pastries, cups, and other supplies to order each day. The numbers you come up with may depend on the day of the week, the time of year, the weather, any special events in town, and so on.

You also need to know and follow health department regulations for handling food and know how to hire employees who have a gift for gab to keep customers engaged.

Where to get them: Turn to Chapter 20 for advice on how to use sales records to estimate future needs. We also advise you on how to reduce shrinkage—both waste and theft—on a daily basis so your inventory counts stay consistent.

We offer tips on preparing and storing food in Chapter 17. It's smart to check in with your local health department for handling procedures specific to your area. Finally, in Chapter 12, we give you the scoop on hiring a crew.

Work of the Week

Depending on the day of the week, we may have one or more special tasks to tackle. Maybe they're too time-consuming to do every day, or perhaps they only need doing once a week. Our list of special tasks includes cleaning the light fixtures, dusting the air vents, hosing out the garbage cans, emptying the ice machine, and taking down all the coffee pots and French presses for sale and wiping down the shelves.

Another of these tasks is to create a work schedule for the next 1 or 2 weeks. Some employees can work only certain days and times—almost never the same days and times they said when we hired them—and some have given us special requests for time off. We also have to consider the needs of the shop itself: when are sales fastest, for example, and which days do we receive the most deliveries?

Counter *Talk*   When Melissa had fewer than 10 employees, she used the free Google Calendar app to create and distribute the weekly schedule. Now that she has 25 employees, she uses a workforce scheduling tool called Deputy (deputy.com), which helps her handle her larger staff more efficiently. The software also serves as a way to communicate with general managers, get daily updates on how employees are doing, and document interactions with employees—which is important when it comes to unemployment claims.

The skills you need: The capability to create a schedule and adjust it as needed. Based on your sales records and other data, you might want to schedule two and a half employees for the morning rush—wait, how do you schedule *half* an employee? (More on this coming up.)

You also need to know your staff: who works well together, and who stands around all day flirting with other employees? Schmoozing is another required skill because sometimes you have no choice but to deny a request for time off. Then you have to turn on the charm, and make your employee understand how much you need her.

Where to get them: We cover scheduling, along with everything else you need to know about hiring (and firing) employees, in Chapter 12.

As for how to sweet-talk employees into doing disagreeable once-a-week tasks—a topic we cover along with other cleaning clarifications in Chapter 22—you'll learn with experience what works best with different individuals. Some are swayed by money, some by gratitude, and some by sympathy.

Closing Shop

Three hours before closing, we start stocking up for the next day. Eventually, we switch into full-on cleanup mode. Instead of merely wiping up crumbs when we take a pastry out of the case, for example, we empty the entire case and wipe down all the shelves and walls. We also clean the bathrooms during this time.

While we do all this, we're still serving customers, being sure not to rush them despite our desire to focus on cleaning and getting out of there. About 10 or 15 minutes before closing, we politely give customers a warning so they can start getting their things together and heading out the door.

Then we take on the tasks that can't be done until after closing, like breaking down the espresso machine and coffee brewer, counting out the cash drawer, and sweeping and mopping. We have two employees in the shop at night, and they stay a half hour after closing to complete these tasks. For safety reasons, we try not to have an employee alone at opening or closing.

Most importantly of all, we deal with the money, counting the cash in the till and reconciling the total with the records from our payment app. (There are penalties if the drawer is off by more than $5.) We put everything in the safe, and the general manager makes a bank run every couple days during the bank's business hours so they can deposit the earnings and replenish our cash at the same time.

Finally, we take one last look over the store, ensuring everything is cleaned out, locked up, or turned off as needed. Then we lock the doors and say good-bye until tomorrow.

The skills you need: Math, math, math! Even though payment systems do a lot of the work for you, you still need to be able to make sense of the numbers and understand voids, over-rings, and payouts. You also need to compute weekly and monthly sales figures to guide you in ordering supplies.

Where to get them: Chapter 20 has all you need to know about tracking sales, managing inventory, setting sales goals, and recording the numbers.

As far as planning for the future goes, Chapter 25 discusses why and how to adjust your menu as you develop a sales history. We also look at how to prepare employees to serve as supervisors and ways to scout for new locations should you feel ready to move on to bigger challenges.

If reading about Melissa's day as a coffee shop owner has gotten you excited about starting a shop of your own, turn to the next chapter, where we help you build a business plan that will take you one step closer to making your dream a reality.

Getting Started

Before you pour your first cup, you need to do some prep work. In Part 2, you get the scoop on creating a business plan that'll help you successfully start and run a coffee shop, not to mention impress potential lenders. You also learn how to hire professionals, such as an accountant and a lawyer, to build a strong team.

Branding your coffee shop, from choosing your colors and logo to coming up with the perfect name, is essential for business success. We explain everything you need to know to get started in the following chapters.

Finally, where you decide to set up shop can make or break your business, which is why we discuss the pros and cons of different locations—mall, city street, strip mall, office building, and more.

Building Your Business Plan

Before you lease a location, before you start marketing, and before you brew your first cup, you need a plan—a business plan, that is. Writing a business plan forces you to confront such tough questions as "Why do I want to start a coffee business?" and "How can I ensure my business will succeed?"

Having a business plan is essential for two reasons. First, it gives you guidelines to keep your business on track and ensure you're reaching your goals. Second, and more importantly, unless you're fabulously wealthy *and* a real estate baron—and if you are, we should have lunch together sometime—you'll need to borrow money and rent property to open your business. With a business plan in hand, you can show lenders and landlords you're serious about your success and a trustworthy recipient of their generosity.

A Road Map for Success

Writing a business plan is rarely a straightforward process. As you answer questions in one section, you might have to reinvestigate sections that seemed settled only days before. For example, you might plan on catering to philosophers and practicing Buddhists, but while investigating potential competition, you run across the Drink and Think on the other side of town. You might now need to reconsider your target market.

Let's look at how to craft a business plan that will impress banks and landlords and help you launch your café with confidence.

Nailing the Who, What, Where, and Why

What do you want from your business? How do you want to live and work? Whip out a notebook and pen, or open your laptop, and answer the following questions to discover the first glimpses of how to structure your business plan—and your business.

* What are your personal goals? Do you want to be your own boss, make more money, enjoy a flexible schedule, build a business to support your family, meet and work with a wide assortment of people?

* Where do you want your business to be in 6 months, 1 year, 5 years from now? Do you want to stay small or expand your business into a major coffee chain?

* Whom do you want to serve? Students, executives, families, tourists?

* What services and products will you provide? Will you offer catering or delivery? Sell coffee-related gifts and accessories? Host live music or corporate events?

* How are you going to let customers know you exist? (We have much more to say about advertising and promotion in Part 5.)

* Why will customers come to you? What will make you and your products better than the coffee shop down the street—or the coffee maker on their counter?

* Will your coffee shop have a theme, like board games or cats? (We have more on this in Chapter 8.)

Don't dismiss spending time on these questions as unproductive navel-gazing. Sure, you could rent the first empty building you see, plug in a Mr. Coffee or two, and open for business, but that's hardly a recipe for success.

Counter *Talk*   Melissa didn't have a business plan for the first Brewpoint location, but looking back, she wishes she did. She would have been much better off outlining a plan beforehand.

You'll have plenty of time for hard labor in the weeks and months ahead. First, though, you need to know how to direct that labor and what you hope to accomplish with this venture. Spend time on these questions, and keep your answers handy as you read the rest of this chapter. You'll refer to them frequently.

Researching the Market

It's important to do some research on the people who will become your customers—and the people who will steal those customers away from you if you let them.

You'll need to know the demographics of the area you're thinking of starting your business in, from the average age of its residents to their genders and average income. This will let you know whether there are enough potential customers in a chosen area to support your business.

A great—and free—way to find details on your chosen market is to check with the folks who write the book on such things: the U.S. Census Bureau. The free Census Business Builder suite of services "offers small business owners selected Census Bureau and other statistics to guide their research for opening or expanding their business." Find it by searching "Census Business Builder" on census.gov.

Another great resource is your local library, especially if it has a business center with a business librarian who can point you to any number of resources, including "paid for" databases, a creative studio, and a list of all the local small business resources in the community.

Finding competition, on the other hand, is much easier. Just look around as you drive through your city and nearby towns. Ask your friends, your hairdresser, and your doctor where they buy their coffee. Search the internet for coffee shops within a certain distance of your home.

Don't automatically assume you'll open the coffee shop in your hometown. The perfect opportunity might actually be 50 miles away, but you won't know—or know about the competition to that opportunity—unless you broaden your scope of research.

Sussing Out the Competition

Before you hang out your shingle, you need to know about all the other shingle-hangers in your area. Scope out the competition, and learn what you can from every operation, both successful and not so successful.

The internet is a good place to start your search, but be sure to also visit a few coffee shops to check out their products and services.

You might feel like avoiding shops that always seem empty, but you can learn as much from them as from the shops that always seem busy. Are they in the wrong part of town? Do they charge too much? Do their products taste "off"? Is the music too loud? Knowledge is everywhere, if you know how to look.

Make a chart or spreadsheet that lists your competitors down the left side, write the items you want to compare (hours, prices, and so on) across the top, and add your research data to the columns. Not only will this keep your findings organized and easy to read, but you'll likely pick up ideas on what will and won't work at your own business as you look at what others are doing.

Be sure to note basic information such as the following:

* What products they offer in addition to plain ol' joe

* How much they charge for various products

* How many employees they have

* How long they've been in business

* Which hours and days they're open

* Whether they offer catering or delivery

* What the décor looks like

* How many customers the shop seats

Finally, be sure to go beyond prototypical coffee shops in your research. Coffee is sold in gas stations, convenience stores, bookstores, restaurants, supermarkets, and many other locations as well. If a business sells coffee—even coffee you'd dismiss as undrinkable swill—it's serving some portion of the coffee-buying public you want to make your own.

Projecting Income and Expenses

You can talk up your dream of coffee shop ownership 24/7, but what tells the real story is the financial data. If you don't include numbers in your business plan, you're leaving out the most important information: the stuff that tells you whether or not you have a chance of making money.

Counting Costs

Much as we hate to bring out clichés, you have to spend money to make money. Starting a business requires much more than the purchase of raw materials, and this section is where we start to see these costs add up.

Expenses come in two types: start-up costs, which are typically one-time payments you make before you open the business, and operating expenses, which roll around on a regular basis, both before and after you open.

Examples of start-up costs include the following:

* Business registration fees

* Business licensing and permits

* Rent deposits

* Purchases (equipment, promotional materials, uniforms)

* Utility setup fees (phone, electric, water)

Your list of start-up costs will vary widely depending on what you want your coffee shop to look like; the regulations in your state, county, and town; and so on. Want customers to sit in vibrating chairs at solid marble tables? Write that down in your business plan. Be sure to note which expenses can be altered (in case marble tables turn out to be a wee bit expensive) and which can't, such as registration costs.

Counter Talk

One of the biggest start-up costs (and headaches) is the build-out you may need depending on the space. Brewpoint's first location was a turn-key: it cost $36,000 for the built-out space and leftover equipment and stock. Cheap! For the third location, Melissa built out a 4,000-square-foot loading dock to be a coffee shop and roastery—which cost $225,000.

As with start-up costs, your list of operating expenses will start small and grow as your vision of the finished coffee bar becomes clearer. Operating expenses you definitely need to account for include the following:

* Payroll for you and your staff

* Rent and loan payments

* Phone and utility bills

* Advertising

* Janitorial and food-handling supplies

* Food and drink

Adding up these expenses lets you know how much money you need to get the doors open and how much you need to make each month to keep them that way.

Forecasting Income

As you can see from these lists, the cost of the food and drinks you sell is only a tiny part of your total expenses—and yet the sales of said food and drink must support everything else. Quite a job for a brown beverage and a few bagels!

While your sales revenue naturally starts off at $0, a market-based sales forecast—that is, a formula that estimates how much your business could sell—gives you and your banker a rough idea of your income in the months and years ahead. (Don't have a professional banker yet? In Chapter 5, we tell you how to find one.)

To figure out the numbers in your market-based sales forecast, use this formula:

Sales forecast = market size × growth rate × market-share target × average sale × average number of visits

This formula has a lot of variables for you to fill in. Here's what the terms mean in more detail:

* Market size is the number of potential customers within your area.

* Growth rate is an estimate of how much the industry is expanding each year. This will be expressed as a percentage.

* Market-share target equals the percentage of the entire market you expect to capture.

* Average sale is how much a customer typically spends each time he or she purchases something.

* Average number of visits is an estimate of how often a customer enters your store in a specific time period (week, month, quarter, and so on).

Don't overestimate your sales forecast by thinking you're going to nab half of your competitor's customers or that your store will be so wonderful people will visit at twice the national rate. Be realistic, and accept that business growth takes time. Your forecast might indeed be accurate for sales a year from now, but at first, business will be much slower than you'd like.

The best thing you can do with your conservative forecast, in fact, is make it even more conservative by cutting it by another 25 percent. Yes, a whole quarter of your expected income. Better to be pleasantly surprised than unfortunately undercapitalized.

Digging Up Data

Now it's time to fill in those blanks. But how do you figure out the market size, growth rate, average sale, and average number of visits? To dig up these details, check out coffee trade associations, industry suppliers and distributors, market research firms, the Census Bureau, online industry forums, and even other coffee businesses in noncompeting areas.

Here are a few coffee industry organizations and a sample of the information they have available to members and the public:

* The National Coffee Association (NCA; ncausa.org) offers members free monthly market sizing reports, a weekly industry newsletter, and more. Nonmembers can purchase annual reports like "National Coffee Drinking Trends."

* The Specialty Coffee Association (SCA; sca.coffee/availableresearch) offers free email newsletters and helpful infographics. Members get free market and financial reports like "Specialty Coffee Consumer Behaviors, Motivations, and Perceptions" and "U.S. Coffee Market Retail Value Report." Nonmembers can purchase these reports.

* The CoffeeTalk Media (coffeetalk.com) group of products for the coffee industry includes free webinars that can help you learn more about the business.

For other coffee-related organizations, turn to Appendix C.

Securing Start-Up Costs

To pay for start-up costs, you'll need to dip into your savings or, more likely, take out a business loan. Your ability to pay off that loan, as well as all the rest of your operating expenses, will depend on your sales revenues.

Thinking of asking your family for a loan? Even if your family boasts several rich aunts and uncles, think twice before you borrow money from relatives to start a business. You'll risk turning every holiday gathering into a discussion over whether you're running the business properly and using their money wisely.

Asking for Help

You'd think a solo business owner would do all the initial grunt work, well, solo. Not so. No matter how much of an independent self-starter you are, you can and should rely on lots of other people—like lawyers, accountants, bankers, insurance agents, and mentors—to get your business up and running.

It's not a sign of weakness to ask others for help. Think of it as doing everything possible to make your business succeed. Big-name entrepreneurs might stand alone on the stage at their TED talks and SXSW appearances, but they have a million assistants behind the scenes who have helped them get there.

Counter *Talk*

Some of the most helpful people are your suppliers, especially in the case of coffee suppliers. Some reps have owned or managed coffee shops themselves—or, at the very least, have seen a lot of successful (and not-so-successful) coffee shops. Take advantage of their knowledge and experience if you can.

We explain how to hire lawyers, accountants, and other professionals in Chapter 5, but thankfully, some advisers don't charge by the hour for their advice. Your personal life and the business community at large abound with individuals willing to help an up-and-comer like you start off on the right foot.

Making Use of Mentors

Whenever you're beginning a new venture, it's helpful to have someone who has gone through what you're going through or who can share advice while helping you avoid pitfalls. Enter the mentor.

A mentor is someone you trust, who has an interest in you and your business and will tell you he likes this logo over that one or urge you to drop a troublesome supplier. A mentor can be a friend, spouse, sibling, parent, local business owner, professional (like a lawyer or accountant), or even another coffee shop owner.

If it's not your style, there's no need to create a formal mentor-mentee relationship. All you need is someone—or a few someones—whose opinions and experience you trust and whom you can contact when you have a problem or a question. Keep their numbers handy, and touch base often.

Positive Peer Pressure

Peers are those people who are already doing what you long to do. They're running their own companies and trying to make a living outside of big business. "Peers?" you grumble. "You mean *competitors!* Why should I network with them?"

Why? Because they've been there, done that. If they're in business, they've either done things right or learned from their mistakes. (Okay, they could just be really, really lucky, but let's give them the benefit of the doubt.)

Any business owner, whether a coffee shop owner or not, can be a valuable resource for an emerging entrepreneur such as yourself. Other business owners have been through the start-up phase and may have tips on how to hire good employees, deal with suppliers, handle difficult customers, and market a small business.

Being active in the business community and networking with other business owners keeps you up-to-date on industry happenings, generates new ideas for running your business, and gives you sympathetic ears to bend when your friends are sick of hearing about the supplier from hell.

To get in on the networking loop, you can …

* Attend networking events such as those put on by your local Chamber of Commerce.

* Talk to other business owners in your area.

* Participate in online discussion groups for business owners, whether coffee-centric or more generally focused.

* Join associations like the ones discussed earlier.

* Attend coffee industry conferences like CoffeeFest (coffeefest.com) and the National Coffee Association's annual convention.

If you're feeling shy about your status as a business newbie, remember this: every entrepreneur started in your position and received lots of help on the way to a positive bottom line. All you have to do is ask questions, and they'll gladly overwhelm you with tales from the front lines.

Even if you gain no useful information from your peers, talking with them spreads the word about your business, and they in turn might plug your coffee-klatch skills to their own customers, friends, and family.

Going Before the Board

More momentous than a mentor, and more pressing than your peers, we advise you now to create an advisory board.

Advisory boards aren't solely for international conglomerates with more money than they know what to do with. An advisory board is simply a group of people who offer advice on running a business, and because you plan to run a business, it wouldn't hurt to have a bunch of these smart people watching your back.

An advisory board might include your lawyer and accountant (folks we discuss hiring in Chapter 5), professionals in related fields (such as restaurant owners), mentors, public relation experts, and other small business owners.

How do you form an advisory board? Just ask people you trust and whose opinions you value whether they'd like to serve on your board. You're already paying your accountant and lawyer for their advice. If you feel bad asking others to advise you gratis, offer them free gift certificates or catering in exchange for their time. Whenever you meet as a group, treat them to a cup of coffee or a nice meal.

When asking for a person's help, be sure you both understand what this responsibility means. Will you contact him only when you have a question, or do you want to meet at regular times? Unlike large companies that force the CEO to speak before the board, you can make your advisory board as formal or informal as you like.

If you do opt for something more formal and corral these folks in the same place at the same time, play the role of professional businessperson to the hilt by …

* Creating an agenda that outlines the major points you want to cover.

* Sending your advisory board copies of the agenda beforehand.

* Giving an overview of the points you want to cover at the start of the meeting and then discussing them one at a time.

* Allowing a certain amount of time for table talk over each issue, tabling the issue for a later date if it's not resolved in that time.

* Using a recorder or having someone take notes.

Writing Your Business Plan

If you've followed along with everything in this chapter so far, you should have a mountain of information at your fingertips. Time to transform that material into a presentable business plan.

A business plan typically has seven parts. Let's look at each.

Executive Summary

The executive summary gives an overview of your entire plan, highlighting the key strategic points. You typically write this section last but present it first.

Company Description

The description of your company includes your vision and mission statements, a company overview, and its legal structure (discussed in Chapter 5).

Products and Services

This section details which products (specialty coffee, biscotti, homemade donuts) and services (catering, delivery, custom baking) you'll provide customers, as well as how much they'll cost and what research and development you've done to support these offerings.

Marketing

Here you define the market you'll be operating in (the coffee-drinking public), the type of client you expect to serve (your target market), your competition (The Bitter Cup Coffeehouse), and your strategy for attracting clients (handing out flyers to customers of The Bitter Cup when the owner isn't looking).

Operations

This section describes your business's physical location, any equipment and inventory you need, and any other applicable operating details such as a description of your workflow—that is, how your business will perform its day-to-day activities.

Management

Here you outline your key employees (starting with you), external professionals (accountant, lawyer), the members of your advisory board, and your human resource needs (how many staff members you'll need to start operations).

Financials

The nitty-gritty of the business plan, this section contains your financial projections for expenses and income and how long it will take your business to become profitable—that is, to pay off your start-up loans and support itself.

Although this is the end of the business plan chapter, you haven't necessarily reached the end of your business plan. Every other chapter in this book contains information and advice that will affect your plan. If you need more help, the U.S. Small Business Administration website (sba.gov) offers tons of information on how to write a business plan, including downloadable sample plans.

Start your plan now, and by the time you work through the rest of the book you'll have everything ready to go. Then, keep reading to find out about the professionals who can help you get your business off the ground, plus make your job easier when you're there: accountants, lawyers, and more.

CHAPTER
5

Partnering with Authority

We're going to assume you didn't earn a law degree, work as a banker, study accounting, and master the ins and outs of insurance before you set your sights on opening a coffee shop. If you aren't fluent in those worlds, you need help from those who are. Managing a business on your own is one thing, but handling all the legal nitty-gritty that comes with managing a business can be an enormous time suck that pulls you away from doing what only you can do.

By hiring professionals in these fields, you can focus on your core business while knowing that everything behind the scenes is on the up-and-up. As your business changes and grows in the years ahead, you'll return to these pros again and again to reevaluate how you keep records, file taxes, hire employees, and more.

The Pros of Pros

You do need help from professionals, but don't just run out and hire the first ones you find. You must do some research in this area, too. After all, the work these folks will do for you is very important—we're talking finances, insurance, taxes, and even potential lawsuits.

Ask family, friends, and acquaintances if they can recommend the type of professional you're looking for. After you have a few names, call and ask to meet with the professional for a consultation—many will do this for free—and be sure he or she has experience with small businesses like yours. Expect the professional to pepper you with questions: Where do you want to be in 5 years? What are your goals? How do you expect to reach those goals? What are your major concerns? What do you expect from a lawyer/accountant/banker/insurance policy?

These questions aren't tip-offs to a nosy personality. If the pro is going to help your business succeed, she needs to know what you want to succeed at. (And if a professional doesn't grill you, that could be a sign they either don't know your industry or can't be bothered to find out more about you. Neither situation is good.)

Don't be afraid to ask a few questions yourself. You're the one writing the checks, so consider asking the following:

* **Are you experienced?** Has the professional done any of the tasks you're asking them to do, or is this new ground they'll be learning on your dime?

* **Are you well connected?** It's unreasonable to expect the pro to know every single fact in their field, but do they also have a network of peers to turn to for those times they're in the dark?

* **Do you have other clients in my industry?** Having other coffee shop clients is good (as long as they're in different towns) because the pro will be able to offer you better advice.

* **Can you teach me what I need to know?** You're hiring this person for his or her knowledge, but you don't want them to keep it all to themselves. Can they explain things so you know what's going on?

The professional should explain her fee structure so you understand it, and she should have time to address your concerns. Be wary of any professional who keeps interrupting your meeting to answer the phone or deal with other tasks because they might not treat your work as a priority. Ask the professional for referrals, and call at least two of them to be sure the pro is up to doing the job.

Finally, be sure you feel comfortable working with the professional. Her brilliance might be awe-inspiring and the referrals outstanding, but if she's brusque and unpleasant, you might be reluctant to call and ask for help when you really need it—which defeats the purpose of hiring her in the first place.

Landing a Legal Eagle

On TV, lawyers spend their time chasing down murderers, protecting orphans, or representing town folk who sue evil corporations for poisoning the local drinking water. In real life, lawyers create and interpret contracts and leases, defend their clients in legal actions brought against them, offer legal advice on topics such as hiring and firing employees, register and ID clients' businesses, and help clients choose the right business structure. (More on these last two topics later in this chapter.) In other words, lawyers spend much of their time doing those tasks you might find incredibly difficult or boring on your own.

By hiring a lawyer, you can release responsibility for much of the legal work your small business requires and focus instead on running your coffee shop.

Not sure where to inquire to find your legal eagle? Start with the internet and recommendations from friends and family. If these don't pan out, contact specialized organizations with attorney listings such as these:

* The American Bar Association (americanbar.org)

* Lawyers.com, which specializes in lawyers for small businesses

* FindLaw (lawyers.findlaw.com), which also sells legal forms for business formation and more

With any lawyer you hire—or any of the other professionals we recommend in this chapter—keep accessibility in mind. Can you consult her by phone, or will you have to visit her at her office? If the latter, how far away is the office, and do the business hours clash with when you need to be behind the counter?

Finally, try to find a lawyer who has experience with small businesses like yours. She'll be more familiar with your needs than a lawyer who works mainly with large corporations and can offer better advice on hiring employees, choosing the right business structure, and more.

Accounting for Taste

Think you can get by with QuickBooks or another accounting software platform and don't need an accountant? Think again.

While you focus on running your coffee shop, an accountant can compile and explain financial statements, design an accounting system to ease your year-end financial reporting, keep Uncle Sam off your back by helping you pay the correct type and amount of taxes, tell you whether that fancy new home coffee maker is a legitimate business expense, and work with your lawyer to decide what type of business structure you should have.

Counter *Talk*   Originally, Melissa and Angelo hired an accountant to do the business's taxes and took care of most of the bookkeeping themselves. Every 6 months they'd realize they messed up the bookkeeping and had to do it all over. Finally, after 3 years, they asked their accountant to handle the task for them. They wish they'd done that from the beginning!

Good accounting can't save a coffee shop that serves bad coffee, but a good coffee shop can still go bust if the owner doesn't know how to handle money. Costs can rise above income, for example, so each sale brings a loss instead of a profit, or tax penalties for misfiled forms can plant a business so far in the hole that recovery is highly unlikely.

As with your search for a lawyer, start online and with recommendations from friends. If those sources don't help, use the "Find Accountant" link on the Professional Association of Small Business Accountants' website (smallbizaccountants.com).

Insuring Success

You may be the most careful coffee shop owner there is, but one claim of personal injury, bodily injury, or sexual harassment can empty your bank account in a flash.

Comedians might have mocked the woman who sued McDonald's for serving overly hot coffee in the early 1990s, but the lawsuit itself wasn't a frivolous matter. The jury ruled that the fast-food giant had engaged in reckless conduct and issued a $2.7 million punitive damage award. The award was later lowered to $480,000, but that's still enough to wipe out almost any small business.

Protecting your personal and business finances requires insurance, and an insurance agent can tell you which types and how much coverage you need—both before you open and as your business changes over time. Agents are typically independent businesspeople who work for several companies that provide different types of insurance. One agent should be all you need to find liability insurance, health insurance, and other policies.

Again, ask around for recommendations.

Storming the Banks

If you're like most small business owners, you have a bank but no banker. We encourage you to change that. Bankers handle accounts for bank members and assist members in getting credit, avoiding fees, and enhancing business opportunities.

Counter *Talk*

Big banks may promise you they can secure a loan, but unless you have a lot of assets coming into the business, you're not likely to be approved for much more than a bank account. Melissa changed banks three times before landing with a community bank, where she was finally able to get a loan and a credit card. The bank's tech is a bit archaic, but at the end of the day, she'd rather have a small bank that really believes in Brewpoint than one where she can deposit checks via an app.

The best way to find a banker who will help keep the money flowing is to ask other coffee shops, restaurants, and small business owners whom they use and then research the banks to be sure they fit your needs. How long does it usually take to approve a loan? How much red tape will you have to go through to, say, replace a missing debit card? Does the bank have a good app? Interview bankers at your banks of choice and then pick the one you feel the most comfortable with.

Many small business owners don't bother with bankers, and when they do, they don't understand how to cultivate an alliance with them. Follow these tips to build a good relationship with your banker—after all, a good rapport is like money in the bank!

* Invite your banker to tour your facilities. Although you want the banker to be familiar with your business and its particular needs, don't invite them to tour the shop immediately before applying for a loan. You don't want to look like you're pleading for sympathy or special favors.

* Let your banker know when something important happens, such as gaining new market share, reaching a profit goal, or facing a new competitor.

* Don't ask for favors at the beginning of your relationship. Create goodwill first by giving the bank your business and trying to bring in other accounts.

* If business setbacks occur, try to determine the cause and develop a plan of action before contacting your banker. When you have a plan, then give your banker a call. He'll want to know about potential financial problems (and your plan to solve them) ASAP, not months after they develop.

Many small business owners feel (wrongly) that they need to "fight" their banker to win approval for loans and credit. Try to avoid creating such a relationship. Instead, recognize that a banker who trusts you and your business is on your side. He'll go to bat for you to get lower interest rates or a credit line extension, for example. You're not fighting an institution; you're working with a business partner to achieve a goal.

Should You Go It Alone?

So let's jump back to the beginning of the chapter when we considered your past work history. Maybe you did take one of those tax-preparation classes from H&R Block, or perhaps you were a lawyer before you decided you'd rather pull drinks than push papers. Will you save money by handling the accounting or legal tasks yourself?

It depends. Every hour you sweat over tax filings or contracts is an hour you're not building your coffee shop business. Sure, you may save $50 by filing that form yourself, but in effect you're *losing* money at the same time because you could be thinking up ways to sell more products or network with other business owners.

Even more importantly, when you're dealing with employees and customers, you're building good-will. When you're struggling with a legal form, you're building nothing but a headache.

If you're cash-strapped when you first start out, it might make sense to do as much on your own as you can. But as soon as you're able, we suggest hiring professionals to do their thing, so you have time to do *yours:* sell coffee and build your business.

Structuring Your Business

Businesses don't append titles like *Inc.* and *LLC* to their names because they sound cool. Those are shorthand for the business's legal structure, which affects how much the business pays in taxes, the amount of paperwork the owners have to do, the personal liability they face, and their ability to raise money for their business.

> **Counter** *Talk*   No one business structure works best for every coffee shop. Brewpoint Coffee is an LLC—actually a series LLC, which is much more complicated—but Melissa has seen other coffee shops operate as all the other options.

The business structure you choose initially doesn't have to be the structure your coffee shop has for all time. You can move from one to another, although the ease with which you do this will depend on what you're changing from and what you're changing to.

Liability, taxation, and record-keeping are the most important factors to keep in mind when choosing among business entities. The following sections offer a brief look at how the most common forms of business entities differ.

Sole Proprietorship

A sole proprietorship is the simplest and most common way entrepreneurs organize their businesses. You are the only proprietor, or owner, and you have complete control over managing every aspect of the business.

Control is good, right? Well, yes and no. Control can come back and bite you because financial control of the business is also your responsibility. You are personally and solely liable for all financial obligations, which means that if someone sues your business and wins, your business *and* personal bank accounts have to ante up the dough. If the business goes bankrupt and you still owe money, your future wages, even if they're from a completely unrelated business, must pay off your debts.

Now, with that warning in mind, let's consider the benefits. First, handling tax matters under sole proprietorships is fairly easy because you can file a Schedule C with your individual income tax return. Tax-filing software can make this process so simple you might be able to complete the tax forms on your own. You should still run them past your accountant so she can double-check your work, but this will save you money.

The second real benefit of being a sole proprietor is the ease with which you can start and end a business. Sure, you need all sorts of licenses to sell food and drinks—a topic covered later in this chapter—but the business itself exists as soon as you say it does. If you want to use your child's college fund as business capital, you don't have to write yourself a loan; you just use it. (Convincing your spouse this is a good idea is an exercise we'll leave to you.)

Partnership

A partnership is akin to two or more sole proprietorships combined with the "sole" aspect tossed out. Partners share the profits (and suffer the losses) together, and they typically sign contracts that detail how to split funds among them.

As with a sole proprietorship, partners enjoy ease of tax filings but suffer from the threat of being personally liable for all financial obligations of the business.

Of greater concern is how partnerships change over time. A year or two after opening, one partner might feel he's doing all the work while netting only half the earnings, or the partners might disagree on how to expand the business, who to promote to manager, or what to add to the menu.

To avoid these pitfalls, partners need to decide who will handle which responsibilities long before the business opens. Ideally, the partnership contract they sign should spell out exactly who does what, for how much of the profits.

More importantly, the contract should include a method for revising the contract should the work situation change over time. If, for example, one partner is hurt or dies, what happens to his share of the business? If a partner decides a coffee career doesn't suit her any longer, how much will it cost to buy her out? By confronting these issues early, preferably with a lawyer to get everything in writing, you'll avoid arguments and lawsuits in the long run.

Corporation

By legal definition, a corporation functions just like a person. When the owner of a corporation buys something by using money from the business, the item purchased is owned by the corporation itself and not the business owner.

Similarly, it's the corporation itself that makes a profit or loss, is taxed on earnings, and is held legally liable for its actions. If the corporation is sued, only items owned by the corporation are at risk, not the personal finances of you and the other co-owners.

You're not completely off the hook, of course. The corporation pays you a salary and you still owe taxes on that income, you can be personally sued for wrongdoing, and so on. What's more, running a corporation requires an intense amount of paperwork, which is best handled by legal and accounting experts.

Limited Liability Company

A limited liability company (LLC) walks the line between incorporation and sole proprietorship. Profits and losses pass through to the owners—thus avoiding the "double taxation" corporations deal with—yet owners are shielded from personal liability for business debts.

Just as you share benefits, however, you also share drawbacks. LLCs require more paperwork than sole proprietorships or partnerships, and they expire with the owners—unlike corporations, which can "live" beyond a single owner. If you dream about going public in the future and selling shares of stock, you're best off forming a corporation instead of an LLC.

Securing IDs, Licenses, and Permits

As a business owner, you must apply for numerous licenses, permits, and ID numbers. The exact requirements vary depending on your city and state, but we've included an explanation of the most basic licenses and numbers here.

Employer Identification Number

The employer identification number (EIN), or federal tax identification number, identifies your business in its current legal structure. If you formed a sole proprietorship, you can use your Social Security number as your EIN; if you chose a different structure, the EIN effectively serves as the business's Social Security number.

Apply for an EIN online with the U.S. Internal Revenue Service (irs.gov). The website also offers information on how to apply by mail if you prefer.

Business License

No matter which part of the country you live in, you'll almost certainly need to secure a business license. If the business falls inside the borders of an incorporated city, for example, you need to contact the city for a license; if it lies outside city limits, the county government is likely your license source.

Certificate of Occupancy

While setting up your coffee shop, you might take over an existing business and use it exactly as is. If you want to set up in a new building, however, or renovate an old one for your needs, you need to apply for a certificate of occupancy from the building or zoning department. Contact your local city or town hall to find out how to do this.

Fictitious Business Name

In their quasi-person-like status, corporations already have a name under which to do business—that is, the name of the corporation itself.

You, as an individual, are not doing business under your name because few people would enter a store labeled "Herbert Terwilliger" and expect to find coffee for sale. Because you're doing business under a fictitious name, you must apply for a license to do so from the appropriate local government office. The fictitious business name license is also called a DBA or "doing business as."

Food License

If you sell perishable foods, such as fresh coffee instead of canned, or baked cookies instead of powdered and freeze-dried ones, you need to obtain a food license from the city or state (or both).

Zoning Compliance Permit

We talk more about finding a location in Chapter 7, but now's the time to mention that many cities require you to get a zoning compliance permit before you open shop. Be sure to ask city hall whether you need this permit before you sign the lease; otherwise, you could be liable for a location where you can't even do business.

Reseller's License

Because you're purchasing items from a wholesaler—such as coffee beans or bagels—to resell to others, you first need a reseller's license, which is also known as a seller's permit or sales tax permit. That's right, you have to collect sales tax on (nearly) everything you sell. (We cover the tax topic in detail in Chapter 20.)

These licenses and permits will get you started, but consult your lawyer (that pro we suggested you hire a few pages back) or speak with the appropriate government agency in your area to find out exactly what's required to open for business in your town.

You've taken care of all your banking, legal, licensing, and other business needs. Now let's get creative and think about your business branding.

Branding Your Business

Can you imagine customers referring their friends to "that coffee shop … oh, what's it called? … the one on Main Street"? Probably not. That's why you need a name for your business that will be easy for your customers to remember and share with their friends.

Similarly, a strong logo, a graphical depiction of your business, also helps customers remember your business and what you stand for.

Your business name and logo should convey everything that's good about your business—what makes you unique, why customers should buy from you instead of anyone else—while at the same time telling potential customers that you sell coffee. It may sound hard, but we show you how it's done in this chapter.

The Importance of a Brand

Starting in the 1990s, businesses began paying more and more attention to their brand, or corporate identity, which is the essence of who they are, what they do, and how they do it. Examples of popular brand images include the Nike swoosh, the red-and-white Coca-Cola "wave," and yes, the green-and-white Starbucks siren.

Why do these businesses and thousands of others care so much about making their brand well known? First, it helps differentiate their brand in the marketplace. If you see a swoosh on a product, whether it's a sneaker, a shirt, or a golf club, you know the item is a Nike design. Not Adidas, not Reebok, not anyone else. Whether that's good or bad depends on your past experience with Nike, your concern over sweatshop labor, and other factors, but the important thing from Nike's point of view is that every consumer can recognize its products.

That ties into a second benefit of branding: if a company creates a coherent image and packages it into its advertising and product design, it can create more effective marketing campaigns that will likely result in better sales.

To continue using Nike as an example, the company used the phrase "Just do it" so regularly in its advertising campaigns it's now impossible to use the phrase without thinking about the company. Writers even write sentences such as, "As Nike says, 'Just do it'"—as if no one else in the history of the English language had ever uttered that phrase. Say "the next generation," and Pepsi comes to mind; mention "I'm lovin' it" in the same sentence as a hamburger, and who will think of anything other than McDonald's?

Brands are so powerful that they can be worth beaucoup bucks all on their own, even beyond the products they sell. In 2018, the Coca-Cola brand itself—not the soda-producing machines, factories, or any other equipment, but simply the *essence* of the brand—was worth close to $80 billion, according to statistics portal Statista (statista.com).

While large, international companies spend millions of dollars to create a brand image, you as a small business will likely budget a tad less. That's okay—no one expects you to compete with the big boys in terms of dollars spent. As long as you offer quality products, you'll be well on your way to success.

That said, your business name, logo, colors, advertising, and more will work together to make up your business's brand and its image in the marketplace and surrounding community. This means you need to consider the following sections carefully, with an eye toward long-term use and consistency.

The Name Game

Step number one in creating a business name that will have customers lining up outside your door is deciding what you want your name to communicate.

While you were building your business plan in Chapter 4, you focused on the target market you want to serve and researched the size of that market. Now it's time to decide how you want to position yourself within that market.

What do we mean by "position yourself"? You need to position your coffee shop in the mind of the buying public. Is the coffee you offer exclusive to the area? Do you make your own blends? Are your products expensive, modestly priced, affordable, cheap? Are you open before dawn, after midnight, around the clock? Will you provide live music, a place to study, a shelf of books or games to borrow?

These are just a few of the questions you can ask yourself as you consider how you want to be viewed by the market at large. Ideally, your name will convey all this information in as few words as possible so customers know what to expect when they enter your shop.

Counter *Talk*   The name *Brewpoint* was at the top of Melissa and Angelo's list, but before running with the name, they checked that it wasn't already trademarked by anyone in the United States. They'd heard stories of other coffee shops that had to change their name a few years in because there was another coffee shop in the United States with the same name. You can check your candidates using the U.S. Patent and Trademark Office's search tool at uspto.gov; go to "Trademarks" and then "Search Trademark Database." Don't forget to see if the domain name is available as well, which you can do at Whois.com.

Asking Yourself Some Questions

Continuing in our Socratic vein of self-examination, we have more questions for you to ask yourself. As you do, write down at least 10 names that reflect your answers.

* What problems do I solve for my target market? (Do I help them wake up and warm up in the morning? Provide them with affordable indulgences? Help them brew the perfect pot at home? Offer types of coffee they can't find anywhere else?)

* What words or phrases appeal to my target market? (For example, *hot, brewed,* or *fresh?*)

* What are the biggest benefits my business brings to customers?

* What kind of atmosphere should people expect to find in my shop?

* What kind of name would differentiate me, in a positive way, from my competitors?

Be cautious about choosing names that limit you to a certain location or type of business. If you name your business Boston Beans, for instance, how might that name affect you down the road if you expand to nearby towns or move your business out of Boston? What if, after opening The Cheap Cup, you discover that customers are hankering for pricey gourmet beans?

When you have a list of names written down, run them by friends, family, and potential customers. You even can create a social media survey to get a wider sampling of opinions and ideas. (We find that the promise of a small freebie or prize drawing helps entice people to fill out the survey.) Which names make people want to come to your shop and sample your wares? Which names make them scrunch up their brows in confusion?

If possible, ask people for an opinion on your chosen names without offering other information about the business. You might love "The Perfect Pot" for your business-to-be, but they might wonder whether you're opening a coffee bar, a pottery store, or an establishment that sells cannabis products.

Say the names out loud, and ditch those that don't roll off your tongue. Imagine the name on business cards, on a sign, on letterhead, or in a newspaper article. Pretend someone at a party or on an elevator asks the name of your business. Can you imagine answering the phone with this name? If not, forget it and move on to the next.

Many naming experts recommend your business name use real words instead of made-up monikers like Kodak and Skechers. Why do some companies get away with invented names while you have to stick to boring ol' real words? Simple—you can't afford it. Those firms have multimillion-dollar marketing budgets to plant their invented handles in the minds of consumers. You, on the other hand, probably lack the millions of bucks needed to get customers to remember that Drinqs or Zelpod is a coffee shop.

Speaking of naming experts: if you're still having trouble coming up with the perfect handle for your business, consider hiring a professional naming or branding company. These can be costly, but they'll help come up with a name that has impact, show you how the name will look on signs and promotional materials, and assist you with trademarking and registering.

Marking Your Territory

When you finally find the perfect name for your coffee pot of gold, consider whether you want to trademark your creation. A trademark is any word, image, or combination of words and images used to distinguish your business or service from any other business or service.

Trademarks are why people named McDonald shouldn't name a business after themselves. In 2003, for example, nationwide lingerie retailer Victoria's Secret sued a small adult novelty and gift shop named Victor's Little Secret. This despite the fact that one of the co-owners was actually named Victor! The U.S. Supreme Court eventually ruled that there was no confusion between Victor and Victoria and threw out the lawsuit, but it's unlikely that you want to risk a drawn-out court battle simply to name a business after yourself. (We're talking to you, Duncan Pete Starbuck!)

You don't *have* to trademark your name, but doing so ensures that other businesses in the same industry can't use it for themselves. This exclusivity might not be important to you now, but if you want to expand your business later, you don't want to unexpectedly find competing shops with the same name where you plan to expand.

To submit a trademark application, visit the U.S. Patent and Trademark Office (USPTO) at uspto. gov. First, check out the "Trademark Basics" page for information on how the process works and ways to avoid common pitfalls. Then you can apply online. Application fees range from $225 to $400 for each application.

Keep in mind that in addition to trademarking your business name, you also might apply to trademark your business logo or even individual recipes, and each is an individual trademark application.

If you submit the application without the help of a lawyer, you're responsible for complying with all requirements of the trademark statute and rules. If you do use a lawyer, you'll avoid this grunt work as the USPTO will correspond with only the lawyer—but of course, this will cost you more.

Logo Logistics

If you're driving with kids down a Florida highway and spot a sign that has a black circle with two smaller black circles above it, be prepared for lots of screaming from the back seat. You're getting close to Disney World, and the kids can hardly wait.

A business's logo is visual shorthand for the business itself. The silhouette of Mickey Mouse is one of the world's most recognized logos, and as soon as most people see three black circles in a certain arrangement, they automatically think about Disney, vacations, overpriced souvenirs, and very long lines for amusement park rides.

As a coffee shop owner, you can use a logo to give your business an image of substance and stability while grabbing past and future customers with a visual hook that connects the act of drinking coffee with your business. Although not essential, a logo gives a business a more professional look.

Counter *Talk*   Just like people do, brands evolve as they discover who they are. Brewpoint has rebranded three times. The first logo, which Melissa and Angelo created by hand, was hard to read. The second was more visible but much more "in your face" than they wanted. The final logo is more delicate yet represents the brand's values. It's key to rebrand carefully, though, and to have a good reason for switching things up. Brewpoint's final rebranding happened when the company expanded to three spaces and a roastery.

What Makes a Logo?

There's more to designing a logo than pasting a stock image of a steaming coffee cup onto your business card. Your logo needs to convey important information about your business beyond "I sell coffee." A gym, for instance, might use a vibrant design to convey health and vitality, whereas an accountant will choose something more conservative to radiate seriousness and trustworthiness.

You want your logo to reflect the true image of your coffee bar—the image you developed earlier in this chapter while deciding on a name. Ideally, your logo will work with your shop name to reinforce the perception you want customers to have about your business.

Keep in mind, though, that a logo has its limits. You might decide the perfect logo is a four-color design of an Italian woman quaffing espresso and holding a croissant, and only later discover that when you copy your logo on a black-and-white copier, it ends up looking like a big coffee stain.

To be successful, a logo must be appropriate to your business. Beans, coffee cups, coffee pots? Good. Flowers, puppies, power tools? Bad. (Unless those fit with your theme. More about theme shops in Chapter 8.)

Your logo should be readable and memorable, too. When potential customers see your logo, they have to be able to understand what they're looking at, read the name of your business, and remember what the logo stands for. If you plan to open near a busy road, your logo needs to be simple enough that drivers can understand it, even while in motion. If you're located in a pedestrian mall, something a bit fancier and more eye-catching might be appropriate.

Be sure it's reproducible at all different sizes and looks crisp whether in color or black and white. The more colors and detail you have, the harder and more expensive it will be to reproduce on napkins, in advertisements, and anywhere else you want your logo to appear. Test your logo to ensure it will look good on business cards, menus, signs, social media, and your mobile website.

Ensure it's unique. If your logo resembles the logo of, say, a business that rhymes with *Farbucks,* customers might have a hard time distinguishing your products from a competitor's—until the lawyers shut you down, that is. Fonts and graphics used need to be uniquely yours, too, or legally available for you to use.

Finally, be sure your logo is professional and not trendy. You don't want to look like a here-today-gone-tomorrow business, so be sure your logo conveys stability and professionalism. Don't mimic a design or color that's popular now, or your logo will quickly become dated—and make your business look out-of-date as well.

Remember, you don't have to highlight all the key points about your business in your logo. It would be difficult, for example, to express the concepts of Italian, fresh pastries, coffee, coffee gifts, and gourmet in one simple design.

Getting Design Help

Déjà vu time—as we said in the previous section, there's more to choosing a logo design than pasting a stock image of a steaming coffee cup onto your business card. Unless you have a background in graphic design, it's a good idea to hire a professional designer if you want your logo to look, well, professional.

Don't think you have to lay out a huge wad of cash, though. You're not Coca-Cola looking for a new concept for an international marketing campaign; all you need are a few designs based on the concepts you already have. You can even contact art and design schools to find a student who may design a logo for you cheap or perhaps in exchange for an endless supply of "study fuel," a.k.a. coffee.

Another option is to look into one of the many online marketplaces for graphic designers, such as 99designs (99designs.com) or Fiverr (fiverr.com). You need to be very selective about who you hire because the designers' credentials can vary from "I know how to use Canva" to "I'm a long-time pro," but you can get a solid design without breaking your budget. (Keep in mind that on sites like these, cheaper isn't always better! More experienced designers charge higher prices, but they're more likely to give you an on-point design than someone who charges bottom-of-the-barrel rates.)

No matter who designs your logo, be careful to not use fonts or images that you don't own or that aren't public, or you can get into legal trouble.

What Color Is Your Business?

Colors convey emotions, so the color you choose for your logo and your shop is an important aspect of your image. To help you select the best colors for your logo, letterhead, signs, tables, floors, and so forth, check out this list of popular colors and the emotions they convey:

* Red is an attention-grabber that makes people look immediately. Red symbolizes fire, heat, passion, excitement, power, and aggression. It can elevate blood pressure and respiratory rate. Hmm, sounds a lot like caffeine!

* Blue is peaceful and tranquil, and it relaxes the nervous system. At an extreme, the color represents solitude and depression, such as in the expression "feeling blue."

* Green is a neutral, relaxing color and can communicate the idea of life, renewal, hope, vigor, nature, or money. This could be a good color for an environmentally friendly shop that sells, say, free-trade coffees and uses recyclable paper goods.

* Black is the color of authority and power, but in large doses, it can represent somberness and mourning—not necessarily a good mix with coffee, no matter how black you serve it. However, black also conveys elegance and class, which could be a smart choice for an upscale coffee shop.

* Yellow conveys brightness, playfulness, creativity, and warmth. It's the most visible of all the colors, which is why traffic signs are this color.

* Purple, the color of royalty, conveys luxury, wealth, and sophistication as well as passion and romance. This may be a good color for a shop selling pricey luxury items.

* Brown, the color of earth and wood, is solid, reliable, neutral, and comfortable. It also symbolizes credibility, strength, and maturity. Oh, and it's the color of coffee!

For more color inspiration, take a look at Pantone's tools for designers at pantone.com. The Color of the Year is always fun to play with—although, again, you don't want to be too trendy. The company also offers trend forecasts and informational articles and case studies.

As with your business name, you can trademark your logo to ensure no one snatches your awesome design; the trademark application process is the same. Some companies have even gone so far as to trademark a particular color! This makes sense when, in the public mind, brown equals UPS delivery, for example, but you have nothing to worry about—at least until you start delivering coffee coast to coast.

When you have your brand image set, from your business name to your brand colors—keeping in mind that these are likely to change over time, and that's okay—it's time to find a good place to settle down in. In the next chapter, we go into detail about all things location.

Location, Location, Location

One of the most important business decisions you'll make—after deciding to start your business, that is—is where you'll base your operations. How much space do you need? Do you want to be in the suburbs or the city? How much rent can you afford? Do you want to be in a mall, in a strip mall, on a city street, or in an office complex?

The future success of your business depends on finding a good location. If, for example, your downtown location ends up with less foot traffic than you expected, you'll have to pour money into marketing to get folks to stop by. If you set up in a strip mall with a supermarket that shuts down 6 months later, you might have to contemplate shutting down your shop as well.

All this may sound like way too much thinking for someone who hasn't had their morning cup of coffee yet, but that's okay. In this chapter, we tell you how to develop criteria to analyze locations and prepare a proposal for the landlord.

Where to Get Started

In the movies, the budding entrepreneur passes by a building with a "For Rent" sign, walks in, and starts her business—with great success, of course! In real life, you'll rarely find your perfect location with a "For Rent" sign conveniently hanging in the window.

Deciding where to start can be daunting. After all, you have a whole city or town (or more) to choose from! We suggest you start by mapping out a large area to determine where the most profitable locations lie—and by *profitable* we mean "bearing lots of potential customers."

In your "war room" (that is, your office or living room) put up a large map of your city or town. Armed with a bunch of stickers in different colors, and your computer with a search engine open in your web browser, place stickers of one color on the map for businesses that attract the same sort of clientele you're hoping to target. For example, if you want to attract families, put stickers on baby stores, toy stores, and family restaurants. If you want to target students, put stickers on colleges, bookstores, libraries, hip retail stores, and so on. Put stickers of another color on businesses that compete with yours.

Do you see any areas where a bunch of stickers seem to converge (even competitor stickers—we talk more about this later in the chapter)? These are the areas where you want to start looking for your perfect location.

Choosing a Type of Location

Now that you know where to start looking, the next step is to decide what type of location you're looking for. Not all locations are created equal; they differ by rent, traffic patterns, accessibility, upkeep costs, and more. Here are the pros and cons of the various options.

Shopping Malls

You'd think a place with all that walk-by traffic would have great potential for a coffee shop. Sadly, that isn't so. You can't count on gaining a loyal clientele at a mall, unless it's the employees of the other stores.

First, with the rise of online sales, shopping malls don't have the same allure they used to.

Second, when people do shop at malls, they tend to do their shopping *after* the peak coffee-drinking time of the day, since malls usually open no earlier than 9 A.M., which means many people won't be tempted to stop shopping to enjoy a cup of coffee in your store. And unfortunately, those disinterested people who are already in the mall are your main market—after all, would *you* fight traffic, find parking, and navigate the mall just to get a cup of coffee?

But that's merely the beginning of the drawbacks. Rent, which is typically charged on a price-per-square-foot basis, can be extremely high in the mall because it's a very competitive place to be. If the rent is low, there's probably a good (and by *good,* we mean *bad*) reason for it. You have to contribute to the mall's media fund for advertising and marketing, too, and that fund goes toward marketing the mall in general, not your store in particular. You also have to pay for common area maintenance (more on this later), which can be pricey. With their fountains, landscaping, and huge parking lots, malls are expensive to keep up.

On top of everything else, the mall's hours are set in stone, and you must obey them. Are they open 7 days a week from 9 A.M. to 9 P.M., including most holidays? Then so are you—and you have to pay for the labor to staff the store every hour the mall is open, even when it would be more profitable for you to close your doors.

Despite all the doom and gloom in the preceding paragraphs, malls can sometimes support a coffee shop based solely on the volume of traffic, especially during the holidays. Few other retail organizations draw thousands of people to one location on such a regular basis. Rather than set up an entire store, though, you might be better off running a coffee cart only during certain times of the year. We discuss cart opportunities a bit later in this chapter.

Counter *Talk*

Brewpoint has three different locations, each with its own pros and cons. Brewpoint Founders, in a retail storefront, is the busiest shop and gets the best bang for the buck in regards to rent and the number of patrons who come through. The Brewpoint Workshop and Roastery is in the side area of a strip mall. It's hard to find but is marketed as a "hidden gem" with a strong social media presence. Brewpoint Lexicon is inside a public library. The rent is cheap and the spot is visible and busy, but it's small and offers little control over hours.

Strip Malls

Strip malls are shopping centers in which all the stores are set along a strip and are accessible from the outdoors. Strip malls have great potential for coffee shops because the storefronts are usually visible from the street, and there's ample parking. The foot traffic is generally good, too, especially if the strip mall has a popular anchor (that's the big store at the end), such as a grocery store or a good bookstore.

Rent and maintenance costs at a strip mall are lower than at a traditional shopping mall, and you're usually free to set your own hours. By giving up a portion of the foot traffic generated by traditional malls, you also give up almost all the drawbacks of these malls. Sounds like a good deal to us!

Office Buildings

An office building can be an awesome place to start a coffee business, especially if the shop has access to the outside for additional walk-by traffic. You have a built-in customer base, and you can expand your profits by offering catering to the businesses in the building; for example, some companies may want you to supply coffee and pastries for their Monday morning meetings. You can also offer gift baskets, which are popular gifts from businesses to their clients and from employees to bosses and vice versa.

One disadvantage might be hours. If you're limited to being open when the building is open for business, you may miss out on key coffee-drinking times of the day, such as before work, especially if you have outside access and rely on walk-by traffic from people who don't work in your building.

Storefronts

Storefronts—that is, businesses in a building that faces the street—are excellent for coffee shops. You can open and close when it works best for you, you benefit from walk-by and drive-by traffic, the rent is often cheaper than in a mall, and you can do cross-promotions with other businesses on your street.

One sticky point may be parking. If there's no separate parking area for your store, look at how street parking is during your hours of operation. No one wants to circle the block five times to get a cup of coffee.

For either a storefront location or a strip mall, think about the possibility of including a drive-thru to catch customers on the go. You might be able to overcome a shortage of parking spaces simply by letting customers stay in their cars.

Carts and Kiosks

You can dip your toe into the coffee business, so to speak, by opening a trial location in a mobile cart or semipermanent kiosk. Many shopping malls, for example, rent cart space during the holiday season to take advantage of the increased foot traffic. Kiosks are a little larger than carts and are usually located in a secure permanent location such as a park or next to an office building downtown.

Whether or not the landlord supplies the kiosk depends on your location and your agreement. They may supply the basic kiosk with electricity and plumbing, for example, and expect you to outfit it with your own brewing equipment, refrigerator, and so on.

These locations have very limited space, so you'd need little more than an espresso machine, a couple brewing carafes, a stocked refrigerator, and supplies to get started.

Your initial investment costs are far lower for carts and kiosks, perfect while you get the hang of the business. According to Bellissimo Coffee Advisors, it costs $20,000 to $25,000 to start a coffee cart and $25,000 to $75,000 to start a kiosk. Compare that to the $200,000+ it costs to start a sit-down coffee shop!

Although these locations cost far less for the initial setup, they offer poor working conditions because you're confined to a very small space for most of the workday—not to mention dealing with the weather if you're outdoors. You tend to work alone, which increases boredom, and you lack real opportunities for growth. Finally, expanding from a cart to a brick-and-mortar location requires almost as much work as starting from scratch.

Inside Other Businesses

Some coffee shops start within other businesses. For example, you can open a shop in one of the following spots:

* Gourmet shop

* Superstore

* Convention center

* Gym

* Theme park

* Hospital

* University campus

* Bookstore

* Tourist stop

* Hotel lobby

* Museum

You're guaranteed walk-by traffic in these locations, and you don't have to worry about competition. The main business usually has vast parking facilities, although you might be required to contribute toward their upkeep.

Because you're relying on their customers for *your* business, the disadvantages can come if the business or organization you're affiliated with is weather-dependent, such as a zoo or theme park; is slow during certain seasons, such as a university; or just isn't doing very well. Sure, a university campus will supply a steady stream of caffeine-deprived students during the semester, but how will your business survive the summer months when they've all gone home?

Evaluating Locations

It would be nice if finding a business location were like finding an apartment. Big rooms, lots of natural light, free utilities? We'll take it! But in reality, many important criteria must be considered when judging a potential location. Let's look at a few.

Size

Sure, the location might seem like the perfect size now. But keep in mind that you may want to expand your business sometime down the line so you'll need someplace with the potential for expansion. You'll also need plenty of room for storage, a workspace for you and your employees, and restrooms. Do you plan to host entertainment or hold workshops (which we discuss in Chapter 13)? If so, you'll want to be able to rearrange the seating area to accommodate such uses.

Experts at Total Food Service (totalfood.com) recommend allowing for about 15 square feet per person and keeping in mind that 60 percent of the floor space will be the dining area and 40 percent will be for food prep, storage, and so on. So if you're eyeing a 2,000-square-foot space, your dining area would be 1,200 square feet and you could seat 80 people.

Atmosphere

Sunny, spacious, and clean? Great. Dank, dark, and gloomy? Not so great. Of course, you can change a lot of the characteristics of your chosen space with cleaning, remodeling, and redecorating, but you don't want to spend thousands of dollars trying to turn a completely inappropriate location into a space that's cozy and inviting for your customers (and your employees).

Counter *Talk*

Be sure to have a consistent look in your coffee shop. (Although your look can vary among different shops if you open more.) If your shop's look is haphazard, customers will feel it even if they don't consciously notice it. Even if your look is "thrift store chic," you can harmonize it with a common color or time period. Brewpoint's Founders location, for example, uses a travel theme to pull together an eclectic look.

Rent

Industry experts at Total Food Service say rent should be no more than 8 to 10 percent of sales. But you don't have any sales yet, so how can you know what a reasonable rent is?

This is where your business plan, which we talked about in Chapter 4, comes in. Take a look at the average price per square foot for café and restaurant locations in your area, do some math to find out what your monthly rent will be on the size of space you're hoping to have, and calculate how much you'll need to earn per month in sales so the rent is no more than 8 to 10 percent of those sales. If the number scares you, you may need to adjust your plans.

Don't automatically discount a place with high rent, though. Many desirable locations have high rent because business is so good in the area that competition keeps the rates up. If your rent is $1,000 per month and you can count on 1,000 customers who spend an average of $3 per visit, you have $2,000 after rent (not including food costs). If your rent is $10,000 per month and you can count on 10,000 customers who shell out an average of $3 per visit, suddenly you have $20,000! Makes the higher rent worth it, doesn't it?

To take away some of the rent burden as you start up, negotiate for 90 days of free rent while you set up shop. Most landlords will agree to this.

Counter *Talk*

Melissa has heard of cafés bringing in anywhere from $25 to $800 on their first day of sales in the Chicagoland area. To calculate what numbers you need to hit to make the rent worth it, though, it's not necessarily the revenue you'd expect to hit the first month that you need to consider, but the revenue you'd expect to hit by month 6. When Melissa took over the turnkey coffee shop, the sellers claimed sales were about $200 per day, and that's what they started at. Brewpoint's sales grew by 500 percent in the first 6 months!

Term

The term is how long the lease lasts. For example, you may have a 1-year term or a 2-year term. You probably don't want to get stuck with a very long lease in case you have to close your business. At the same time, you don't want to go for a very short lease and then find out the landlord won't renew it, or you want to sell the business but can't find a buyer because your lease is about to expire.

A good bet is a shorter lease with a renewal option (say a minimum of 3 years to offset the cost of improvements you made) and a guaranteed rate for rent increases over a set period (such as 5 to 10 years).

The term that's best for you also depends on how much money you'll put into the space as a tenant. If you're not investing a lot into building out your shop, a short lease could be good because it means you may be able to sell the space if you need to get out quick and not lose too much of your initial investment. You wouldn't want to have a 3-year lease on a $250,000 build-out, though, because that means the landlord could hike up the rent at the end of year 3, making your time to return on investment even longer.

Visibility

The nicest coffee shop in the world won't succeed if no one knows you're there. You usually need a location that's visible from the street, preferably one that's right on the curb.

When you find a potential location, walk or drive down the street and see from how far the shop is visible. Can you see the store? How about the signage? When you walk by the store, are there nice, big front windows that show you what's inside? A store that's 70 feet wide and 10 feet deep requires a far different approach than one that's 10 feet wide and 70 feet deep.

Convenience

Would you take a left turn across busy traffic to score a cup of joe? No? A lot of other people wouldn't, either. That's why you need a location that's convenient to the types of customers you want to attract. For example, if you want to cater to busy execs on their way to the office, you should be on the right side of the street on their way to work. If you want to cater to students, be sure your shop is convenient to pedestrians so they don't have to dodge traffic going from the campus to your store, and try to have room out front for bike racks. In most cases, you need ample parking as well.

To place your store right in the path of customers, you can visit the city or county planning department and review traffic flow maps that show how many cars travel on which streets at what times. (Those black rubber cords stretched across the street you've probably driven over dozens of times record such data.) The maps are public information, so make good use of the information you and thousands of other drivers created.

You can often find traffic flow maps online, too. Check your local Department of Transportation website, or do a web search for "traffic flow map" and the name of your city to see if one is available online.

Competition

You need a location with no other coffee shops around, right? Wrong.

If there are no other coffee shops around, there's probably a good reason for it. Maybe the citizens in that area aren't interested in gourmet coffees and teas, or maybe there's not enough walk-by or drive-by traffic. In any case, you want to see thriving businesses in the area you plan to inhabit.

Don't worry about the competition. As we discuss later in this chapter, you can stake them out to uncover their strengths and weaknesses and use that knowledge to your advantage.

Take a tip from the big guys: many times competing businesses feed off one another, which is why you'll often see Burger King, Wendy's, and McDonald's all in a row, or three gas stations at one intersection. If this strategy works for the big chains, you might want to consider it as well.

Signage Laws

Some cities have signage bylaws that require you to keep your signs at or below a certain size, or restrict you from using certain types of signs. How awful would it be to spend $2,000 on a sign only to be told you're not allowed to put it up? Check city bylaws for signage restrictions, and talk to a sign company in your area that's created signs for local businesses. Chances are, they have a good knowledge of city bylaws.

Electricity

Be sure the electrical capacity in your chosen location can handle your coffee equipment, like brewers and roasters. You probably need an electrical system that can handle at least 220 volts because most espresso equipment requires a lot of juice. Talk to an electrician to find out if a location you have your eye on has the potential to handle your electrical equipment.

Tenant Improvement Allowances

Tenant improvement allowances (TIAs, or TIs for short) are funds a landlord gives to you, the tenant, to build or improve your business. These improvements—a resurfaced wall, perhaps, or updated insulated wiring—stay behind in the building if you leave, providing the landlord with a more attractive space for later tenants.

Landlords who have many people bidding for their space are less likely to offer TIs, but it never hurts to ask when you're considering a location.

Common Area Maintenance

Common area maintenance (CAM) is money you pay to maintain the building site. This includes such services as window washing, trash removal, and security. The contract your landlord offers should spell out exactly what the CAM pays for so you know what you'll receive for this money. The contract should also detail procedures to follow in case you find the services haven't been provided.

Ideally, you want to keep the CAM as low as possible. In some cases, you might be able to arrange for window cleaning and other maintenance services yourself, which will allow you more direct control over the look and cleanliness of your business.

Courts in some states have ruled that landlords must reveal the costs behind CAM fees to their tenants. The idea behind this ruling is that landlords can't use CAM fees to boost their own profits; they must use the fees only to cover their own (reasonable) costs for the upkeep on their facilities.

Scan contracts from your landlord to find out whether CAM fees and other expenses are charged on a leased or leasable basis. If the fees are based on a leasable formula, your costs will be the same no matter how many other stores he owns are vacant. If, however, the fees are based on the amount of space currently leased, you'll pay more if one or more locations are vacant as the landlord spreads the maintenance costs among his remaining tenants. Argue for a leasable formula so your costs don't fluctuate due to circumstances outside your control.

Real Estate Taxes

As with CAM fees, the landlord will charge you a portion of the entire real estate bill based on the percentage of space your shop occupies.

Restrooms

You'll probably be required by city health codes to have at least one restroom, and some areas require you to have two. Be sure the area either has the restrooms you need or has the space to build them, taking into account the need for disabled-accessible stalls.

Using these criteria plus the map you created in your "war room," narrow down your selections to five or six potential spaces for your coffee shop. You'll probably have a first-choice location, but it's a good idea to have backups in case that one falls through.

Scoping Out the Competition

As we mentioned, a location that has some competition is a plus because it indicates your chosen area can support a business like yours. Just keep in mind that you can face two kinds of competitors: direct and indirect.

Direct Competitors

Direct competitors are those competing for the same coffee dollar you're going after. This means other coffee and tea shops.

Search online on sites like Yelp (yelp.com) and local business directories, and make a list of direct competitors in your area. Read online reviews and also hit the pavement and visit these shops in person, asking yourself these questions:

* What are the competition's strengths? Do they have excellent customer service, superior product, great prices, a wonderful location?

* What can you do in your own business concept to combat these advantages?

* What are the competition's weaknesses? Do they have surly baristas, ugly décor, bad coffee, a location that requires customers to go through an obstacle course to reach it?

* What can you do in your own business concept to take advantage of these disadvantages?

* What's the most common complaint about the business in online reviews, and how can you use it to your benefit?

* What's the most common bit of praise in online reviews, and how can you build your concept so this competitor's strengths don't diminish your business?

Every business has a weakness, no matter how profitable it is or how popular it seems. Don't be afraid to take on one of the big-league coffee chains if you can provide customers with a better retail experience, whether in terms of atmosphere, taste, price, or convenience.

Indirect Competitors

Indirect competitors are those competing for the same general food and beverage dollar, like doughnut shops, bakeries, and sandwich shops. Find the indirect competitors in your area, and ask yourself the same questions you asked about your direct competitors.

Don't forget that these competitors can actually become your customers in some cases. Perhaps you can sell fresh-roasted beans at wholesale prices to a sandwich shop. As another example, if a local bakery doesn't serve coffee, or if the coffee it does serve is less than ideal, approach the owner with an offer to provide coffee for the business. Perhaps you can even work out a comarketing agreement where he sells your coffee and you feature his pastries.

If you focus solely on the individual customer, selling only one cup of coffee at a time, you'll miss opportunities to sell lots of coffee in places you never would have thought possible.

Counter *Talk*   When Brewpoint started, four other cafés operated within two blocks. Melissa and Angelo visited these and scoped out their prices to see where Brewpoint might fit in. They noticed that none of the shops offered coffee from big-name roasters, so they used that as their point of differentiation before starting their own roastery. It was a little pricier than going with a smaller, lesser-known roaster, but it was worth it.

Dealing with the Landlord

Once again, we wish renting a business space was like renting an apartment, with nothing but a simple application to fill out: if your references check out and you haven't actually destroyed any of your former dwellings, you're in.

But a business landlord has a lot more to worry about than an apartment landlord. An apartment landlord wants to be sure you'll take good care of the apartment and pay your rent on time.

A business landlord wants to know that, too, but he also needs to be sure your business will benefit the other tenants in his building; he'll recoup any money he gives you for improvements; and your business won't fail, leaving him to find another tenant ASAP.

Writing Your Proposal

Although it's not required, a proposal will answer the landlord's burning questions and also help you stand out from the other businesses that want to rent the space. Here's what to address in your proposal:

* Your business concept

* What your business will look like (For this section, you can include photos and illustrations of how you'd like your space to look. We talk more about kitchen and restroom layout in Chapter 11.)

* How your business will add to the value of the site and the other tenants

* What types of customers you plan to attract

* What products and services you'll be offering (For this, you can include a copy of your planned menu with products, services, descriptions, illustrations, and prices.)

Don't try to reinvent the wheel here. You can lift much of the information for your proposal straight from your business plan, which we talked about in Chapter 4.

Dropping off or presenting your proposal to the landlord in person is a great opportunity to make a positive impression. Dress to impress, and don't press the landlord for an immediate answer. If he has any doubts whatsoever, he'll be likely to answer with a big, fat no. Instead, give him a chance to internalize all the information you've offered and get back to him at a later date.

> **Counter Talk** Before you send your proposal, interview other renters to find out what kind of landlord you're dealing with. These conversations can give you ideas for items you may want to add into your lease.

Drafting Your Letter of Intent

Along with your proposal you'll want to send in a letter of intent (LOI), which you would create with either your real estate agent or lawyer. This document outlines the terms under which you're willing to commit to a lease. To learn more about LOIs, and how to draft one yourself if you want, check out "Commercial Leases: Letter of Intent" on Nolo at nolo.com/legal-encyclopedia/clb-commercial-lease-letter-intent.

Negotiating the Lease

Congratulations! You've found the perfect place, and the landlord is interested in negotiating a lease with you.

Hand the landlord a list of things you'd like him to supply you, such as CAM waivers, TIs, free rent for the first month (or first few months), and so on. The landlord will likely cross off some of the requests, but not all of them, leaving you both happy.

Keep these negotiation tips in mind to ensure you and the landlord both get the best deal:

* Never be the one to offer to split the difference. Wait until the landlord offers and then do so.

* Never negotiate by phone or text. It's easier to communicate in person.

* Don't haggle too much. A frustrated landlord may just walk away.

* Get everything in writing, right now.

* Give yourself enough time to negotiate. If you're in a rush, you may not get the best deal. Also, never reveal any deadlines you may have.

* If you make a concession, ask the landlord to make one, too.

* Keep an open mind. If the landlord can't offer something you want, maybe he can offer something you'll like just as much that you hadn't thought of before.

* If this is your first business, don't be surprised if the landlord asks for a personal guarantee.

* Be sure the lease is assumable—which means someone else can take over the lease—in case you decide to, or need to, sell the business.

Remember that lawyer we suggested you hire in Chapter 5? Well, bring her back into the picture because she can help you understand and negotiate the lease.

You've learned what makes a profitable location, how to find one, and how to handle the lease. Now let's talk about what goes *inside* that location, from the theme of your coffee shop to your crew.

Setting Up Shop

Now that you have a plan, it's time to act on it: deciding whether you want a theme for your shop, planning the layout, building the counters and shelves, arranging the tables and chairs, and buying the equipment that will make your drinks (and your *dreams*) come true. Part 3 explains the principles to keep in mind as you bring a two-dimensional plan into three-dimensional life.

No matter how enthusiastic you are, though, you can't do it alone. You need a well-trained crew to handle all the business you're hoping to get, so we also explain how to hire, train, and—should the situation arise—fire employees.

To Theme or Not to Theme?

You've got the perfect location for your new coffee shop, whether that's on a city street, in a strip mall, or tucked away in a hotel lobby. But you're not alone. As of 2017, 33,000 coffee shops were operating in the United States, according to the Specialty Food Association (specialtyfood.com). When you've got that many shops vying for coffee drinkers' dollars—not to mention that some of these shops belong to chains with multimillion-dollar marketing budgets—how can you make yours stand out?

Some clever owners are turning to themes. Giving your coffee shop a fun and unique theme can help draw customers, but themed shops are not for everyone. In this chapter, we look at what exactly themed coffee shops are, some ideas for themes that work, and how to know if this is a good option for your business.

From Cats to Cookie Dough

Start looking around at themed coffee shops, and you might be surprised at the wide variety of concepts others have chosen for their shops. You can choose a tried-and-true theme for your coffee shop, or you can invent one that resonates with your particular demographic. It might be hard to find an idea that hasn't already been done, though, as you'll soon learn.

It's up to you how far you take your theme. You may want to add the theme to your business name, hang related images on your walls, and call it a day. Or you may want to go all out with a theme that dictates everything from your furniture to the food and drinks you serve.

Let's look at some popular categories of coffee shop themes.

Food Themes

Many coffee shop themes revolve around the type of food served—or not served. These concepts can definitely garner attention, not to mention simplify your menu:

* **Cookie dough.** A café in New York City serves scoops of raw cookie dough. (Don't worry—pasteurized eggs and heat-treated flour are used to make it safe to eat raw.)

* **Marshmallows.** At a Chicago shop, you can buy marshmallows in all kinds of unique flavors or order them incorporated into a dessert latte.

* **Cereal.** In a London café, cereal is the only food on the menu, but customers can splurge on limited-edition cereals and ask for add-ins like candy or colored milk.

Animal Themes

Want to enjoy your java while petting a furry friend? Shops with animal themes like these appeal to critter-loving coffee drinkers:

* **Cats.** You've likely heard of cat cafés. As of 2015, two dozen were open in the United States, and more may have opened since then. They're also located in Singapore, Russia, Japan, Spain, Canada, and other countries. Details vary from shop to shop, but in general, they follow strict rules to help keep the kitties happy and safe.

* **Owls.** Tokyo, which seems to be the epicenter of unusual themed cafés, boasts a coffee shop where owls fly free. Customers can help themselves to drinks from a vending machine and pet or hold the owls (with the help of a trained owl handler).

* **Meerkats.** This one is in Seoul, South Korea. Once customers purchase a drink, they have 10 minutes to pet and cuddle with meerkats inside a glass enclosure.

Popular Culture Themes

Some themed shops draw on movies, books, comics, music, and art. Here are a few examples:

* *Titanic.* Los Angeles is home to a themed shop based on the blockbuster film and shaped like the doomed ship.

* **Comics.** These cafés appeal to a wide audience, and depending on the shop, offer comics, geek merch, or superhero-themed treats for sale. Comic-based cafés have already popped up in Malaysia, the United States, and other countries.

* **Board games.** Game-related shops may be the most well known of the themed cafés. Enjoy a game of *Settlers of Catan* or *Exploding Kittens* while you enjoy your skinny vanilla latte.

Décor Themes

Some themes are all about the furniture, feel, or interior design of the shop. But don't automatically assume they're easy to implement. Consider about the planning and expense that go into themes like these:

* **Hammocks.** Many people go to coffee shops to relax. And what's more relaxing than a hammock? Hammock coffee shops are operating in the United States, Japan, and elsewhere.

* **Minimalist.** A theme based on a *lack* of décor? Yep. One café in Singapore boasts a minimalist theme, with gray walls and sparse furnishings. The theme takes advantage of the shop's small size and shines the spotlight on its food and coffee.

* **Travel.** Brewpoint's Founders location was started with a travel theme, with maps on the walls and drinks named after explorers.

Counter *Talk*

Brewpoint's travel theme is a play on the company name. When Melissa and Angelo chose the name *Brewpoint*, they were thinking of it as a play on the words *brew* and *view*—so it would be "Brewpoint—expand your brew(view)." It was all about expanding your exposure through travel, through reading, and ultimately through great coffee.

This is far from an exhaustive list of possible themes you can employ for your coffee shop. Others that currently exist include maids, Nutella, crafts, avocados, Harry Potter, Siberian huskies, sewing, vampires, snakes, treehouses, and *Alice in Wonderland*. Oh, and the prison, butler, sheep, and poop cafés we mention later in this chapter? They're real.

Deciding If You Should Theme Your Shop

Now that your mind is spinning with ideas, let's talk about some important considerations that might help you decide if a themed coffee shop is right for you. We go over the advantages and disadvantages, plus share some questions you should ask yourself before you commit to ensure you stay on the good side of your landlord—and the law.

The Pros and Cons of Themes

Before you start buying hammocks or getting too invested in peanut butter sandwiches, let's first look at the advantages of themed coffee shops:

* **You can sell theme-related merchandise.** For example, if you're a board game coffee shop, you can sell games. An art-related theme lends itself to selling products like customized mugs and T-shirts.

* **You'll stand out in a crowded marketplace.** There's probably more than one place in your town where people can get good coffee, but you'd likely be the only coffee shop in your area where customers can pet cats, lounge in a hammock, or nosh on artisanal toast.

* **Your word of mouth will skyrocket.** An unusual theme encourages people to talk up your coffee shop to their friends, and some motifs are incredibly Instagram-worthy. After all, how many people can say they've visited a prison-themed coffee shop?

* **The press will eat it up.** The local media might not care about yet another coffee shop, but they *will* care about a local shop that gives customers the unique opportunity to dip poop-shaped cookies into lattes served in a mug shaped like a toilet bowl.

It's not all sunshine and roses, though (but wouldn't that be a good concept for a theme?). Here are some reasons a themed coffee shop might not be your best bet:

* **It can be expensive.** For example, board game coffee shop owners can spend thousands of dollars building up their stock of games.

* **Your customers might mishandle your products.** If your theme deals in any damage-prone items like board games or hammocks, you may find yourself having to order replacements frequently. In a coffee shop, spills happen!

* **It might be harder to find good staff.** You'll want employees who are at least interested in your theme, if not an expert in it. For example, your cat coffee shop will be a turn-off for potential hires who are allergic to cats or who just don't have experience handling them.

* **Customers may sit all day and not buy.** If your coffee shop theme is books, chess, cats, or popular board games, you might get people who come in to enjoy the theme but not purchase any coffee or snacks. (As one example, the board game *Puerto Rico* can take more than 2 hours to play.) Some coffee shops have mitigated this problem by enacting a minimum purchase rule or charging by the hour, but that creates more work on your end.

* **Tastes change.** Your customers might be clamoring for a butler coffee shop *now,* but will the trend die down in a few years, leaving you with a lot of butler costumes and no sales? Also consider that even if your customers don't tire of your theme, *you* might.

Keep in mind that a heavily themed coffee shop could be harder to sell. If you're looking to sell your shop down the road, it may be smarter to stick with lighter themes like travel, minimalist décor, or something food related than, say, banking on the TV show *Friends* or filling your shop with exotic animals.

Considering the Law and Other Factors

Before you get your heart set on a themed coffee shop, you must first find out if your idea is (1) even possible and (2) legal. Ask yourself the following questions:

* **Will your landlord allow it?** This may be the question that puts an immediate stop to your theme idea. If you already have a contract with a landlord and they don't want you to build a treehouse or let sheep roam free inside the space, you can ditch that idea right now.

* **Do you have the right kind of space?** Hammocks take up a lot of room, especially when people are actually sitting or lying in them, and you need something to hang them from. Some animals need special enclosures. Board games require a lot of shelf space. Before committing to a theme, be sure the space you have (or will build out) can accommodate it.

* **Will the theme comply with the law?** Say you want to start a fox-themed shop. There are health regulations regarding animals in restaurants, and animal cruelty and wildlife laws may govern how you must house, feed, and treat wild animals—and whether you're even allowed to keep them in a coffee shop at all. Even if your theme *is* a possibility, it still might be too much of a financial and legal hassle to turn into reality.

* **Is the theme free from any potential for harm?** If your woodworking-themed coffee shop exposes customers to circular saws, for example, you may need to spend more on legal help and insurance to ensure you won't lose your shop if someone suffers a flesh wound.

* **Will the demographics of your area support your theme?** The young families that make up your market may not be interested in a cigar lounge/coffee shop, and the customers who stream in from the local business district probably won't be excited about a *Minecraft* motif.

If you get all "Yes" answers, research your market and your idea, talk to owners of noncompeting themed cafés, ask your lawyer for advice, and start brainstorming how you can bring your idea to life. If your answer to any question is "No," consider whether it might be better to try a different theme or to make your coffee shop stand out in some other way—like unusual coffee concoctions or fun events.

In the next chapter, we talk about décor and design principles that work for any coffee shop, whether you have a theme or opt to go with a regular—but still amazing!—shop.

Planning Your Décor

Every business, whether the owner has thought about it or not, has a style—a look that tells first-time customers and passers-by what to expect when they come through the doors. That's especially true if you have a themed coffee shop, which we covered in the preceding chapter. The style might not be obvious to customers, but it's there all the same, shaping the image of the business in their minds.

Let's look at a couple examples: Walmart presents a no-frills style that embodies its low-cost approach. Its buildings are supremely uninteresting, saying to customers, "We don't spend any more than we have to on our look, and we pass those savings on to you."

The restaurant chain Longhorn boasts dark wood everywhere, steer horns, and old-timey black-and-white photos of cowboys and cowgirls, presenting customers with a frontier-town feel that complements the hearty steaks and chops on the menu. The manly man nature of the restaurant is evident even in the small details. Buttering bread isn't normally a task for tough guys, but the impressively wide knives given to customers—knives that look capable of skinning a buffalo—make it tough and cool.

We can't tell you what style to choose for your coffee shop, but we can advise you on what to avoid and what to keep in mind as you plan and design your dream domain.

Design Principles

To begin with, let's assume you want to create a style rather than randomly assemble whatever's closest at hand. You could, of course, buy a half dozen mismatched couches and tables at Goodwill, throw velvet Elvis paintings on the walls, and call it a day. For some coffee shop owners, adopting a haphazard (and dirt-cheap) style is completely satisfying—and this style might be perfect for the market of college students and night owls they're trying to attract.

For the rest of us, however, we need to take more care with our choices because we want customers to view our shop in a certain light. We want our business to be comforting, inviting, energizing, efficient, or any of a hundred other adjectives. And of course, if we've decided to open a themed café (see Chapter 8), our décor needs to reflect that. With these goals in mind, let's cover a few design basics before we get down to the details.

What's Easiest to Clean?

If you're torn between two or more choices, take our advice and pick the one that's easiest to clean. You might not realize it now, but you're going to do a lot of cleaning in the months and years ahead. You'll clean tables, chairs, floors, windows, espresso machines, bathrooms, counters, garbage cans, napkin holders, and much, much more.

Your business serves things to eat and drink, after all, and if the furniture and accessories aren't clean, customers are unlikely to stick around to find out if the food and drinks are equally unclean.

Your design decisions will directly impact how easy or hard it is to keep your coffee shop clean and inviting. Pick a textured surface for tables, and you'll need more elbow grease to keep them spotless. The more decorations you put on the walls, the more dusting and wiping down you'll have to add to the cleaning schedule.

How do you know which materials are the most cleanable? Ask manufacturers for sample fabrics, tiles, and whatever other design elements you're considering, and run the samples through a gauntlet of spilled drinks, mashed-in chocolate cookie crumbs, and concentrated floor cleaner to find out which items resist stains best.

Counter *Talk*

The sofas and chairs Melissa chose for Brewpoint's Workshop location looked amazing, but now she regrets that she prioritized looks over commercial-grade functionality. Furniture that can withstand hundreds of people plopping down on it is a lot different from the furniture you'd choose for your home.

Buying for Tomorrow

Unless you plan to serve 10 million customers the first year and then retire, it's important to think about how the design you choose now will affect the decisions you can make in the future.

If, for example, you choose an unusual table design, how easy will it be to find that same design should a table fall apart or you move to a bigger location? Can you buy this table from more than one supplier so you're not stuck if the original supplier goes out of business?

You might like the look of a particular kind of mug, but the edges might chip easily or the special glaze might require that the mugs be hand-washed. Does the coolness of the design outweigh the potential replacement costs in future years, or the added cost of labor needed to hand-wash the mugs?

Outside Looking In

Everyone knows that first appearances can be deceiving—and yet we judge people, places, and things on first appearances all the same.

Prospective customers will approach your coffee shop the same way. If the outside of the shop doesn't welcome them, they'll never experience your rich-tasting coffee or the comfy lounge chairs you spent so much time looking for. They lose; you lose; everybody loses but your competition.

With this thought in mind, approach your location from every possible direction and consider what you can do to make your shop more inviting.

Sign of the Times

If you followed our advice in Chapter 7, you've investigated the town's signage laws and know how many signs you can put up for your coffee shop and in what sizes.

Laws give only a starting point, of course. Ask yourself a few questions to determine what you really need for signage. How will customers approach your business? If they drive down a one-way street, perhaps you can tilt your largest sign so it faces traffic. If you have a mix of car and foot traffic, place a sign in the window at a height where both pedestrians and auto passengers can see it. You can also consider neon "Open" signs or custom boxed signs that are lit from within.

Does your town allow sandwich boards on sidewalks? If so, you can use them to advertise daily specials or simply tell the world you're open for business.

Signs are all about being visible, so be sure to include your logo on any signs you purchase to give customers a visual hook. Use the same lettering style on your sign that you plan to use in the rest of your marketing materials, and choose a color scheme that can easily be read from a distance. If you're not sure what type of design will work best for your coffee shop, or where to get signage made, check out the "Signage" section in the list of products and services at the Sign Builder Illustrated Directory (signbuilderdirectory.com).

Window Dressing

Signs in windows help passers-by learn about your business, but covering up every inch of glass with come-ons and pitches is a bad idea. By letting people see into your shop, you're inviting them in and giving them a taste of what you have to offer.

Walk by the windows of your coffee shop and notice what parts of the store are visible from the outside. Be sure whatever you put in those locations—a stage for musicians, comfy chairs, or a cat bed for your cat-themed café—will draw customers in. Restaurants do this by always filling the tables by the windows first. They seem to be saying, "See, other people eat here—why not you?"

A final tip about windows: keep them sparkling. Clean windows show customers that you take care of your surroundings. You can easily hire a window washer to come by once or twice a week, or you (or an employee) can clean the windows yourself just as easily with nothing more than a squeegee, a lint-free cloth, and a bucket of soapy water. If you don't know how to get a streak-free shine, search YouTube for videos that demonstrate the process.

Dining Room Design

Once customers pass through your doors, what will they see? The counter with your smiling face behind it? Precisely arranged rows of tables and chairs? Shelves brimming with board games? A potted plant that blocks off a quarter of the room?

Again, the details of the room will depend on the style you want to present, and your coffee shop's theme, if it has one. Some examples of choices to make include the following:

* Solid wood tables that call to mind home comfort, or smaller metal and plastic tables that customers can push together

* A drink bar where customers can watch your employees do their magic, a refrigerated dessert cabinet customers can eye while waiting for drinks, or both

* The elements of your theme, such as comic books or craft supplies, on shelves, in a cabinet, or in baskets on each table

* Wallpaper, wainscoting, or a simple paint job

Whatever you choose, keep in mind the need for easy cleaning and long-term use. This means, for example, that carpets are definitely out because spills are a sure thing in a liquid-heavy environment; however, small carpets are welcome (and less likely to attract spills) in the entryway or a kids' play corner. The same goes for hardwood floors, which are difficult to install, scratch easily, and don't play well with liquids. Porcelain tiles, luxury vinyl tile, and laminate are your best bets for quick cleanups and a long life span.

<table>
<tr><td>**Counter** *Talk*</td><td>If you ever run more than one coffee shop, don't think they have to be exact duplicates of one another. Each Brewpoint location has a different type of décor. The Founders location has a travel theme with maps and globes. The Lexicon location, housed in a library, features simple dark wood and a logo. The Workshop location rocks an industrial chic interior. Each location boasts its own personality but has the same mission and product.</td></tr>
</table>

Pull Up a Chair

Depending on the space available, you'll need a combination of tables that accommodate two, four, and sometimes six customers. To mix things up you might place raised bar tables in one area, and upholstered chairs with small side tables in another.

Sit in the chairs as you're shopping and test them for comfort. Do they have enough back support? Will customers stick around long enough to order a second cup, or will they squirm uncomfortably in their chairs until they finish their drinks and bolt from your shop?

Whatever furniture you choose, if you have fixed seating—meaning it's attached to the walls or floor—the Americans with Disabilities Act (ADA) requires restaurants to make at least 5 percent of those tables accessible. By law, the tops of these tables must be between 28 and 34 inches above the ground with a minimum of 27 inches of clearance for legs and knees. Similarly, at least one section of the serving counter must be no higher than 34 inches.

For more information on how to make your coffee shop accessible, visit the ADA Guide for Small Businesses at ada.gov/smbustxt.htm. Your lawyer (remember her from Chapter 5?) can also advise you on the sections of the law that are relevant to your business.

To satisfy both the easy-clean and long-life provisos at the beginning of the chapter, be sure the feet of tables and chairs are padded so they don't scratch the floor. More importantly, laminate the tables (and counters) so they don't expand, contract, or absorb stains.

Climbing the Walls

Walls usually aren't too exciting, and that's okay because they don't need to be colorful or eye-grabbing. They're merely the backdrop against which business is conducted and drinks are drunk.

When it comes to dressing your walls, wallpaper can be a fine choice if you install a chair guard in all seating areas to minimize damage and you keep an adequate supply of replacement rolls on hand for the damage that will inevitably occur.

To avoid the time and cost of replacing wallpaper, you might opt for an old-fashioned paint job or perhaps a faux finish to add depth to your walls. Decorate with framed artwork or posters that match your café's theme, if you have one, and the mood you want to create.

Another possibility is to install a shelving unit, or slotted wallboard that holds brackets and shelves, to show off retail wares, such as French presses, teapots, mugs, or bags of whole roasted beans. (We cover retail possibilities in more detail in Chapter 17.)

Feeling lost? Pinterest (pinterest.com) is full of boards users have put together of coffee shop décor ideas. And if you're *really* feeling lost, consider adding a commercial interior designer or an interior decorator to your team of professionals.

Creating Ambiance

With the right approach, your coffee shop will be more than just a place to grab a cup of joe to go. As you plan your shop, think about how you can personalize all the details of a business that might normally go unnoticed. Let's look at some factors that can add to, or subtract from, the environment you're trying to build.

Designing with Color

At the end of Chapter 6, we discussed colors and the emotions they convey. Aside from your logo, perhaps you can add your brand colors to the edges or tops of tables, around doorframes, in pictures and artwork on the walls, or on the aprons your employees wear at work.

A good design principle is to use three colors, with 70 percent of the space being one color, 20 percent a second color, and the final 10 percent reserved for an accent color. Working within this plan keeps a space from having a monotonous checkerboard look with colors alternating regularly, or from having a room dominated entirely by one color.

Playing Music

When you think about setting a mood, whether romantic, festive, or hip, you often think in terms of music. The right tunes can go a long way toward cementing the style you want, and you can go all out with an installed multispeaker system or as low budget as an MP3 player dock and speakers.

A great source of coffee shop music is streaming music platforms like Pandora, Spotify, or Apple Music. These options don't subject your customers to radio ads like traditional radio might, and some subscription types let you filter out songs with explicit lyrics. Platforms like these have thousands of premade playlists, many of which are highly specialized in the type of music they play. Want to stick with alternative country, early twentieth-century blues, or lounge-style electronica? No problem.

Or maybe you want to offer live music on certain evenings or weekends. If so, in addition to creating a stage area, you'll need to consider equipment like speakers, mics, and special lighting.

Whatever music setup you decide on, remember that the goal is to make customers feel welcome. Keep the volume low enough that they can talk, study, and place orders.

Counter *Talk*

Be sure to comply with music laws. You need permission from the copyright holders to play music in your business; otherwise, you can be sued for copyright infringement. Streaming platforms like Spotify and Pandora offer business accounts that have the licensing built in. They're more expensive than personal accounts but cheaper than getting sued. Also, keep in mind that having the license to play *streaming* music doesn't give you the license to play *live* music. That, you have to get directly from the licensing companies. (See Chapter 13 for more details on live events.)

Lighting Your Shop

If you've ever worked for a long period of time under fluorescent lights, you already know you should avoid using them. Naturally, you'd prefer to use natural light, a.k.a. the sun, to set your shop aglow, but not every location comes blessed with large windows. Besides, natural light won't do much for you in winter months or during the late-night "hanging-out" hours.

To supplement whatever natural light you have, choose comfortable, soft lighting that allows patrons to read for hours without eyestrain. If you have a theme shop where customers need good lighting to take part—such as a board games, sewing, or books—task lighting is something else to consider.

If you install a drop ceiling to cover wires or avoid heating a large unused space overhead, you can install light fixtures at the same time to hide the wiring.

Don't forget that lighting can be more than merely functional. Many eating establishments use hanging lights with fancy glass sconces or elaborate painted paper shades, turning a functional item into a stylish feature.

Clearing the Air

Ideally, customers will enter your shop, breathe in the aroma of heated cinnamon rolls or your latest bean blend, and exclaim, "Mmm—that smells good!"

To keep those smells fresh and at the forefront of your customers' noses, ask employees to forgo perfumes and colognes that might compete with the smell of your goods. (You'll have the added benefit of avoiding possible allergic reactions from sensitive customers.)

Smoking in eateries and coffee shops is now forbidden in most states. If smoking isn't taboo in your state, you need to decide whether customers can light up after their lattes or whether the practice will drive off more people than it will attract.

Outfitting Your Employees

You've set the stage and have the props in place; now what about the actors? Many coffee shop owners are comfortable allowing their employees to wear whatever they want. After all, coffee shops are meant to be relaxing, right?

There's nothing wrong with that attitude, but imagine if you did require employees to wear some type of uniform, whether something as simple as black pants, a white shirt, and an apron, or a more elaborate custom-designed outfit.

To begin with, customers would always know who to approach with questions or orders, whether your employees are behind the bar or cleaning tables. The bigger effect, however, might be on the employees themselves. By requiring them to wear uniforms, you enforce a more professional standard and remind them they're there to serve others, not to goof off.

Counter Talk

As an example of what a typical coffee shop employee dress code looks like, Brewpoint's rules specify that employees must be well groomed, keep their hair pulled away from their face and eyes, wear an apron and close-toed shoes, avoid clothing that can snag on equipment, and limit jewelry to plain wedding bands. This dress code not only helps employees look professional but also keeps them safe. (You can find Brewpoint's full dress code in Appendix B.)

How far you want to go with a uniform depends on your budget and your desire to create a unified look. Employees can be expected to provide their own black pants and white shirts, for example, whereas you would have to spring for those customized T-shirts bearing your coffee bar's logo.

Aprons are a worthwhile expense, both to provide employees with a visual hook customers can easily recognize and to protect staff from spills while working. You can have the shop's logo embroidered or silk-screened onto the aprons, or you can simply adorn them with custom-engraved or -printed name pins or buttons, which you can easily find online.

Now that you know what your coffee shop will look like, let's talk about what goes in it—the equipment you'll use to brew the goods and also to grind, measure, and refrigerate those goods.

Equipping Your Shop

You've decided whether or not to go with a theme for your coffee shop, and you've started to plan your shop's design. That's important because customers love a coffee shop with an attractive style and comfortable atmosphere. But if you don't also plan for your coffee shop's equipment and supplies, you won't have anything to serve in that shop with an attractive style and comfortable atmosphere.

Operating a coffee shop requires a wide variety of machines and tools to satisfy your customers' desires. It can be overwhelming to think about everything you need, so in this chapter, we share the essentials you should acquire as well as some bonus items you might like to have.

Essentials You Can't Do Without

Some equipment and furnishings are more essential than others. The exact list of equipment you need for your coffee shop varies depending on which food and drinks you decide to serve (topics we cover in Chapters 14 through 17), but some pieces of equipment are absolute must-haves.

As you shop for the items in this chapter, be sure to consider the following:

* **Electrical requirements.** Espresso machines, for instance, can require 115, 220, or 240 volts, and high-volume, high-power dishwashers also might need more juice than the 120 volts available from a standard American outlet. Consider these electrical requirements when you design the kitchen and create counter space (a topic we cover in Chapter 11).

* **Warranties and service plans.** Does the retailer or wholesaler that sells the equipment also service it, or will you have to ship the equipment to them for service? Can the retailer recommend local shops that can help you out in a pinch? (Not that your machine will ever desert you in a time of need, we say with fingers crossed while knocking on wood.)

* **Color, design, and cost.** Now that you've decided on a style, you need to consider the look of the equipment plus whether it fits your budget.

* **National Sanitation Foundation (NSF) certification.** The NSF has standards for commercial foodservice equipment for sanitation, electrical safety, and energy efficiency. All equipment you purchase for the coffee bar should bear an NSF label to show that the design was inspected and met NSF standards. For more information on these standards, visit nsf.org.

Now, on to the equipment and supplies you need to get your shop up and running.

Coffee-Brewing System

If you want to make a living running a coffee shop, you need a coffee-brewing system with a bit more *oomph* than a single 12-cup machine.

You could go the old-fashioned route and buy two or three brewers with hot plates that hold multiple glass carafes. This setup is still common in convenience stores, all-night diners, and other locations that don't rely on coffee sales for their main source of income. Coffee made this way tastes fine—for a while—but the air contact and constant heat quickly ages the coffee, leading to a lot of waste on slower-selling decaffeinated and flavored coffees.

A better choice is a system that brews directly into airtight thermal carafes. Coffee brewed this way retains its original flavor for up to 3 hours, which reduces both waste and labor costs because an employee won't have to remake specialized coffees every hour or so.

Brewing systems are either *in-line,* hooked directly into the plumbing system so they can draw water as needed, or *pour-over,* which works exactly like it sounds. Choose between the two options based on, first, your potential remodeling costs if you need to run water lines to accommodate an in-line system, and second, your expected level of sales. Pour-over systems are more hands-on, so if you're setting up in a high-volume location, you might prefer in-line.

Purchase at least twice as many carafes as the number of coffee types you plan to offer each day. So if, for instance, you'll serve a medium roast, a dark roast, a special blend, and a flavored coffee each day, purchase at least eight carafes so you can brew a second batch of each before the first carafe runs dry.

Espresso Machine

You have two major choices when purchasing an espresso machine—how many *groups* the machine handles, and how automatic it is.

Espresso machines typically come in two-, three-, and four-group models, which means the machine can make two, three, or four servings of espresso at one time. Choose the number of groups based on your budget and expected sales volume.

The machines also vary in how much attention they need while making espresso. Manual espresso machines require you to heat the water separately and then squeeze the water through the coffee by pulling down on a lever—this is where we get the phrase "pulling a shot." Unless you're working on your upper body strength, we suggest passing on these machines, as the quality of the espresso will vary from shot to shot.

Semiautomatic machines take the hard labor out of the process. You push a button to both start and stop the flow of water through the grounds, which makes for reliable water pressure and also lets you control the extraction time. This is the most common type of machine used in specialty coffee shops. After you've learned how to use it correctly, it provides the best espresso consistently.

Fully automatic machines require only one button push because both the water pressure and the extraction time are regulated. These machines generally come with buttons for single espresso, double espresso, short espresso, and so on, so you can pick the serving to match the order. Restaurants that don't hang their reputation on the quality of their espresso tend to favor these machines because they're easiest to operate.

Superautomatic machines grind the beans, pump the water, and (in some cases) clean themselves. This sounds amazing, but you probably don't need to purchase a machine this elaborate. A semiautomatic machine should be perfect for your shop.

The espresso machine comes with at least one steaming wand and a hot water tap. We tell you how to pull the shots in Chapter 15.

Counter *Talk* Wondering what kind of espresso machine Brewpoint uses? It's a semiautomatic machine with two groups.

Grinder

To make superb coffee, you need to grind the beans in-house each day because the beans lose their flavor quickly after being ground. A *batch grinder* holds exactly the right amount of beans to make one pot of coffee, but if you opt for a thermal carafe brewing system, you should verify that a batch grinder will work for you.

As with the coffee carafes, it's a good idea to purchase two grinders so you can reserve one solely for use with flavored coffees. What's more, espresso grinders grind the beans much finer than coffee grinders, so you might need yet another grinder, depending on the model you choose.

Counter *Talk*   Choosing between a fancy espresso machine and an extra-nice grinder? If you can splurge on only one item, Melissa recommends buying the better grinder and skimping on the fancy espresso machine. Good grinders have more impact on the quality of your espresso shots than the extra bells and whistles on a pricey espresso machine.

Scale

If you sell coffee beans, whether roasted or green, you absolutely need a scale. It should be labeled "legal for trade" so there's no question about proper measurements and shaped so you can easily pour beans into the bag for delivery.

Even if you don't sell beans, a scale is still vital for measuring beans each time before you grind them. For most people, repetition is boring; for great coffee, repetition is the key to success.

Counter *Talk*   Brewpoint employees uses their scales for three tasks: to measure the weight of espresso grinds, to measure the weight of espresso shots, and to weigh batches of coffee for the brewer.

Refrigerator/Cooler

You need at least one refrigerator up front to hold the milk and cream you'll use while making drinks. If you plan to offer food, you might need a larger fridge to hold meat and sandwich fixings that aren't being kept in the prep area.

If you sell soda and other bottled drinks, decide whether to purchase a second, grab-and-go cooler to place near the counter so customers can pick out their own drinks, or use one refrigerator for both purposes. The first option costs more, yet encourages spur-of-the-moment sales because the sweet, refreshing drinks are right in front of your customers. The second option is better for tight budgets or tight operating quarters.

Counter *Talk*   Melissa recommends having as many fridges as you can fit. Brewpoint's original location goes through 20 gallons of milks a day, so imagine how many refrigerators are required to hold enough milk for a couple days.

Freezer

Depending on your menu, you also might want a freezer. For example, if you decide to offer fruit smoothies, you'll need one to store frozen fruit. Brewpoint has a freezer for the pastries that are delivered weekly; when the shop runs low, a staff member pulls out more to defrost.

You can find freezers in all sizes to meet your needs, from short refrigerator/freezers with a worktop for the most efficient use of space to large walk-in freezers—although you'd need to be selling an awful lot of smoothies to need one that big!

Food Display Case

Any business that sells coffee should also sell tasty treats, such as pastries, chocolate-chip cookies, cannoli, or cheesecake. Your choice of foods for sale will determine what type of display case you need. (See Chapter 17 for more on food, plus noncoffee drinks you can sell.)

By sticking with cookies and biscotti, brownies, and other room-temperature-safe goodies, you can use countertop displays or plates covered with glass domes. (In general, stick with glass over plastic because glass is more scratch-resistant and holds up better over time.) For cheesecakes and pies, you must use a refrigerated display case, preferably one that circulates air to prevent condensation inside the case.

Dishwasher

You'll use paper cups for to-go orders, but if you're going for a nice sit-down atmosphere inside your shop, you'll have plenty of plates, mugs, glasses, and other dishes and silverware to clean. Realistically, the number of spoons you'll use behind the counter alone might be enough to merit a dishwasher.

You can try to get away with an employee in rubber gloves and an apron, but that's hardly cost effective. Invest in a high-temperature, fast-running automatic dishwasher that can handle your needs. Choose high temperature over low because these machines have a shorter drying cycle, use less water, and remove grease and lipstick without resorting to chemicals.

An automatic dishwasher is yet another item that needs access to water lines, drainage, and (in some cases) high-voltage wiring, but the benefits are worth the trouble.

Cash Register

Sure, you could run a business with a calculator and cash box, but the harm done to your business would cost far more than the price of a good cash register or point-of-sale (POS) system (which we discuss in Chapter 20).

In addition to automatically determining sales tax and showing the proper amount of change a customer receives, electronic cash registers and POS systems allow you to generate data reports that divide sales into categories you determine. Want to know how many iced coffees you sold in July? How sales of mochaccinos compare to those of cappuccinos? Whether your brownie inventory matches the number of sales? What sales were like between 11 and 11:30 A.M.? The sales tape or POS system can tell you everything you want to know.

What's more, once you program it, the system will charge (or not charge) sales tax as appropriate and let you know how much to forward to your state tax bureau. Many cash registers also can be used as a time clock, which makes it easy for employees to punch in and out and you to determine who's owed what.

Security System

We hate to say it, but crime happens. Burglars break into shops to steal money, equipment, or products, and thieves pinch products off the shelves—or even attempt to reach over the counter and grab cash when the barista isn't looking. (We have more on dealing with robberies and other emergencies in Chapter 21.)

That's why it's crucial to have a good security system. Your landlord might have one already installed for you, in which case all you need to do is learn how to use it. Otherwise, it's on you to select a system, have it installed, and teach your employees how to use it.

Here are some security suggestions to consider:

* **Good lighting.** Be sure your coffee shop, the entrances, the parking lot, and the area around your shop are illuminated at all times to deter burglars, vandals, and other criminals who would rather carry out their bad deeds under cover of darkness.

* **A burglar alarm.** A good alarm system on the doors not only emits a loud alarm sound, but also alerts the local police station.

* **Video surveillance.** A video camera enables you to review footage to help police catch a thief after a crime and also serves as a deterrent. Criminals likely will think twice before stealing or creating other trouble in your shop if they know they're being recorded. (And staff will think twice before taking cash from the till.) Some businesses even set up dummy cameras just to serve as a deterrent.

No single security system is perfect, which is why experts recommend layering different types of systems for the most protection. Installing good lighting, a burglar alarm, and video cameras in and around your shop goes a long way toward preventing crime.

If you have any particular concerns about protecting your business not covered here—such as smash-and-grab burglaries where thieves break through the front window to get in—talk to your local police and bring in a retail security consultant to make suggestions based on your shop and your area.

Counter *Talk*

Brewpoint has a Nest camera system, and Melissa pays for the ability to save all the data to the cloud. This has allowed her to look back on customer/employee disputes. Although she can't hear the discussion (the recording is visual only), the video gives her a good idea of whether the staff member was out of line or the customer was just having a bad day. The security system also deters theft, gives Melissa the ability to check in with staff and see how busy the shops are, and helps her document issues the landlord needs to fix.

The Best of the Nonessentials

Certain types of equipment are essential for anyone entering the coffee shop business, but other machines and systems depend on what and where you sell. We cover the foods and drinks you should consider offering in more detail in Part 4, but for now, think about whether the following might fit in—or break—your budget.

Water Treatment System

The bulk of your coffee shop sales will be from coffee and espresso, and the bulk of coffee and espresso is water. Coffee's flavor comes from the essences extracted from the beans, but that flavor can be destroyed if you make the drinks with bad-tasting water. To counteract water woes, consider using a water filtration system that uses a paper and carbon filter to screen out foul-tasting and odor-carrying particles.

Hard water, which contains a high mineral content, is another concern for coffee shop owners because as the water passes through your espresso machine, it will leave mineral deposits that eventually clog the pipes.

You can call the town's water department to ask whether you need to be concerned about hard water damaging your machines. If that's a possibility, you might consider attaching a water softener, either one with disposable cartridges or a rechargeable device, to the water intake on your espresso machine.

Smoothie and Juice Machines

The range of smoothies you can offer is limited only by your imagination—and, of course, the sensitivity of your customers' palates. Blended frozen coffee drinks are a natural choice for a coffee shop, especially if you're located in a part of the country where the sidewalks sizzle in the summertime.

If you have room to set up a second smoothie machine, you could offer fruit smoothies to give caffeine-avoiding or health-conscious customers another choice on the menu.

You also could opt for a juice machine to create vitamin-packed juice beverages. We talk about juice, smoothies, and other noncoffee drinks you can add to your menu in Chapter 17.

Blender

Milkshakes, both caffeinated coffee-flavored ones and the more traditional ice-cream kind, are another cool option you can offer customers. Some milkshake makers can cost up to $200, but you can probably make do with a blender priced in the low double digits because milkshakes will comprise only a small fraction of your business.

Caveat emptor though: if you go low budget on a blender, avoid adding chunks of ice or large ice cubes to the blender whenever possible. Ice can destroy inexpensive blenders quickly.

Oven, Microwave, and Grill

To capture the crowd that wants more than drinks and treats, you might consider selling more substantial food like sandwiches and wraps. Depending on how heavily you want to get involved in food preparation, consider purchasing a toaster oven (for mini pizzas or grinders), a grill (for grilled cheese and other toasted sandwiches), or a microwave (to melt cheese and heat deli meats). These appliances don't need much space and require nothing in the way of electricity beyond a standard outlet. Larger ovens naturally take up a larger space, not to mention require access to natural gas or propane.

Depending on the foods you plan to serve, you should check in with your local health agency to find out what the regulations are regarding the disposal of grease. Carefully consider these drawbacks before jumping into this side of the food biz. (We lay down the legal nitty-gritty of food sales in Chapter 17.)

Finding Equipment Suppliers

You could go to your local department store and purchase an espresso machine off the shelf, but that's probably not the best way to equip your coffee shop. For one thing, the consumer-grade machines sold in department stores aren't made to handle the high volume you're going to demand of them in your commercial coffee shop. Two or three shots a day, yes; two or three hundred, not really.

Of greater concern is the level of support the manufacturer of this equipment can offer you. If your home coffee machine breaks, you probably just do without until you can go to the store to buy a new one. If the coffee-brewing system that pumps the lifeblood of your business breaks, you need a repair or replacement, and you need it now.

When you start talking with equipment suppliers, begin evaluating the supplier from the first "Hello." Everything the supplier does tells you about the level of service you can expect. Does the supplier answer the phone in a courteous and professional manner? Does he answer politely, even when you're only calling to ask questions, or does he bark, "Call me when you're ready to buy," and hang up? Does he return your phone message after an hour —or after a week? Is he more concerned with his bottom line than yours? If a supplier tries to pressure you into making a deal, even going so far as to offer a special discount if you sign that instant, walk away.

Also, insist on a demonstration. Whether you meet with a supplier in a retail location or at a showroom, try out the machines so you can see how each one handles. Have him demonstrate the different features and explain how they benefit you. Ask whether your employees can receive training directly from his company instead of secondhand through you.

Be sure to ask for references—and call them. Any supplier with a good track record has satisfied customers he can offer as references. Don't just take him on his word, though. Call these folks and find out how the supplier has treated them throughout their relationship, especially in emergency situations.

Remember, too, that price is only part of the picture. Suppliers who boast of nothing more than low, low prices usually have nothing more to offer. The thought of saving a few—or a few hundred—dollars might be enticing, but don't think of this purchase as a one-shot deal.

Besides the need for servicing and maintenance, think of yourself as partnering with the supplier to build a stronger company. If you move to a bigger location or want to open a second store at some point, your supplier will be ready to help you upgrade equipment or otherwise support the expansion. When you win, he wins, too, and a sole focus on low prices usually undermines this relationship.

Counter *Talk*

If you buy equipment online, the warranty often covers only major issues upon delivery, or it covers parts but not the labor on the repair. When Melissa buys online, she resigns herself to the fact that if the equipment needs repairs, it comes out of the business's pocket.

Buying, Leasing, or Renting?

For some equipment, the decision to rent or buy is obvious. After all, paying interest on a $50 scale doesn't make much financial sense. (You could ask your accountant to verify this, but that would also set you back a few bucks you didn't need to spend.)

Costlier purchases, such as a decent-size refrigerator or a top-of-the-line espresso machine, run into the four figures, and that might be hard to cough up all at once. You can cover these costs in a few different ways.

You could borrow funds for all equipment purchases. In Chapter 4, which covered how to create a business plan, we included equipment among your initial costs. If you've followed this example, you should have the funds for equipment already on hand.

You also could take out individual loans with equipment vendors. Vendors may or may not be as competitive as banks and other financial institutions when it comes to setting interest rates for loans. We've seen cases where equipment vendors charge 0 percent interest over the first 12 months of the loan, and other cases where the interest rates would make you dizzy.

You might be able to work with a vendor that offers free equipment. Some food and drink vendors provide free equipment, but naturally there are strings attached. These start with the requirement that you carry that vendor's products, usually on an exclusive basis, and post the vendor's brand on the equipment and possibly the outside of your store.

The vendor might set sales goals that require you to purchase a minimum amount of product every sales period. If you don't sell enough, say, bottled iced tea to meet the quota, too bad—your contract says you have to buy it anyway (or that you have to pay a monthly fee if you don't hit your quota). The contract will also require you to stick with the vendor for a certain number of months. Combined with the purchasing requirements, this nets the vendor a certain amount of money, thus paying for the "free" equipment he provided.

You could lease your equipment instead of buying it outright if that works better for you. You don't have to pay for your equipment all at once, and you could decide to lease certain items on a month-to-month basis, which would likely be cheaper than the monthly cost of repaying a loan. At the end of the lease period, you typically have the option to buy the equipment at fair market value or for a token $1 payment. Leasing is cheaper on a monthly basis compared to a loan, but the cost is generally higher in the long run because if you don't buy, you'll have spent a lot of money with nothing permanent to show for it. And if you do buy, you'll pay more than you would have if you had bought the equipment up front.

Renting equipment might make sense if you're unsure of how large a cooler you need or whether you need a two- or three-group espresso machine. If you can test out this equipment for a while as you determine whether it meets your needs, it might be worth the added expense of a month or two's rent on top of the price of the equipment itself.

Counter *Talk*

Coffee shop equipment is expensive, and even if it's under warranty, you may need to send it out for a repair if it breaks, which means you're without a grinder or an espresso machine until it's fixed. It makes sense to learn how to repair your own equipment whenever you can. Some manufacturers offer free classes that teach customers simple maintenance and repairs. Angelo took some of these classes, and now he can maintain and repair equipment after hours so it doesn't affect business operations.

Now that you have the equipment you need, it's time to figure out where to put it. In the next chapter, we talk about how to set up your counter space, lay out a prep area, find the best spot for your espresso machine, and make other layout decisions.

Kitchen and Restroom Layout and Design

Ideally, customers at your coffee shop will be able to enjoy their drinks and snacks and relax in an inviting environment in the company of their friends. When designing your dining room, which we talked a bit about in Chapter 9, this means focusing on style and comfort.

Style and comfort are also important when you design the kitchen and counter areas, but here *comfort* has a different meaning—one that doesn't include plush chairs. In this case, it means your customers can quickly and easily see where and how to order, pay, and pick up their drinks. Customers hate having to guess where the line ends or where they should stand while their drinks are being made. If you do a good job laying out your counter area, you can keep the customer line flowing smoothly and put their minds at ease.

The same goal applies to the space *behind* the counter. Your employees should be able to work around each other with ease so they can serve customers quickly and safely.

Designing safe, efficient, and user-friendly prep areas and counter space creates a good layout that helps you run your business. Potential landlords will want to see your layout before they offer you a lease, too, so let's look at some smart ways to set up your shop.

Designing Your Counter Space

Whatever the size of your shop, most of the action—both monetarily and physically—takes place in an area roughly 50 square feet in size: the counter and the space on both sides of it. This is where customers order food and drinks and employees make them. If you design the counter well, this system will flow smoothly and make everyone happy.

For Your Customer

From your customer's point of view, three things happen at the counter: she orders a drink, she pays for the drink, and she picks it up.

This process needs to flow as smoothly as possible, which means dividing the counter into clear, distinct regions. Pick one end of the counter to be the place to order, preferably the end nearest the door because that's where customers will naturally drift, and deliver the goods at the other end of the counter.

The menu should be fully visible to customers whether they're approaching the cash register or waiting in line to order. You don't want any customer to have to move back and forth along the counter to see the menu. This disrupts the flow and pace of business and makes it more difficult for arriving customers to see where the line is.

You can locate the register at the one end of the counter or a bit farther down toward the prep area. The idea is to keep customers moving, so if one customer moves to the side to pay, the next customer can place her order, depending on how many employees are working.

As with the tables and chairs in your business, which we discussed in Chapter 9, the Americans with Disabilities Act requires that your counter be accessible to everyone. In particular, this means making a portion of the main counter no higher than 34 inches and at least 60 inches long. The counter where customers pick up food must be similarly accessible.

When customers order, tell them where to wait for their goods, which encourages them to move down the counter, or invite them to sit and you'll bring their order to them.

Counter Talk

Depending on your sales and customer base, you may want more than one register. If Brewpoint had the space, Melissa would love to have two registers to help the line move faster. For the location near a train station, a self-checkout kiosk for grab-and-go items or a second register just for simple coffee purchases would help commuters get in and out fast.

For You

Although you want customers to find their way around the counter quickly, you also want to use this space to sell goods. You can achieve this in a number of different ways.

You could use this space to feature the food. Display cookies and other nonrefrigerated goods on the counter in food display cases, which we describe in Chapter 10. Opt for different-size cases so you can rearrange them often to make the choice of offerings look fresh each day. Having many cases also allows you to easily adjust the goods you offer based on sales. Caramel brownies not selling? Wash out the case and try rocky road brownies instead.

Also arrange beverage coolers and refrigerated display cases so customers pass them as they approach the counter. Customers won't automatically buy everything they see (sadly), but if they never see goodies—or see them only after ordering—you probably won't get the sales you expected.

From time to time, set out samples. Cut some cookies and coffee cakes into small portions and offer a plate of samples where customers order. Sure, they know you're doing this to boost sales, not out of the goodness of your heart, but sometimes the samples taste so good they happily succumb to your mercantile desires.

As tempting as it may be, don't try to pass off day-old goods as samples. If what your customer tastes isn't the very best you have to offer, you risk turning away future sales.

Advertise other services you offer, too. Do you host classes on how to roast coffee beans? Will you create a custom blend for a wedding present or corporate gift? Tell customers about these services by placing flyers in a small counter display. These displays are also good for hiding the ugly backsides of cash registers where other displays won't fit.

Whatever you place on the counter, be sure to leave obvious spaces open where the customer is to order, pay, and pick up their goods. Design the counter so they know where to go. Don't make them guess.

Laying Out Your Prep Area

Now let's look at the space behind the counter. You and your employees will spend most of your working hours in this area, which makes it imperative that the space be well organized. You don't want to have to say "Excuse me" every time you turn around because you bump into someone—especially someone carrying a hot beverage!

What's more, the space needs to facilitate speed and efficiency so customers get their drinks and food quickly. The slower your delivery time, the lower your sales volume.

Front and Center

The most important question to start with when designing your work space is also the easiest to answer: where do you put the espresso machine? The answer: on the main counter between where customers order and where they pick up their drinks. Placing the espresso machine here eases the flow of customers down the counter while allowing the employee working the machine to hear orders as they're placed and start working on the drinks.

Don't place the espresso machine on the back counter. Employees will have to turn their backs on customers to make drinks, and your customers will be able to see exactly what goes into making an espresso. (We're not worried about protecting trade secrets here, only that the process is messy and seeing it might diminish the romance of the finished product.)

Along the same lines, place the coffee carafes on the front counter so employees can pour drinks and hand them directly to customers. The shelf holding the carafes might need to be lower than the counter so employees and customers can see each other eye to eye.

Keep espresso cups, coffee mugs, and saucers close at hand so employees don't even need to take a step as they prepare drinks.

Milk, cream, sugar, and other coffee condiments should be placed either on the main counter, past the area where customers pick up drinks, or at a separate station nearby. Whichever you choose, make this area wide enough so more than one customer can use it at once. Put a garbage can inside the counter with a hole over it so customers can dispose of their stirring sticks and teabags without having to touch or see a garbage can.

On the Back Counter

Once you know where to put the espresso machine, it's time to find a spot for the coffee-brewing system, grinder, and scales. Unlike the espresso machine, the brewing system can go on the back counter because employees won't be attending to specific customers while using it. The brewing system requires special electrical and plumbing hookups, so keep that in mind when deciding where to install it.

Blenders, smoothie machines, microwave ovens, grills, and other food and drink preparation equipment can all go on the back counter. Each of these machines requires an electrical outlet, and some require more than the standard 120 volts, so work closely with your contractor or electrician to meet these needs. Keep grills and ovens separate from other machines so you have all the hot stuff in one place.

Store mugs, plastic cups, plates, and so on next to the machines where they'll be used. Employees shouldn't have to walk back and forth for supplies, which slows delivery time and increases the risk of bumps and spills.

In addition to the plumbing hookup for the brewing system, have a sink installed in the back counter so employees can wash their hands regularly and clean up spills more easily. Installing a hand sink isn't just a good idea by the way—it's the law. Contact your local health department for advice on where hand sinks should be placed in relation to food preparation areas.

Resist the urge to fill every available space with equipment. Leave room for food and drink preparation and for people to set boxes when they're bringing goods and supplies out from the back room.

Stored Away

The espresso machine, the brewing system, the cash register, and everything else in the prep area is on counters, ready to be used. But what's underneath those counters? Well, pretty much everything you don't need immediately on hand, such as paper products, straws and stirrers, napkins, paper towels, and much more.

Use the under-the-counter space for cabinets and shelves to hold extra supplies. Just don't use open shelving because a single spill—and there will be a lot more than just one—could ruin a lot of goods.

Label the cabinet doors with what's inside. Sure, you may know the contents of every cabinet, but new employees won't, and making them hunt for extra napkins so they can refill dispensers is a waste of time.

Depending on the counter layout, you might also place a small refrigerator or refrigerator/freezer combo under the brewing system or espresso machine so milk, cream, half-and-half, and fruit for smoothies are always within reach. Again, the goal is always to improve efficiency and lower the customer's wait time between order and pick-up.

Counter *Talk*

Layout and equipment regulations vary depending on your location. Do you need a grease trap? Is the plumbing compliant? Melissa suggests contacting your city's economic development director, who might be able to point you to the people who can help you parse out the rules.

Planning Your Back Room

The goal of the front and back counter layout is to have the equipment accessible, the supplies organized and labeled, and the employees working smoothly without interruption. All this should apply to your back room as well.

Thinking Practical, Not Pretty

At the heart of the back room is possibly the least glamorous, yet most needed element of any dining establishment: the sink and dishwasher. We don't recommend serving everything in disposable packaging unless your shop has more of a grab-and-go vibe—sit-down customers prefer the solid feel of ceramic, glass, and plastic—so you'll be dealing with a lot of dirty dishes.

As with the hand sink in the prep area, contact the local health department to see how many and what type of sinks you need to install in the back room. Triple sinks are commonly required, with the sinks divided into washing, rinsing, and sanitizing stations. The local health department likely has rules on where to locate the mop sink as well.

In addition to cleaning dishes, you'll use the back room to store many other supplies: paper towels, toilet paper, and everything else that's too big to fit underneath the service counters. Again, label every shelf so employees know where to find supplies as well as where to put items when restocking.

Keep black markers handy, perhaps on strings hanging from different shelves, so employees can mark boxes that are otherwise unlabeled. This makes it easier to quickly find, say, plastic lids for large cups versus small ones. Labeling also speeds the counting during inventory time.

Designating a Break Room

Depending on the size of your location, you might devote space to an office or break room. An office gives you a spot to write checks for vendors, interview applicants, or make phone calls without interruption. A break room gives your employees a place to escape the sales floor during their meal breaks. Also, many health departments require lockers or some type of secure area where employees can safely store their coats, handbags, and backpacks.

Keep in mind that you can't treat an office the same as a break room. If employees can eat lunch in your office, for example, you need to keep business and employee records under lock and key so they can't peruse information they shouldn't see, such as a coworker's rate of pay. If the office is locked when you're not in it, you don't have to worry about such things.

Whether or not you set up an office or a break room or both, you need a safe place to store money: rolls of change, the day's receipts, and paychecks. What could be safer than a safe? Find room for the safe in the office, if possible, but if you don't have an office, the break room or back room will have to do.

Whatever you decide, don't forget that you won't be selling anything from the office and you can't seat customers in the break room. Sure, you'd ideally like to create spaces for yourself and for your employees, but be sure to devote enough space to the business end of your business first.

Installing a Restroom (or Two)

Finally, we arrive at the room no one wants to think about but all of us turn to in time of need. As with an office or a break room, restrooms take up space that could otherwise be devoted to customer seating or merchandise shelves. The main difference is that restrooms are essential to keeping customers happy.

You could set up a restroom that's accessible only to employees, but this only annoys customers, who will leave instead of sticking around for refills and treats, or annoys you, when customers inevitably request access.

Although it requires more time, planning, and money, do yourself, your employees, and your customers a favor and install a customer restroom. Depending on the size of your location and the percentage of customers you expect to dine in-house, you might even have separate restrooms for men and women.

Counter *Talk*   Even better might be to have two gender-neutral restrooms—the kind that are a single room with a lock on the door. This setup helps solve the problem of the ladies' room having a long line while the men's room is empty. Brewpoint has gender-neutral restrooms, but because of local regulations, one of them has to have a urinal in it.

Once again, be sure to contact the local health department to find out what's required in a restroom in terms of size, handrails, and so on before you actually start to build. Also get in touch with your city code officials to find out how to ensure your restrooms comply with the Americans with Disabilities Act.

Don't let the restroom look like an afterthought compared with the rest of your shop. Carry the style and design of the coffee shop into the restroom, too, repeating colors, for example, or using mirrors that match those in the seating area. Whatever design you choose, though, remember to use materials that allow for easy cleaning.

You've now set the stage for your customers to buy their drink or snack in an inviting but functional space and for your employees to do their work quickly and safely. What's missing? The people who will help make it all happen. In the next chapter, you learn how to hire the employees who not only make and serve the amazing coffee drinks you'll sell day in and day out but also help arrange events, interact with your customers, and generally keep everything humming along in your coffee shop.

Hiring a Crew

When it comes time to staff your coffee bar, you'd probably prefer to clone yourself a half dozen times and be done with it. After all, you know how you want customers treated, you know the cleaning and restocking procedures, you know everything that needs to happen to make your shop a success, and you know you'd do a great job. But because you can't do that, the next best thing is to hire other people and train them on how to treat customers, clean and restock the coffee shop, and all the rest.

In this chapter, we help you interview prospects, train them, determine what to pay them, and—should they not prove to be your equal—nudge them on to greener pastures.

Finding Help

Believe it or not, it's bad form to walk into a competing coffee shop and shout, "Who wants to quit this dump and come work for me?" Besides, anyone who would leave their current employer that way would likely turn traitor on you just as quickly.

You'll have much better luck finding potential employees by spreading the word through newspaper ads, online job boards, social media, and word-of-mouth.

There's an art to writing and placing job ads that attract qualified applicants—especially in a tight labor market, and *especially* if you can't pay top wages. Here's our advice for making it happen.

Compiling the Ad

Potential applicants need to know what the requirements of the job are. Before that can happen, *you* need to know what the requirements of the job are. It's helpful to make a list of all the elements you'll want to include in a job ad, including the following:

* The job title

* Where the coffee shop is located

* If the job is full-time or part-time

* A description of your ideal candidate

* The salary range

* Your company's mission and values

* What the employee's responsibilities will be

* The availability you require, such as mornings or weekends

* The non-negotiable skills and experience the employee has to have (Running a cat-themed shop? Only cat lovers need apply.)

Include as much of this as possible in your job ad, and applicants won't be surprised later.

Something else to include in your ad: a little of yourself. To help attract good candidates, add personality to your job postings. This helps you find employees who are a good match for your personality, your work style, and your coffee shop. If you're the jokey type, include a joke in your ad. If you're more serious and want your shop to have an upscale vibe, use industry jargon and a more serious tone.

Covering Your Bases

Be sure to post your job ad in all the usual places:

* Place a classified ad in the local newspaper.

* Post your ad on job-finding platforms like Indeed (indeed.com) or Monster (monster.com). Most job sites charge job posters, so do some research to figure out which is the best site for you.

* Post your ad on craigslist (craigslist.com), which costs $25 for each category you post in; select "food/beverage/hospitality." Because craigslist is specific to your area, you'll be reaching out only to applicants near your place of business.

* Try the Nextdoor app (nextdoor.com). Before being accepted into Nextdoor, you need to become verified as actually living in the neighborhood you want to join. Then you can post a help-wanted ad that reaches people in that area.

* If you're looking for a particular type of person, post where they hang out. For example, when looking for coffee shop staff, you might hang a help-wanted flyer at the local university, post your job ad in a LinkedIn group for baristas, or tweet it out on Twitter with relevant hashtags. Looking for a store manager? Try LinkedIn and Facebook groups for the restaurant industry, industry websites, or trade magazines.

* Place a sign in the window that says you're hiring. Some of your best future staff members are current customers who love what you do!

Of course, you may not need to post your jobs in all these suggested spots. If the job market is tight and you don't want to be inundated with applications, try one or two at a time.

Gathering Applicants

Each potential employee should fill out an application before you even consider hiring them, whether through an online application system or a paper application in your shop. The application should include contact information, employment history, education, and pay expectations.

The application is your first step toward dividing applicants into two categories: "Maybe" and "No Thanks." If an applicant can't fill out the application properly, for example, she probably won't be able to handle a payment system or juggle multiple orders. If his past jobs all lasted less than a month, he might be too flaky to trust with the responsibility of opening or closing the shop.

Luckily, the internet abounds with free application templates, including restaurant-specific ones from websites like Template.net. Just be sure to run any applications you plan to use by your lawyer to ensure you don't run afoul of any employment laws.

Interviewing Candidates

Now, it's time to invite the applicants on your "Maybe" list in for an in-person interview. You can interview applicants anywhere, but if you meet them in your coffee shop, they can see where they'll be working and how things are run. This gives them a chance to ask questions, potentially impressing you with their smarts and curiosity, or ignore what's going on around them, which will give you an entirely different (but just as valuable) impression.

You've probably been in the interviewee hot seat a number of times. Now it's your turn to ask the questions and try to determine who's telling you the truth and who's just telling you what they think you want to hear.

Contact all the applicants who sound promising, even if you have fewer positions to fill than the number of applicants. After all, you never know who will have found a job in the meantime or who won't work out.

Not sure how to conduct an interview? Don't worry—the applicant will likely be more nervous than you, and by following our advice, you'll learn everything you need to make the right hiring decisions for your business.

Counter *Talk*   To save time, Melissa conducts 10- to 15-minute phone interviews with the "Maybe" applicants. If she feels they're a good fit, she passes them on to a general manager for an in-person interview. If they do well there, they spend an hour or so interacting with customers at the register as a final trial. This also lets the applicant bow out if they decide the job isn't what they were hoping.

Planning Your Questions

When interviewing candidates, ask questions that explore an applicant's work history while simultaneously answering how the applicant will help you. Avoid asking questions that can be answered with a simple "yes" or "no." Sample questions might include the following:

* What experience do you have in food service and customer service?

* What was your worst working experience, and why?

* What are your two main strengths and weaknesses?

* Why are you interested in this job?

* How would you describe your current job and supervisor?

Write down your questions as you plan for the interviews. Refer to them while you speak to applicants so you remember what to ask and ask everyone the same questions, making it easier for you to compare apples to apples later.

Feel free to go off-list, too. Having the application as well as an applicant's work history in front of you can inspire questions during the interview you might not have thought of beforehand.

Gathering First Impressions

Don't feel you have to jump into the interview right away. Try some small talk first to break the ice and put the applicant at ease. One way to do this is to describe your business and the positions for which you're interviewing. Explain what traits are most important to you: customer service, for example, or teamwork and mutual support. Remember, in a tight labor market, you're selling the job as much as the applicants are selling themselves!

While you're chatting up the applicant, notice the details. Is he groomed and dressed appropriately for your business? Does he smile and look enthusiastic about the job? First impressions don't always tell the whole story, but they help you build a complete picture of an applicant.

> **Counter Talk**   Melissa recommends hiring for values over skill. You can always train someone in coffee skills, but you can't train them to have values that fit your brand.

Asking Your Questions

After you ask each question you wrote down, and any that occur to you while you chat with an applicant, pause and give the applicant time to formulate an answer. Don't run together several questions at once because you probably won't get answers for all of them. Ask follow-up questions such as "Why did you do that?" and "How did that happen?" to draw more out of an applicant as needed.

Be sure to take notes during the interview because days later you'll have a hard time remembering who said what. Try not to be too obvious with your note-taking, though. You don't want the applicant to feel like you're grading her on everything she says.

Keeping It Legal

While you're thinking about what you should ask applicants—the applicants' skills and experiences as they relate to the job—you should also keep in mind things you *can't* ask about.

Don't ask whether the applicant plans to have children, whether he's married, whether he's ever filed a workers' compensation claim, whether he's a citizen, when he was discharged from the military, whether he's been arrested, or what his race/creed/color/religion/national origin/age is. These types of questions can be considered discriminatory, and federal laws prohibit discrimination against job applicants based on gender, race, disability, religion, marital status, and so on.

Turning the Tables

Near the end of the interview, ask the applicant whether she has any questions for you. This not only gives the applicant a chance to clarify the job in her mind; it gives you a chance to learn more about her, too. Does she ask intelligent questions about the training process, or does she ask what you do when a worker's till constantly comes up short?

If you hire this person, you're going to be spending lots of time with her, and she'll be representing your business to customers and the community at large. You can't learn everything there is to know about a person in a 30-minute interview, but you often can learn enough to know whether this person is someone you want to work with day after day.

> **Counter** *Talk*
>
> Be sure to ask why the applicant wants to work at your shop versus, say, the mega coffee shop down the block. During a phone interview, if an applicant tells Melissa they've never been to Brewpoint, she asks them to go visit and then get back to her. It's important that your employees be interested in your brand and enjoy your shop's vibe.

Learning Labor Law

Labor law, or employment law, is the collective name for thousands of federal and state statutes that govern the rights and obligations involved in any type of employment situation. Labor law regulates everything from the initial hiring process and job duties to minimum wage and collective bargaining rights.

The field of labor law is enormous—far more than we can cover in a few pages. Consult your lawyer for advice, or explore the U.S. Department of Labor (DOL) website and elsewhere online to learn about your obligations as an employer.

> **Counter** *Talk*
>
> For details on which states require paid breaks and how long those breaks must be, consult your lawyer for the lowdown on local labor law, or check the DOL site at dol.gov/general/topic/workhours/breaks.

Paying Wages and More Money Matters

Job applicants will naturally be curious about payment. They're not volunteering for this position, after all. They rightfully expect to be reimbursed for their effort, and you should have a figure in mind for each position you're filling.

There's more to paying wages than handing out a simple per-hour rate, though. Workers' compensation insurance, unemployment taxes, Social Security taxes, and more all figure into the equation.

Giving the Government Its Due

Government taxes add an additional 20 to 35 percent onto the cost of an employee's gross wages, so the more you offer an employee, the more you'll hand over to Uncle Sam as well.

You'll have to pay for workers' compensation insurance. Workers' comp covers your employees' costs if they get sick, injured, or even killed on the job. The benefits of workers' comp include medical expenses, lost wages, vocational rehabilitation, and death benefits.

Workers' comp protects you as much as your employees. Before workers' comp existed, a serious injury to an employee could shut down the business. Now, lost wages, rehab, and so on are paid for by the insurance, no matter who's at fault.

Workers' comp requirements vary from state to state, so contact your state's insurance commissioner for more information. Your insurance agent also can help you with the details.

Then there's Social Security and Medicare taxes. Not only are you required to withhold about 7.5 percent of your employees' paychecks to pay for their Social Security and Medicare taxes, you must match those contributions dollar for dollar. If one employee pays $30 a week in Social Security taxes, you pay that amount as well. Add up that cost for all your employees, and you're talking about some serious spending.

Don't forget federal unemployment taxes. Most employers have to pay federal unemployment taxes because the qualifications aren't that hard to meet: you either pay wages totaling $1,500 to all employees in one quarter, or have at least one employee working on any given day for 20 (not necessarily consecutive) weeks in a year.

If you meet either of these standards, as of 2019 you must pay a flat rate of 6 percent on the first $7,000 paid to each employee. This tax covers unemployment compensation for workers who have lost their jobs. States often have their own unemployment tax, so contact your accountant or your state's department of labor for more details.

Keeping Employees Healthy

What about health insurance? As of this writing, businesses that employed an average of fewer than 50 full-time equivalent (FTE) employees during the previous calendar year do not have to offer health insurance, according to PeopleKeep (peoplekeep.com). Full-time employees are those who worked an average of 30 or more hours per week in a given month. You also must calculate the FTE of your part-time employees and add them to the total. To do this, add the hours worked by your part-time employees and divide the total by 120.

If you have more than 50 full-time employees, including your FTEs, you need to offer Minimum Essential Coverage, which is any insurance plan that meets the Affordable Care Act's requirements for coverage.

Check, Please

Okay, the government taxes tell you how much to add on top of what you pay your staff. Now for the harder question: how much *do* you pay? The trick is to offer an hourly rate that makes your employees happy without putting your business in the red.

To begin, go back to your business plan (developed in Chapter 4) to see how much you allocated toward the cost of employees. If you offer, say, $8 per hour—and government taxes push that figure to $9.50 per hour—how many hours of help can you afford? Is that realistic? Are you offering too much per hour? Did you underestimate how much help you'll need?

Contact coffee bars in noncompeting areas to find out how much they pay and how many employees they use during each shift. Use this information to adjust your business plan (if needed) and guide you in determining a per-hour rate for each employee.

Remember that you must offer at least the minimum wage. The federal minimum wage as of this writing is $7.25 per hour, but some states mandate higher minimum wages. Use the Department of Labor's interactive map (dol.gov/whd/minwage/america.htm) to determine what the number is in your state.

Also keep in mind that a barista is a tipped role. Research tip pooling laws especially as they relate to minimum wage when considering how much to offer your baristas.

Insourcing or Outsourcing Payroll

Should you handle your coffee shop's payroll on your own, or should you hire an outside payroll company to handle the burden? As with the issues of hiring a lawyer and accountant (which we discussed in Chapter 5), the answer is: it depends.

Have you researched the federal and state tax issues thoroughly and know exactly how much needs to be withheld from each employee's check? Do you save more money handling the payroll yourself than it would cost for an outside company to do it? Do you file payroll taxes with the Internal Revenue Service promptly? If the answer to all these questions is "yes," perhaps you should keep hold of the checkbook.

If the answer is "no"—or if you want to offer employees direct deposit or track sick hours and vacation time easily—consider hiring a payroll company that's national in scope and can assign an account representative to work with you.

Or split the difference by using payroll software for small businesses such as these:

* Square Payroll (squareup.com/payroll)

* QuickBooks Payroll (quickbooks.intuit.com/oa/payroll)

* Patriot Payroll (patriotsoftware.com)

Payroll software companies generally charge a flat fee per month plus an additional fee per employee. Check software review sites like Capterra (capterra.com) to view details and read reviews on different payroll platforms.

More Than Money

Money is good for lots of things, such as being exchanged for goods and services. But motivating employees and keeping them happy takes more than just cash.

Even if you pay sky-high wages, if you let customers treat your employees badly or you don't praise them for a job well done, they will be miserable. And they won't be miserly with their miserableness; they'll generously share it with customers, who will soon feel equally miserable when they think about coming to your coffee shop.

Don't let this happen to your shop. Keep your business a pleasant place to work with a private, clean space where employees can take breaks, and offer a small fridge to store their lunches. Keep the surfaces clean and the air fresh. (Admittedly, they'll be doing much of the cleaning and freshening, but do give them the tools to work with.)

Take the attitude that employees are working *with* you, not *for* you, and treat them as equals as much as you can. Start football pools, if they're interested, or let them come to work in costume on Halloween. Be flexible with the work schedule to accommodate unusual circumstances instead of dogmatically insisting everyone work the same hours and the same days no matter what. Ask them for suggestions when problems arise.

Offer generous praise when they do good work, and if you want to go a step further, put the praise in writing or reward them with gift cards to local businesses or extra time off with pay. Provide employee discounts on the products you carry. Sure, they might prefer to have a permanent pay increase, but these steps will make your appreciation clear and keep your employees on your side.

Barista Baccalaureate

Training your employees is the best business investment you'll ever make. It's the ol' "teach a man to fish" parable writ large. Once you train an employee, she'll have that knowledge forever. More importantly, she'll be able to pass on that knowledge to new employees, leaving you free to do other things.

Reaching that point of autonomous and self-perpetuating systems doesn't happen overnight, though. You must have a willingness to train employees from the moment they start working with you. Don't half explain a task and then say, "Never mind, I'll do it," or your employees will take the wrong lessons from your training: that you don't trust them, and that you'll take over any job that's slightly difficult.

Train them right, and they'll have confidence in their abilities. What's more, their confidence will be deserved because they will have mastered every task you ask of them.

Creating a Training Manual

Imagine taking an 8-hour crash course on how to run a coffee shop. How much do you think you'd remember about steaming milk, refilling the supply cabinet, running the register, cleaning the tables and floors, and rotating the baked goods? Not enough to do it all correctly the next day, most likely.

That's why it's key to write an employee training manual that spells out your business procedures. Whenever an employee wonders how to maintain a piece of equipment or void a transaction, he can flip open the book and find the answer without having to stop and go find you or someone else who knows how to do it.

Writing all the procedures of your business for a training manual also shows you where your processes might be lacking. Maybe you don't have any procedures in place for handling customers who get ill, for instance, or perhaps you'll discover the need for a chart that shows who's responsible for cleaning what each day. Sometimes you learn what's missing only by writing down what you already know.

Here are a few of the procedures to include in your training manual:

* **How to clean.** Who is responsible for cleaning each section of the coffee shop? How often should cleaning take place? What are the cleaning procedures for tables, floors, bakery cases, and so on?

* **How to maintain equipment.** Who cleans and repairs equipment? How often does maintenance take place?

* **How to take money.** What are the procedures for taking cash versus credit cards? How do you handle register mistakes?

* **How to answer the phone.** What's the procedure for taking messages? Do you want your employees to answer with "Good day, this is Tony at The Best Brew. How may I help you?" If you do, write it down.

* **How to handle an unsatisfied customer.** Do you give her a free cup of coffee? Issue a refund? Call in the supervisor? Call in the Marines?

* **How to deal with safety concerns.** How do you handle medical emergencies in the shop? How do you respond to dangerous storms or other weather incidents? We discuss these and other safety concerns in Chapter 21.

Your training manual should also contain information on benefits like vacation time and medical leave, policies on drugs and weapons in the workplace, details about lines of authority (i.e., who reports to whom), rules regarding lateness and attendance, info about disciplinary actions, expectations for your employees (such as how often they'll be reviewed for job performance), and information on regulatory compliance (like the policies you have in place to comply with the Americans with Disabilities Act and other regulations).

In short, the training manual should detail the goals you have for your business and explain the policies necessary to make them happen.

Tips on Training New Employees

There's more to training employees than explaining a procedure once and leaving them on their own to perform that procedure. Different people learn in different ways, and for you to succeed as a trainer, it's essential to find what works for each person. For one employee, you might be able to simply give verbal directions; for another, you might have to draw a diagram; for a third, you might have to lead him through the procedure the first time. Once you're aware of each employee's learning style, you'll know how to teach him—and you'll know how others can teach him as well.

Role-play is one specific training technique you might try. By *role-play*, we don't mean Dungeons and Dragons; we mean acting out with an employee situations that might arise during a workday, such as a peeved customer who received whipped cream he didn't want or a customer who complains about the music playing in your shop. Acting out these types of situations gives the employee a chance to discover (or remember) the right solution before he's faced with it in real life.

Role-play also helps you evaluate the employee's strengths and weaknesses, so he can share the former and work on the latter.

Shadowing is another training technique you might use. Have the new employee closely follow a more experienced worker (or you), copying everything to learn how things are done. It never hurts a table to be cleaned twice, and you can always give away the practice drinks he makes, thereby building customer satisfaction at the same time!

Switch roles after performing a task twice so the new employee leads the master, talking his way through the procedure out loud in case the master needs to jump in.

It's usually a good idea to assign a mentor to new employees. Ask an established employee to become the new guy's best buddy until he can work on his own. In addition to freeing up your time for other tasks, having an employee serve as a mentor shows you value her knowledge and trust her judgment. Give her guidelines on training if she's never worked with anyone before and then send her on her way.

The mentoring experience teaches *both* employees new things. The newcomer learns everything about the business from scratch, and the old hand refreshes knowledge she might have forgotten while also learning how to take more responsibility for others.

Even if you have employees who are experienced enough to be mentors, don't disappear into your office. Work the floor with your employees to see what you can learn from them as well, and to correct them when they take shortcuts that might hurt the business.

Counter *Talk*   At Brewpoint, the training process takes about 3 weeks before a new employee is ready to strike out on their own behind the counter.

Terminating Employees

No matter how careful you are during your hiring procedures, employees don't always work out. Some turn out to be lazy; some steal; some are rude. Whatever the reason, you need to let them go, and by "let them go," we mean fire them.

Don't think you can go firing people willy-nilly, though. That's a perfect recipe for legal trouble. Just as there's a legally proper way to hire someone, the law also dictates when and how you can let people go. We explain the details in this section in addition to giving tips on how to say good-bye in the politest way possible.

Is the Law on Your Side?

When you hire an employee, explain that the position requires the person to do X, Y, and Z. Effectively, you're making a deal with that person: "You do X, Y, and Z, and I will pay you for doing so." If that person repeatedly fails to do any one of these tasks, you have the right to replace him with someone who will.

You're allowed to do this because—unless you've signed a contract stating otherwise—you've hired the person on an "at-will" basis, which means either one of you can terminate the employment agreement at any time for nearly any reason. (We say "*nearly* any reason" because you can't fire an at-will employee if, for example, he files workers' comp claims, reports you to a state agency for violating the law, or breaks up with you after the two of you start dating.)

Even without a written contract, if you told an employee his job would last at least X months, you need justifiable and documented reasons—such as dishonesty, theft, or misuse of trade secrets—for letting him go earlier.

If you're unsure whether you have the right to fire someone, discuss the situation with your lawyer to be sure you're staying on the right side of the law.

"This Will Go Down in Your Permanent Record"

You might have laughed when a high school teacher threatened to include your note-passing in your permanent record, but she actually had the right idea. By documenting your history of insubordination, the school would have a better case against you later should it need to expel you.

As the owner of a small business, take a lesson from that teacher and record employee violations, along with whatever actions you took to fix the problem. If, for example, an employee repeatedly handles food without gloves despite your warnings, you'll have a much stronger case for firing her if you've documented each infraction. Some HR and employee scheduling apps let you record this right in the app.

Don't keep this record to yourself, though. Develop a plan for handling employee violations, such as a "three-strike" policy, and include details of the policy in the training manual. When you hire employees, tell them about the policy so they can never argue that they were blindsided by your accusations.

> **Counter** *Talk*   Brewpoint uses a three-strike write-up system. The first time an employee breaks a company rule, they receive a written warning. If they get three warnings for the same infraction within 6 months, the employee is suspended from work for 1 week. After they come back from suspension, they're on a probation period that requires not receiving any more warnings.

Saying Good-Bye

The day has come. You've warned Cody repeatedly he can't put his lips on the steaming wand, yet he's still doing it. Before you boot him out, though, run through these questions and be sure everything is in order for the firing-to-come:

Have you given him warnings? Be sure you've documented this employee's past violations. If you grumble quietly to yourself and then fire someone out of the blue, you could face legal action for wrongful termination. By noting violations and making other employees aware of such problems, you also make them feel less threatened because they know you've given the employee sufficient opportunity to fix his mistakes.

Is this really necessary? Is the violation serious enough that it warrants firing? Is the employee leaving milk unrefrigerated, which risks bringing health inspectors down on your head, or is he just not stocking the cups in the order you prefer? Firing an employee often has a traumatic effect on the rest of your staff, so be sure this step is necessary.

Are you sending mixed messages? Don't tell an employee he's doing great and is a super nice person to work with and then hand him his hat and shoo him out the door. The employee might feel he's being fired unjustly and file a wrongful termination suit. After all, why would you compliment him so much if he were really that bad?

Lay out the reasons for the termination, and stress the opportunities you gave for improvement, without hinting at anything positive about the employee's performance. Keep calm if the employee lashes out at you or tries to argue about what a good worker he is. Don't argue back; merely restate your decision and let the employee know that's the final word.

Are you being mean? Although this person has disrupted your business through his actions, don't make the firing a personal assault. Keep things on an all-business level. Leave insults and jabs out of the conversation, and stick to the facts of his work violations.

Much as you might dislike it, you will have to fire employees at some point. We hope your good hiring practices will make the practice rare, but knowing how and when to let someone go is an important skill every business owner must learn.

Counter *Talk*

It's never fun to let an employee go, especially in the moment. But Melissa has realized that whenever she does need to fire someone, it ends up being the right decision. Within a week, whatever problem the employee was causing disappears and the environment in the shop improves.

After reading the last few chapters, you're all set for employees and have the perfect design and layout for your coffee shop. Now let's talk about the fun things you can do in your shop besides serving coffee, like hosting live music, seminars, charity events, and more.

Hosting Events

Now that you have your coffee shop designed, decorated, and equipped, what are you—and those new employees you just hired—going to do in your shop? Yes, of course you'll serve incredible coffee and scrumptious snacks, which we talk more about in Chapters 14 through 17. But what else?

To attract new customers, create a sense of community, and bring your business mission to life, you could host events in your coffee shop as well.

In this chapter, we look at all the considerations that go into planning and hosting events. Do you have the space and resources necessary to host? If so, what types of events are best for your coffee shop? And finally, how can you turn events into another revenue stream and not just a "nice to have" extra for your customers? Read on to find out.

Should You Host Events?

Your mind may be swimming with dreams of holding live music events, fun birthday parties, smart educational seminars, or creative maker workshops. But before you start sending out invites, check out these must-dos that will determine whether you can host events in your coffee shop—and, if so, what kinds you should schedule.

Upholding Your Mission

In Chapter 4, we suggested you include mission and vision statements in your business plan. These will come in handy as you decide what events to host. For example:

* Are you all about community? Maybe try a book club in which members read books penned by local authors.

* Is doing good deeds your thing? Charity events could be a good match for your café.

* Is your mission to support creators? Perhaps you could turn your shop into a makerspace/coffee shop.

As we discuss in this chapter, there's no shortage of events that might align with your mission.

Using Your Space Wisely

The space you have will dictate, to a large extent, the types of events you can host. A tiny coffee shop, for example, is probably not the best place for live music, but it could work for a weekly writer's group.

Then again, if your space is big enough, you may be able to rent out the whole thing for large parties or corporate events (more on that later in this chapter).

Matching Your Market

Just as with the themes we discussed in Chapter 8, some events will resonate with your customer base more than others. Try to match the events you host with your customer demographics' interests and needs to draw a larger crowd. If you largely cater to a starving college-student clientele, for example, don't load up your event calendar with pricey VIP nights. How about offering a class on different ways to dress up packaged ramen instead?

Understanding the Legalities of Hosting

Local regulations might dictate how many people you can have in your coffee shop at once, or you might need to hold a special insurance policy for certain types of events. Talk to your lawyer (that helpful professional we recommended you hire in Chapter 5) before committing to any particular type of event.

Deciding What Events to Host

You name it, and you can probably organize an event around it. If you need some ideas, here are 15 types of gatherings your coffee shop can host. We share some common events customers really seem to enjoy plus more unique get-togethers that can help your coffee shop stand out from the rest.

Coffee-Related Events

This is an obvious extension of your coffee shop's brand. You already know the bulk of your customers like coffee, so hold coffee tastings, offer talks on how to roast beans at home, or host latte art competitions where customers can vote on the best design. Brewpoint even has held espresso classes for wholesale clients after hours.

Live Music

If you have the right setup for it, live music events can bring in plenty of foot traffic, whether you have one guitarist strumming away in the corner or an entire band playing on a platform.

Counter *Talk*   One big caveat about hosting live music: if you're a tiny shop that offers live music only occasionally, you may have no problems, but if you're larger, you may come under the scrutiny of music licensing companies. Melissa has had the unpleasant experience of these companies emailing her incessantly, demanding a licensing fee in case the bands she hires play licensed music. Even worse, once you pay, you'll start hearing from other music licensing companies who want to get in on the action.

Open-Mic Nights

How hilarious are your customers? An open-mic night is a good way to find out. Just be sure to either request that aspiring comics keep their acts PG, or make it clear in your marketing that this is not a kid-friendly event.

If you're collaborating with an organization, such as a student-led group from a local college, they could do all the marketing and emcee work. Otherwise, you should emcee the show yourself or give that responsibility to an employee who has experience emceeing.

Poetry Readings

Got an artsy crowd at your coffee shop? Dedicating some evenings to poetry readings could draw in more customers.

You don't have to limit your invitations to poets. You could try other types of readings, too, such as flash fiction.

Book Clubs

Coffee and books are a natural match. Create a book club of your own, or encourage customers to hold their book club meetings in your coffee shop.

If you create your own club, you can choose a different book to discuss each month that matches your coffee shop's mission. Have a book-loving staff member lead the discussion, or invite someone from a local independent bookstore do the job. This bolsters your shop's goodwill in the community and gives the bookstore a chance to promote their wares.

If you do task a staff member with the job, consider whether it's worth paying them to lead the group. Can you recoup your costs by charging a small membership fee?

Writers' Groups

Writers are notorious for fueling their inspiration with coffee. What a perfect match for a coffee shop! You might even have some writers working quietly in your shop already and not realize it. Offer to host a writing group, and they may notice and bring in their writer friends.

If you don't want to host your own group, which might require you to supply a leader with writing credentials, try offering space to a local writers' group that already exists. Its members likely would be thrilled to have a nice place to meet.

Teaming up with your local public library or a nearby college are other great options for cohosting writers' events.

Crafting Clubs

People who are passionate about crafting enjoy meeting like-minded hobbyists—not to mention good places to meet them where they can sit and chat while they work. A group dedicated to knitting, cross-stitching, or scrapbooking may love to use your space for their get-togethers.

Get to know what treats your crafters like to nosh on during meetings so you can be sure to have them on hand. This goes for any type of regular meeting or club held at your coffee shop.

Board Game Days

Gather a shelf full of board games, and turn your slowest day into a board game day. You could ask customers to bring their own games, or feature a different game every month.

Who knows—maybe you can convince your local board game shop to sponsor these events and let you borrow games for the day. See if you can get them to send over an expert to teach your customers how to play the day's game, too.

Two caveats: first, as we mentioned in Chapter 8, some board games take a long time to play— some up to 2 hours long and even longer. To avoid the problem of gamers taking up tables for hours without actually buying food and drinks, you can either require a minimum purchase or offer special discounts on select items to club members. Second, board games can be expensive. If the idea of someone spilling coffee on a $70 game makes you want to weep, stock up on used games or have members bring their own.

Celebrity Events

Invite local celebs like authors, actors, and athletes for book signings, talks, or meet-and-greets. Try reaching out to them directly—many local celebs enjoy supporting their community—or go through their agent. If this proves difficult, or if you want to host celebs often, you can use the paid service WhoRepresents.com to find out who represents these luminaries and how to get in touch. When you talk to the agent, ask if the celebrity charges a fee to appear. If so, you have to decide if the benefits you'll get from having them there are worth it.

Charity Events

Support a charity your customers care about by charging admission for a special event and donating the proceeds to the charitable organization. For example, hold a coffee competition where patrons create their own concoctions, host a special holiday event featuring Christmas carolers, or showcase the wares of local artists who donate a portion of their sales to the cause.

Another idea that works well is to offer all profits over a certain time period, such as a weekend, to the charity. You also could host a talk from a charity representative during that time to boost interest.

Seminars and Talks

Depending on your clientele, you might bring in experts to speak about business or career topics, wellness subjects, political issues, or hobbies.

The good news about these types of events is that the host is often happy to do them for free to promote their own business. Even better, you and the host can comarket the event, each on your own social media accounts, in your newsletters, and so on, bringing new customers to the both of you. Pair up with a host who's well known in the area, and you may see a flood of new faces.

Political Discussions

Roundtables, panels, and meet-the-new-commissioner-of-education types of events will bring in engaged community members.

Counter *Talk*

What if someone wants to hold an event that goes against your values? Melissa tries to be fair and allow events of all political persuasions, as long as they encourage constructive conversations. However, she's ready to say no if an event doesn't make sense for Brewpoint. Luckily, Brewpoint's customers are familiar with what the business stands for, so Melissa hasn't gotten any wildly incompatible requests. Another reason to ensure you have a clear mission—and let your customers know about it.

Corporate Event and Private Party Room Rentals

If you have the space for private functions, all you have to do is advertise that fact, set rules around the use of the space, and help the hosts make their events a success. For example, you may offer catering, decorate the space, or even bring in the entertainment the hosts will need.

For these events, be sure to either have your lawyer write up a rental contract, or find a template online and have your lawyer customize it for your needs.

Counter *Talk*

Brewpoint has five private rooms from two locations that Melissa rents out for $25 to $125 per hour depending on the size of the room. Customers are responsible for providing their own food and decorations, but Brewpoint partners with vendors customers can hire if they want help with food and other party needs. Some venues require customers to work with certain vendors, or set requirements for how much food customers must purchase, so Brewpoint patrons appreciate having control over who they hire.

Whole-Shop Rentals

If you have a lot of space, some customers may want to rent out your entire coffee shop for, say, a wedding reception or a corporate event. Hold these events after hours so you don't have to close down the shop and turn away loyal customers, but do have a staff member on hand to ensure everything runs smoothly.

Drawing Crowds to Your Events

If you think you want to bring more customers into your coffee shop by holding events, you're in good company. Many coffee shops boost their bottom line by hosting gatherings. But there's more to it than adding a flyer to your front door or a banner to your website telling folks to come in for book club Wednesday nights.

Let's look at the steps to creating events that work for you, for your coffee shop, and especially for your customers.

Planning Your Events

Before you host an event, you have to know what it is you're hosting and what kind of help you might need.

The best way to know what functions to offer is to ask your customers what they want. Build an online survey on one of the platforms we suggest in Chapter 21, such as SurveyMonkey, invite your email newsletter subscribers to send you suggestions, or ask customers at the counter in your shop.

Once your coffee shop is established, you'll probably have plenty of people approaching you asking if they can hold an event in your space. When you're starting out, though, you may need to reach out to potential hosts or groups. Post on your shop's website and social media pages that you're looking for speakers, music acts, book club leaders, or whatever it is you need for the type of events you want to offer.

Counter *Talk*

It's easier to let people approach you about holding events at your coffee shop than to seek out event hosts. As Melissa has learned, if you approach the host, he or she will expect you to be the one to bring in people. Events typically don't bring in a ton of revenue, so why take on the entire burden of promoting them yourself? Instead, put the word out that you're open to hosting, and let the hosts come to you.

Depending on the event, you may need a mic, platform, folding chairs, or other types of furnishings and equipment. Ask the host what they need and what they can bring on their own. Then, when you know what you need to supply on your end, shop around for the best prices ahead of time so you're not scrambling at the last minute to locate that one crucial piece of equipment. (This may also be a good time to reflect on whether you really want to hold this type of event. Will it be worth it to your business to spend time and money buying the necessary supplies?)

Then there's the issue of deciding what, and whether, to charge for the event. It's nice when events make your customer happy *and* put some extra profits in your bank account, but determining what to charge for events can be a challenge. Will you charge an entrance fee—and if so, how much? Will you require a minimum purchase? Or will you charge the event host to use your space? Decide now, and make it clear in your event promotions so customers aren't surprised when they show up.

Counter *Talk*

Melissa books a lot more events if she offers a split commission, where Brewpoint splits the profits with the event leader. For example, if a local florist holds a flower-arranging workshop for $40 per person and the supplies cost the florist $10 per person, the florist and Brewpoint each take in $15 per attendee ($40 – $10 = $30 ÷ 2 = $15).

When will your event take place? The day and time you choose depend on a number of factors, from how busy your shop is at certain times of the day to when your customers will want to attend a particular type of event. A "sip and paint" event where aspiring artists enjoy wine while creating a masterpiece would work better in the evening than the morning, for example. You may want to hold live music events during typically slow evenings to bring in more foot traffic. And writers' groups might work better during quiet afternoon stretches so they can concentrate.

Marketing Your Events

There's nothing sadder than when you throw a party and no one comes. That's why it's crucial to market your events so your community can schedule the date in their calendars. Here are some tips for getting the word out about your events. (Chapters 23 and 24 share more publicity and marketing ideas that can help.)

Social media is probably the best place to promote your events—and it's free! Be sure to include an enticing image to attract more clicks, and include all the relevant info:

* The date and time of the event

* Your coffee shop's address

* Details about the event

* The price

* Any restrictions on the event (for example if children are not invited)

Email your subscribers list, too, and send them the same details you posted on social media.

Hang posters in your shop and on local bulletin boards. Stuff flyers or ads into customers' bags along with their to-go orders to promote your event, too.

Spread the word farther by posting the invitation on an event calendar. Eventbrite (eventbrite.com) is a free platform many people use to search for events in their area. If you use the Shopify platform for your website, you can even integrate it with Eventbrite so all your events are uploaded to the site automatically.

Create a calendar of events inside your coffee shop that customers can easily see. Customers might not know you host events until one day, while waiting in line for their coffee, they spot something on your calendar that interests them—knitting group Wednesday night!—and they can make plans to attend. If you plan to hold a lot of events, ask your web designer to add an events calendar to your website where visitors can select a date and see what you have going on that day.

You've got your location, your design, and perhaps even a special theme. You've hired the best staff and decided what events you want to (or don't want to) host in your fabulous space. What's missing? The one very important ingredient to a successful coffee shop: coffee. In the next chapter, you learn all about what's in a bean, the different grades of coffee, and how to choose the right coffees for your shop.

Deciding Which Products to Sell

Now we get to the stuff that goes in the cup. In Part 4, we cover the different types of coffee; the ways beans are sorted, graded, and prepared; and how to create coffee drinks like lattes and cappuccinos. And where coffee goes, milk must follow, so we also discuss dairy options, not to mention flavored syrups and other delicious add-ins.

Not everyone digs coffee (gasp!), so we also talk tea—its history, the different types available, and how to prepare the perfect cup— as well as many other drinks, from soda to smoothies.

Who brings all these goodies to your shop? Lots and lots of suppliers, all of whom you learn about in Part 4. We also look at how to price your products so you can actually earn something from all this effort.

Complete Coffee Compendium

Planning your coffee shop décor and hiring friendly employees to work in it are essential steps to the future success of your shop, but let's face it: what's going to draw customers through the door—and more importantly, keep them coming back—is the smell and taste of your coffee. You sell coffee, they buy it, they like it, they return for more. Sounds simple, right?

If only it were that easy! You have dozens, if not hundreds, of different types of coffee to choose from, each with its own flavor, aroma, and body. So how do you know which one(s) to purchase and use to appeal to the widest customer base? We cover all the essential coffee details here so by the end of this chapter, you'll be well on your way to becoming a coffee connoisseur.

Coffee 101

In our quest for the perfect pot of coffee, let's begin at the beginning, with the bean itself. Each coffee bean is actually the seed of a coffee cherry, the fruit of the coffee tree. Most coffee trees grow near the equator, but with a lot of care they can be raised in other locations.

Coffee beans come in two major types (no, not regular and decaf!): *robusta* and *arabica*.

Robusta beans, which are native to West Africa, grow at low altitudes and are less prone to disease than arabica beans. This makes them cheaper to grow than arabica, but robusta beans have a harsher taste and up to twice the caffeine, so they're used mostly in mass-produced, supermarket blends of coffee.

Arabica beans, by contrast, are grown at altitudes of 3,000 to 7,000 feet above sea level, which makes them expensive to grow and harvest. Despite their high cost, specialty coffee shops prefer arabica beans because they have a smooth, rich taste that can't be matched by robusta beans. Anywhere from 60 to 85 percent of the world's coffee production is in arabica beans.

In addition to arabica and robusta, more than 20 other types of coffee exist, such as liberica, dewevrei, racemosa, stenophylla, and zanguebarica. These other types account for less than 1 percent of the world's production of coffee.

Coffee trees and bushes belong to the botanical family *Rubiaceae,* which is made of more than 13,000 species of flowering plants, including gardenias and cinchona, which produces the malaria treatment quinine. If only coffee cured diseases!

A pound of coffee contains roughly 4,000 coffee beans, so with only 2 seeds in each cherry, 2,000 cherries must be picked for each pound of coffee. That's a lot of picking! Unripe green berries, ripe red berries, and overripe black berries may show up on the same branch, which makes coffee bean picking a very time-consuming task.

A few methods can extract the bean, the part you want for coffee. The quickest is the *wet,* or *washed,* process. Here, machines strip the cherry from the beans, and the beans are soaked to both ferment (a chemical reaction during which yeast and bacteria break down sugars in the fruit) and remove any remaining fruit or mucilage (a sugary, honeylike substance that surrounds the beans). Then the beans are allowed to dry. A longer process, but one that results in a more flavorful bean, is the *dry,* or *unwashed* (or *natural*), process. Here, cherries are dried in the sun or in dryers and then machines strip the dried mucilage from the beans. Then there's the honey process, where the fresh cherries are depulped but dried without fermentation or washing. This creates a cup that's more complex than the washed process but not as fruity as the unwashed process.

Coffee beans can have no more than 11 or 12 percent moisture, so after processing, they must dry anywhere from 6 to 14 days before they are cleaned again, inspected for damage, and packed for shipping.

Decaffeinating Details

Not everyone wants caffeine in their coffee, and thankfully science has figured out how to separate the *cof* from the *caf.* You won't have to decaffeinate the beans you buy from suppliers, but in case you want to explain to your customers what goes on behind the scenes, here are the different decaffeinating processes and how they work:

* **Methylene chloride (DCM) processing.** In most instances of DCM processing, the beans are soaked in DCM, and molecules of caffeine bond with molecules of methylene chloride. The beans are then washed to remove the DCM, which is carcinogenic in large doses. (Roasting the beans burns off any remaining DCM.)

* **Ethyl acetate processing.** The chemical ethyl acetate is found naturally in certain fruits, so using ethyl acetate for decaffeination is sometimes labeled a "natural" process. As with DCM processing, the coffee beans are soaked in ethyl acetate, and the caffeine bonds with the chemical.

* **Carbon dioxide (CO_2) processing.** In this type of processing, the CO_2 is compressed into a near-liquid state and combined with the coffee beans. As with the other processing methods, the caffeine molecules bond with the CO_2 and are removed. Carbon dioxide is found in coffee beans to begin with, and any CO_2 remaining behind has no effect on the taste of the finished product.

* **Water processing (also known as Swiss water processing).** Here, coffee beans are soaked in hot water, which absorbs both caffeine molecules and "flavor" molecules, the oils and other components of the beans that give them their particular taste. The water-caffeine-flavor solution then passes through a carbon filter that removes the caffeine but leaves the other elements untouched. The beans soak in this solution again to reabsorb the flavors and oils.

Calling coffee "decaffeinated" is not quite right, because decaf coffee still contains some caffeine, no matter which processing method is used. Federal regulations in the United States allow products to contain up to 2.5 percent caffeine and still wear the decaffeinated label.

And here's an interesting fact to wow your customers with: the caffeine removed from coffee isn't thrown away. It's added to medicines, soft drinks, and other products. Believe it or not, less than 5 percent of the caffeine in a regular cola drink comes from the kola nut itself. The rest of the caffeine in the drink comes from coffee that has been stripped of its natural buzz.

Judging Coffee Beans

Determining whether a batch of beans makes good coffee or not isn't just a matter of brewing a pot and giving it a taste. Taste alone isn't a true measure of quality. Instead, you have to take a closer look at the beans themselves.

Each country that produces coffee has its own guidelines for quality, but rather than compare dozens of different guidelines, let's look at those created by the Specialty Coffee Association of America (SCAA) for use by member coffee shops that roast their own beans. To start, we have a list of primary and secondary defects to look for when examining a coffee lot (a plot on a coffee farm).

SCAA Green Coffee Classification

Primary Defect	Number of Occurrences Equal to One Full Defect
Full black (over-roasted bean)	1
Partial black	2 or 3
Full sour (bean with a fermented odor or taste)	1
Partial sour	2 or 3
Pod/cherry (whole cherries including shell)	1
Large stones	2
Medium stones	5
Small stones	1
Large sticks	2
Medium sticks	5
Small sticks	1
Parchment (membrane that surrounds the bean)	2 or 3
Hull/husk (dried cherry pulp)	2 or 3
Broken/chipped	5
Insect damage	2 to 5
Floater (lighter than normal)	5
Shell	5
Water damage	2 to 5

So one large stone, although not desirable, does not equal one primary defect in a coffee lot. Eight beans damaged by insects equals anywhere from two to four secondary defects, with the amount of damage to each bean determining the actual number.

In addition to spotting these defects, you need to measure the beans to be sure the coffee hasn't been "cut" with a lower-quality grade. Why does this matter? Beans grown at the highest altitudes—the most *arabica* of the arabica, as it were—are denser than beans grown at lower heights. These beans are also thought to have the best flavor because denser beans contain more sugar. You want your beans to be an overall similar density, quality, and to some extent size so they roast more evenly and consistently and produce a smoother-tasting coffee.

To measure bean size, you filter them through screens of size 18, size 17, and so forth down through size 14, where *18* means "¹⁸⁄₆₄ inch," *17* means "¹⁷⁄₆₄ inch," and so on. Beans in one lot should all be the same size so they'll roast uniformly. (You don't necessarily need to buy screens for your own use, but we want you know what the numbers stand for.)

Don't get hung up too much on bean size and automatically choose larger beans. Good tastes can come in small packages: peaberry coffee, which comes from cherries that have only one seed instead of two, is often a delight in the cup.

Evaluating Taste

A coffee's taste, or flavor, is the combination of several characteristics: acidity, sweetness, aroma, balance, and body.

Acidity is a feeling of dryness at the back and edges of your mouth, which, unlike sourness, is a good thing. Without the bright, pleasing, astringent tartness of acidity, a coffee would taste flat. *Sweetness* is less a measure of how sugary-sweet the coffee is, like when you'd add sugar or a packet of sweetener to your cup, and more a measure of how smooth, mild, and flavorful the coffee is. Sometimes fruity or other flavors like caramel, honey, or chocolate are noted in the sweetness evaluation. *Aroma,* or *fragrance,* adds subtle touches such as nutty or floral to the basic taste sensations of sweet, salty, sour, bitter, and umami (a meaty flavor associated with proteins). *Balance* is an evaluation of how all the coffee's characteristics work together. Are they all harmonious, or does one stand out more? Finally, *body* refers to the weight or mouthfeel of the coffee. Is it light and fluid in your mouth or thick and heavy?

Cup fault is a general term for an overwhelming problem with the taste or odor of coffee. (If it's noticeable but not overwhelming, it's known as *cup taint*.) Examples of faults include grassy (too much nitrogen in the beans while the cherries matured) and hidey (a breakdown of fats during the drying process due to too much heat).

Considering Grades

With all these details in mind, here are the SCAA grade guidelines from best to worst when examining 350 grams of hulled coffee:

* **Grade 1: Specialty Grade.** No primary defects, 0 to 3 full secondary defects, sorted with a maximum of 5 percent above and 5 percent below specified screen size or range of screen size, and exhibiting a distinct attribute in one or more of the following areas: *taste (flavor)*, *acidity*, *body*, or *aroma*. Also must be free of cup faults and taints. Zero *quakers* (that is, unripe, blighted, or underdeveloped coffee beans) are allowed. Moisture content between 9 and 13 percent.

* **Grade 2: Premium Grade.** Same as Grade 1, except maximum of 3 quakers and 0 to 8 full secondary defects.

* **Grade 3: Exchange Grade.** 50 percent above screen 15 and less than 5 percent below screen 15. Maximum of 5 quakers. Must be free from faults with 9 to 23 full defects.

* **Grade 4: Standard Grade.** 24 to 86 full defects.

* **Grade 5: Off Grade.** More than 86 full defects.

These grades are based on 350-gram samples from much larger lots, but they should be good indicators of overall quality. If you do limit yourself to using only specialty-grade beans, you'll pay a premium for the quality, but you can turn that cost into a marketing advantage. Post signs in your coffee bar that explain the grades, and boast about the standards you keep to give your customers the best coffee possible!

Bean Roasting Basics

Roasting coffee isn't like roasting a side of beef—you can't just throw it in the oven for an hour and go do something else. Coffee beans are small and cook quickly, so like people on a caffeine buzz, they have to be in motion at all times. Typically, coffee is roasted in a rotating metal drum over a heat source such as a gas flame. The air temperature inside the drum falls between 400 and 500 degrees Fahrenheit, with the specific temperature being determined by the experience of the roaster, the type of beans being processed, and the desired roast.

How the Pros Do It

During the roasting process, the beans lose more of their moisture, so the finished batch weighs less than when it started. The beans also lose a bit of protein, traces of different chemicals, and roughly 10 percent of their caffeine. Sugars and other carbohydrates in the bean are caramelized—that is, burned—and this darkens the bean and adds flavor.

The roasting process occurs in several stages, most commonly differentiated by the physical changes the beans go through during each stage. Here's how it works:

After the first stage of roasting, while changing from bright green to yellow to light brown, the beans have cracked and swelled in size as the moisture has been driven out. American mass marketers usually stop with this "light" or "cinnamon" roast, with dry, lightly roasted beans.

During the second stage, called "medium" or "city" roast, the beans gain a bit more sweetness as the sugars caramelize.

During the next stage, the interior of the bean reaches 400 degrees Fahrenheit, and an oily film starts to appear on the bean's surface. The sweetness of the caramelized sugars overtakes the bean's aroma, and the oil gives the bean a somewhat spicy taste. This roast, known as "dark" or "French," is common in Europe but only came to prominence in the United States thanks to specialty coffee stores in the Northwest. Fun fact: in France's colonial days, the French roasted their coffee extremely dark to mask the poor flavor of the robusta blends that came out of the country's colonies in West Africa. Today, "French roast" refers to any dark roasted coffee, whether the beans are arabica or robusta.

Farther along in the roasting process, the beans stop cracking and the sugars begin to carbonize—that is, turn to carbon—and taste smoky. The surface of these "Italian" or "espresso" beans looks very oily, and the flavor reaches a nearly burnt intensity.

The roasting machine operators sample the roasting beans continuously—smelling the changing nature of the sugar, listening for the beans' first and second cracks, and so on—and when the beans reach their moment of perfection, the operator dumps the beans into a cooling tray and blasts them with cool air to keep them from cooking any longer.

Counter *Talk*   The light-to-dark continuum isn't as standardized as you might think. For example, Brewpoint's darkest roast is still lighter than Starbucks' blonde roast. If your customers have questions, offer samples of your roasts and explain what you call each one so they understand what you mean by *light* and *dark*.

Roasting Your Own Beans

Learning to roast your own coffee beans takes practice. View your first efforts as experiments, and keep a notebook or spreadsheet to record the type of beans you used, the preheating time, the time in the heater, the chilling method, and so on. You never know which batch will turn out perfect, and when that happens, you don't want to have to guess at how you got it.

You can buy a roaster that handles large quantities of beans—and you'll definitely need to purchase a roaster if you decide to self-roast in your store—but before you make that investment, you can experiment with a much simpler tool: a hot air popcorn popper.

Try to use a popper that heats from the side of the popcorn reservoir instead of the bottom. This reduces the danger of fire that might result from overheated beans. Also, roast outdoors if possible; chaff from the green coffee beans will fly out during roasting, and the roasting smell—while initially delightful—quickly becomes stale inside your home.

With green beans and a colander or sieve at hand, plug in the popper and let it heat up briefly. Pour in green beans until they stop swirling; you don't want to add too many or the ones on the bottom will burn. As the beans start to dry out, they'll start churning again.

Wait for the first crackling of the beans and then listen for the second crackling a minute or so later. Start timing from the start of this second crackling, and roast for an additional 1 to 3 minutes, depending on how light or dark you want your coffee to be.

When you decide to stop roasting, dump the beans into the colander or sieve and swirl them around in front of a fan to cool them down and stop the roasting. In addition to fanning, you could sprinkle them with water, although this shouldn't be necessary. When the beans are cool, you can store them (more on that coming up soon) or turn to the section on grinding later in this chapter and put them to use right away.

Counter *Talk*   Roasting coffee on a large scale is an expensive endeavor. Brewpoint's roaster cost $40,000, although you can get small ones for around $5,000. You'll likely have a lot of regulations to deal with as a roaster as well. For example, some landlords won't let you roast in your shop because the scent will bother other tenants. (Can you imagine being bothered by the smell of roasting coffee?)

Crafting the Best Blends

You'd think that with hundreds of combinations of flavors, roasts, and types of coffee, eager bean buyers would be satisfied. Not a chance. Many types of coffee hit a drinker's sweet spot in, say, taste and acidity but not aroma, or they have body but lack taste. No coffee is all things to all drinkers.

To solve this problem, roasters and coffee dealers offer a variety of blends, or mixtures of two or more coffees designed to create a better drink than any single coffee offers on its own.

Coffee drinkers might not be familiar with the sharp, medium-bodied taste of Yemen mocha or with the smoother, richer java arabica, for example, but they've all surely heard of, if not tried, mocha java, a blend created from one part Yemen mocha and two parts java arabica. Mocha java provides a taste experience that doesn't exist in any single coffee, and that uniqueness is what makes blends popular.

Another reason for the appeal of blends, at least from a manufacturer's point of view, is cost. Mass-market coffees generally offer a blend of better-tasting arabica beans with cheaper robusta beans to lower their costs while still providing a coffee buyers want to drink.

As you become more experienced with the nature of particular types of coffee, you'll likely want to experiment with blends yourself. You'll notice something in one cup that's missing from another, so what's to stop you from mixing them together? The worst that can happen is that you spoil a few beans. The best thing, of course, is that you create a house blend that's available nowhere else in the world. If customers want it, there's only one place to go!

If you roast your own beans, roast each type of bean individually before blending and grinding them. (More on grinding later in the chapter.) This process, although more time-consuming, ensures that each type of coffee is roasted properly. Otherwise, you risk undercooking one while scorching another.

Storing Your Coffee

Roasted beans, when exposed to air, stay fresh for only 7 to 10 days, so you need to get them into storage, preferably something airtight, pronto.

Some roasters solve this problem for their customers by packaging beans in a coffee bag with a one-way gas valve that lets gases escape from the beans—which allows them to reveal their optimal flavor as chemicals from the roasting process escape—but keeps outside air from reaching the beans. If beans aren't packaged in this type of bag, they begin to deteriorate, and dark roast beans are the most vulnerable. This also happens after the airtight bags are opened and the beans are exposed to air.

> **Counter** *Talk*   Green coffee is good for 6 to 8 months before roasting. Brewpoint takes coffee off the retail shelves after 3 weeks, and after a bag is opened, it's used for up to 1 week.

In a retail environment, you're most likely using beans quickly and they're not sitting around for weeks waiting for their moment in the sun. Customers who purchase whole beans from you will go through their supply more slowly, though, so you might offer them these storage techniques so the fine coffee they bought from you will keep its great taste longer:

* **Keep the beans whole until you're ready to use them.** Whole beans stay fresh for a week, but ground coffee starts losing flavor an hour after it's ground.

* **Store the beans in an airtight container.** It's best to use a glass jar with a rubber gasket. When you're ready, take out only as many beans as you need for each grinding and brewing session. Coffee cans with plastic lids aren't airtight, so don't rely on those.

* **Don't store coffee in the refrigerator, even in an airtight container.** The "oils" in coffee aren't oils at all but rather water-soluble substances that absorb surrounding moisture and odor. Refrigerators tend to be both moist and odiferous, so unless you want a "Colombian and Leftover Chinese" blend, keep the coffee out of the fridge.

* **Place coffee in the freezer only if you plan to store it longer than a week.** If that's the case, use freezer bags and squeeze out as much air as possible. Remove coffee from the freezer as you need it, and don't try to refreeze it. Light roasts fare better than very dark roasts, but all types of coffee can suffer from freezing because the oils may break down in the freezing process.

Labeling Your Coffee

You've roasted your beans, maybe created a house blend, packaged your coffee, and are ready to offer it to your customers for sale or in prepared drinks. But what do you call it? Just like you planned out your coffee shop's logo, theme, décor, and overall style, you should give some thought to what you call your coffee and how it's packaged.

Give each coffee a unique name. You want to make it creative, but not so out there that your customers won't know what they're looking at. Also be sure to have a description of the roasts and blends where customers can easily see it.

Many coffee names include the country where the beans were picked. Non-European country names, such as Kenyan, Mexican, or Ethiopian, let the buyer know the beans were all part of one crop in that one country. European names refer to the darkness of the roast and not the country of origin, which is why you can find French Colombian coffees on supermarket shelves.

Market names are another way to label coffee, with the market being a single town, province, state, port, or landmark that somehow relates to the origin point of the coffee. Moshi, for example, is a large city on the south slope of Tanzania's Mount Kilimanjaro, and beans grown on the mountain carry the market name "Moshi."

Even more specialized than market names are estate names, like Nicaraguan Santa Lucia Estate and Jamaican Blue Mountain Mavis Bank Estate. A coffee that bears an estate name has been grown—and most likely processed—entirely on a single farm or estate. A coffee's flavor varies depending on the soil and altitude it grows in, so an estate coffee is prized because buyers know exactly what they're getting from one batch to the next.

A flavoring agent can be added to almost any coffee, and the coffee name will naturally include that flavor to attract the attention of those customers eager for a taste of vanilla, chocolate, cinnamon, raspberry, amaretto, or dozens of other nuts, spices, and fruits.

"Organic," "Fair Trade," and "decaffeinated" are three more labels that might accompany a coffee's place of origin, roast, grade, and flavor. For a coffee to be labeled organic, one of several international monitoring agencies must verify that no harmful chemicals were used during the beans' lifespan. Fair Trade coffee producers promise to pay coffee growers a set price rather than wildly fluctuating market prices, provide credit at fair rates, and develop long-term relationships with growers. The U.S. Food and Drug Administration doesn't specify how much caffeine has to be removed for a coffee to be labeled decaffeinated, but the general rule of thumb is that decaf is around 97 percent caffeine free. Don't get stuck on Fair Trade or organic certifications. Getting certified costs a lot of money for a small coffee producer, so they may not be able to afford the seal of approval even if they comply with all the regulations. It's up to you to find out if a supplier offers organic coffee or complies with Fair Trade practices; you may even want to visit them and see for yourself. It's a good excuse for a trip!

On each coffee's label, note the name of the coffee, the type of blend, the type of roast, the weight of the package, a few brief tasting notes, and the date the beans were roasted.

Counter *Talk*

Brewpoint's blends are named after unique occupations: the Stargazer, the Acrobat, and the Alchemist. Each coffee's label notes the roast type, origin, tasting notes, weight, and roast date. The bags have to state where the coffee was roasted and list contact information. (A website is sufficient.) Brewpoint's blends are year round, and its single-origin coffees are seasonal. If a certain coffee has a special mission, it's highlighted on the label. For example, Brewpoint proudly supports women-owned farms.

When creating labels for your coffee packages, you can make your own with your shop's logo and the key information highlighted in this section, or you can work with a designer. (See Chapter 6 for more on finding a designer.) As you plan your labels, think about which design aspects you want to be consistent across all labels and which can vary. On Brewpoint's labels, for example, the formatting of the text area is largely the same on each label (modified slightly for single-origin coffees), but the background image changes to match the name of the coffee. Although the graphics are different, the labels share a similar look and create a cohesiveness when viewed together.

Grinding Guidelines

You've picked the beans (from the supplier, not from the tree!), roasted them, and blended them. You packed some for retail sale to customers and have some reserved for use in your shop. There's one final step to go before you can drink the fruits of your labor: grinding.

As we mentioned in the storage section, coffee begins to lose flavor only 1 hour after grinding, so it's best not to grind more than you plan to use immediately. This will be tough when you first open your doors for business because you won't be able to predict how much you'll sell any given day, but as you gain a sales history, you'll be able to plan a grinding schedule that provides customers the freshest taste possible and eliminates wasted ground coffee.

Mechanical grinders offer several different grinding levels, and the more experience you get making different types of coffee drinks, the better you'll get at determining what grind size is best for each. But to start, you could grind the coffee as fine as you can without turning the beans into powder or clogging your brewer's filter. The smaller the particles, the more surface area is available between the coffee and the hot water. More contact equals more flavor from the coffee oils being transferred to the water, making a brew that better reflects the nature of the coffee. As with anything else, practice makes perfect, so experiment with your grinder's grind sizes and learn what's best for the drinks you make.

Also be sure to match the grind to your type of brewer. It's your responsibility to taste batches and determine whether your grind is appropriate, whether your grinder needs cleaning and adjustment, and whether you need to change the degree of fineness.

A burr or conical burr grinder will be ideal for your business. This device, which crushes the beans between moving and nonmoving surfaces, allows you to grind the beans to a consistent size, which means your coffee will have a consistent taste. Burr grinders create little heat, so the flavor of the coffee won't be changed during the grinding process.

Avoid blade grinders. Instead of grinding the beans, the blades work like a blender and slice the beans apart. Because the beans move about freely, the blade grinder mashes the beans into a mix of large chunks, small bits, and powder. This varying bean size creates a different taste with each brew. Even worse, the friction of the blades creates a lot of heat, which can start to cook the beans while they're still being ground. Hardly a recipe for success.

If you serve flavored coffees, consider purchasing a separate grinder for these products so the flavors don't taint the regular coffee. Flavored coffees have their fans, but folks who prefer the plain stuff won't welcome an unexpected hit of vanilla or hazelnut.

Making small pots of coffee to test new blends or offer customers sample tastes? Consider grinding the beans old-style—with a mortar and pestle. This tool served humans for hundreds of years, and the personal touch allows you to fine-tune the grinding to perfection.

Even if you feel that hand grinding is too much of a, well, grind, don't shy away from making mortars and pestles available to customers in your retail space. Many people feel homemade cooking is always better, and although they're unlikely to fly to South America to pick their own beans, a hand grinder might be perfect for their kitchen.

Preparing the Perfect Pot

After all that roasting and grinding, it's time to finally make coffee! And what a simple process brewing is at heart: you soak ground coffee in water until the water tastes good. You could get away with just a metal pot, an open fire, and a strainer, but there's probably a law against having open fires in your shop.

A drip coffee maker is fine for home use, but in a retail environment, you need to think in bigger terms. How many roasts, types, and flavors do you want to offer? How much should you make of each type? How do you make coffee on such a large scale? Let's look at each of these questions in more detail.

How Many Types of Coffee Should You Offer?

It's crucial to find a balance between providing all things to all people and wasting lots of money by pouring unsold coffee down the drain. The key is to offer variety without overwhelming the customer with coffees that differ only slightly.

Although you can find or make a dozen different roasts, your best bet is to offer only three: light, medium, and dark. You can name the roasts with more specialized terms (see the earlier section on naming and labeling your coffee), but be sure to post the generic terms as well, so customers know how to ask for what they want.

In addition to reducing customer confusion, offering only a few roasts also makes the job easier for your employees. They'll have just three roasts to match (if you roast your own beans), less chance of mixing up customer orders, and fewer carafes or thermoses to clean.

For the same reasons, stick with only three types or blends of coffee. For variety, you might choose to offer one or two different blends daily, but most customers value consistency and want the same drink every day. You don't want to throw these folks for a loop with a constantly shifting menu, or they'll find some other place for their morning brew.

As for flavored coffee, one or two types should be all you need. This provides customers a taste of the larger coffee world without you sinking too much time and money in brews that lack the widespread appeal of "plain" coffee. What's more, flavors linger in thermoses no matter how much you wash them, so you don't want to invest in 20 separate thermoses for all the flavors you carry. And don't forget you can give customers almost any flavor they want by adding flavored syrups like vanilla, cinnamon, and hazelnut.

How Much of Each Type Should You Make?

The right answer to this question will come only with time. The longer your store is open, the more sales data you'll have to draw on, and the more accurate you'll be when deciding how much coffee to make. (We talk more about how to use sales data in Chapter 20.)

The answer to this question also depends on which type of brewing system you use. The best system for a retail environment might be one that brews coffee directly into a thermal carafe. Because the coffee isn't exposed to air and retains its heat, it can stay fresh for hours, reducing waste and rebrewing time.

How Do You Make Coffee on a Large Scale?

The essence of coffee-making remains the same, whether you're brewing 1 cup or 100:

* Grind the coffee immediately before brewing.

* Use at least 2 level tablespoons coffee per 6-ounce cup, unless your brewing equipment recommends otherwise.

* Clean the coffee maker and grounds basket after each use; rinse the carafes with hot water before each brew.

* Use fresh or filtered water. Coffee is 98 percent water, so if the water tastes like anything at all, that taste will carry over into the coffee.

* Water needs to be near-boiling for the best brew. In-line systems heat the water to a preset temperature before passing it over the grounds.

Coffee might taste strong, but it's actually quite delicate. If you boil or reheat coffee, you cook off elements of the flavor and leave more bitter components behind. Storing coffee over a heat source has the same effect. Mixing old with new coffee is another no-no. Sure, you want to save money by not wasting coffee, but reusing or reviving coffee robs customers of a clean coffee taste—and will cost you far more in the long run.

Congratulations! You now know all about the different types of coffee beans and roasts, plus how to grind beans and brew the perfect pot. A lot more goes into a coffee shop menu than, well, coffee—so next, we talk about specialty coffee drinks, espresso, dairy options, flavored syrups, and other coffee enhancers.

Beans with a Boost

Regular coffee may still be the king of sales, but the world of coffee drinks goes far beyond "I'll take it black." Espresso has been around for nearly two centuries, for example, and in an effort to reach new markets, innovative coffee shops and experimental baristas have come up with all kinds of tasty coffee treats.

Whether you want to create concoctions of your own design or merely be able to satisfy every request a customer throws at you, let this chapter be your guide to the international world of coffee drinks. Assume the role of drink ambassador, and get ready to send your customers on a tasty trip!

The World of Specialty Coffee Drinks

Specialty coffees are usually built on a base of espresso with steamed or aerated milk—although some drinks contain no beans at all. Specialty coffee drinks include the following:

* Cappuccino

* Latte

* Café au lait (This is made with drip-brewed coffee, not espresso.)

* Hot chocolate

* Flavored steamed milk

* Mocha

* Iced coffee, including cold brew coffee

* Blended frozen coffee drinks

And that's only the beginning of what's possible! When you become comfortable making these drinks, you can blend elements from two or more different drinks, search online to find drinks popular in other countries but unknown in the United States, or let customers' tastes guide you in fresh directions.

Deciding on Dairy

Before we plunge into the drinks themselves, let's look at one of their most important ingredients: milk. Many coffee drinks call for steamed, or aerated, milk, which we describe in a bit. Because milk holds its heat, its texture, and most importantly its flavor far longer than espresso, you'll want to prepare the milk first.

Milk is categorized according to its fat content: skim (nonfat), 1 percent, 2 percent, and whole. Do you have to offer your customers all these choices?

Whole milk is the most popular, with nonfat and 2 percent tied for second. If you're in an area with limited competition, you may be able to get away with offering something middle of the road, such as 2 percent. But if you're in a competitive area or have customers with sophisticated tastes, you may want to offer more choices—and even nondairy alternatives like soy, almond, coconut, or oat milks, which are popular options for vegan, health-conscious, or dairy-intolerant customers. Some customers also order their drinks "breve," which means made with half-and-half, so you may want to offer this option as well.

Whole milk is the most common choice for drinks that contain steamed milk. When milk is steamed, its fat content breaks down. So whole milk, which contains more fat, retains more of its fat during steaming and results in a drink that's much more flavorful than one made with skim milk, which has little if any fat that's quickly broken down during steaming. When you offer free samples of drinks to entice new customers, be sure to use whole milk so they experience the richest taste possible!

And then there's whipped cream. Canned whipped cream is bad for the environment and is also inferior in taste and texture to fresh, so invest in a dispenser and chargers, and order fresh pints of cream as you need them. A whipped cream dispenser looks something like an old-time seltzer bottle. It uses nitrous oxide chargers to blast the liquid cream into its smooth, whipped condition and dispense it through the nozzle on top. Load a dispenser with other ingredients, and you can make sweet sauces as well.

Counter *Talk*

Brewpoint offers almond, coconut, and oat milks. As of this writing, the oat milk brand Brewpoint uses is in short supply because it's so popular. The local supplier chose Brewpoint and two large coffee businesses, much to the dismay of other (bigger) cafés because Melissa and Angelo were nice to them. It pays to be nice to your suppliers!

Steaming Milk

Steaming, or aerating, is key to preparing milk for specialty coffees. When you steam milk, you add water, air, and heat to it using the steam wand on your espresso machine.

There are two styles of steamed milk—latte milk and cappuccino milk. The only difference is the texture, which is determined by how much you aerate the milk. Latte milk is heavier and more liquid; cappuccino milk is lighter and more velvety, with that foam we're all familiar with.

Steaming milk has two main stages: first you focus on adding air and then you add heat.

You've seen the baristas at your local coffee shop expertly steam milk. Now it's your turn to learn how:

1. Fill the steaming pitcher with cold milk for the drink you're making (up to a maximum of two-thirds full).

2. Release a short burst of steam from the wand to purge any water and old milk in the wand.

3. Position the steam wand in the milk. The wand should not touch the pitcher, but it should be angled along the curve of the pitcher to create a whirlpool effect when the steam is on. Position the tip of the wand just under the surface of the milk ($^{13}\!/_{64}$ inch/.5 cm).

4. Hold the pitcher by the handle with one hand. After you turn on the steam, you'll place your other hand on the pitcher opposite of where the steam wand is pointing.

5. Turn on the steam and add air. When the wand is on, you should hear short, controlled bursts of air that sound like paper tearing. This is the milk folding over the air that's being added. If it's splashing or creating deep gurgling sounds, submerge the wand deeper in the milk. If you're not hearing anything, your wand is too deep and you should pull it up a bit. To make latte milk, add air for 1 to 3 seconds. To make cappuccino milk, add air until the pitcher is warm to the touch; the extra air creates the foam that sits on top of a cappuccino.

6. After you've added the correct amount of air, submerge the tip of the wand about ¾ inch (2 cm) under the surface of the milk. Don't let the wand touch the bottom of the pitcher.

7. Turn off the steam wand about 2 seconds after the pitcher becomes uncomfortable to the touch. (You'll learn how to get a feel for the right temperature—literally.) Be sure to remove your hand from the pitcher at that point, too.

8. Place the pitcher on the counter and allow it to rest.

9. Immediately wipe down the exterior of the steam wand with a dedicated steam wand towel and purge it by releasing a quick burst of steam. (You need to wipe the wand at this stage, but you don't need to do it before you start the steaming process; only a purge is necessary before.) Take care not to touch the wand with your bare hands. All that steam passing through the wand heats it enough to burn your skin on contact.

10. Firmly tap the bottom of the pitcher on a hard surface to burst any large bubbles of foam. Swirl or fold the milk to ensure a smooth consistency throughout the entire pitcher, and pour.

Practice steaming milk a few times, and soon you'll become an expert at it!

Pulling Espresso Shots

To make many of the specialty coffee drinks we've mentioned, knowing how to pull a great shot of espresso is crucial. The espresso machine does a lot of the work for you, but you still must master the basics.

Espresso 101

A good shot of espresso—which is always pronounced with an *eS* and not an *eX*—is created from freshly ground coffee packed tightly into a portafilter and brewed with hot, high-pressure water.

Most espresso recipes have a dose, time, and yield. The dose is how much dry coffee to use, the time is how long the espresso is brewed, and the yield is how much liquid coffee you get. The measurements and timing may differ depending on who you talk to. Brewpoint, for example, uses 17.5 ounces ground coffee (dose) to make 35 grams liquid coffee (yield) in 28 seconds (time). Sound like high school science? Don't fret—we give you a step-by-step guide to pulling the perfect shot in a sec.

You can make espresso with any coffee you like, and it can be roasted however you like. Whatever you decide on, though, be sure you stick with it, because the consistency of your product is key to keeping customers.

To get the best flavor from the coffee during the short brewing time, espresso is ground very finely. This results in more coffee surface area for the water to come in contact with and extract flavor from. Coffee tastes best when it's made from freshly ground beans, so grind your espresso as the drinks are ordered. To test the grind of your espresso, take a pinch between your thumb and forefinger and slide it around. If it feels like flour, it's too fine. If it feels like sugar, it's too coarse. If it feels like grains of sand, it's perfect. (We covered grinders in more detail in Chapter 10.)

How to Make a Perfect Espresso

When you first try to work an espresso machine, the process will likely seem as clear as mud. Your first pull of espresso might even *taste* like mud! Let's review the terms you need to know, from parts on the espresso machine itself, to supplementary equipment, to what to look for in the cup:

A *doser* is a device mounted on your grinder that measures and dispenses ground coffee into a portafilter. (Not all grinders have dosers.)

Dosing is the act of measuring out espresso from your grinder. It's best to use a scale for this to ensure accuracy.

A *portafilter* looks a bit like a bicycle handlebar grip with a small, round metal cup on one end. The coffee grounds for espresso are dosed into the portafilter basket. Later you tamp the grounds and then attach the portafilter to a group head on your espresso machine.

A *distribution tool* is a round, flat device used to create a uniform brew bed before the espresso is tamped.

A *tamper* is a tool with a mushroom-shaped wood or aluminum handle and a flat metal base that's used to pack the espresso grounds into the portafilter. Avoid plastic tampers because they break and chip when dropped.

A *group head* is the port on the espresso machine where the espresso is brewed. Espresso machines come with one to four groups. Hot water runs through the group head, over the grounds held in the filter insert, and out the spouts on the bottom of the portafilter into the waiting cup.

Crema (also *creama*) is the rich, golden-brown foam that occurs naturally at the top of a good shot of espresso. The characteristics of the crema depend on the grind, the length of the extraction time, and other factors.

Now let's demystify the process of pulling espresso shots.

ESPRESSO

1. Remove the portafilter, and run a short burst of hot water through the group head. This cleans the group head screen of excess coffee and ensures that there's fresh water in the group head ready to brew.

2. Wipe the interior of the brew basket with a dedicated portafilter towel, removing any old grounds and water.

3. Place the cleaned portafilter under your grinder's chute (basket first!), and start the grinder to grind your dose. Brewpoint uses timed grinders that they dial in to grind the correct dose (which, for Brewpoint, is 17.5 grams dry coffee).

4. Tap the outer edge of the portafilter with your hand to even out the ground espresso because it'll often mound under the grinder. Tap the portafilter straight up and down on a firm surface to settle the espresso and ensure no air pockets remain under the surface, or use a distribution tool to evenly and uniformly distribute the espresso.

5. Holding the tamper like a doorknob, with your thumb and fingers on opposite sides of the handle, turn your body parallel with the portafilter handle, place the tamper in the portafilter basket, and hold your tamping arm in an L shape, creating a 90-degree angle between your forearm and upper arm. Keeping your wrist straight, lean on the tamper, applying level pressure to the espresso. Use your body weight for this, not your arm strength!

6. Wipe the exterior lip of the brew basket to remove any dry coffee there.

7. Lock the portafilter into the group head.

8. Immediately start the hot water to brew; at the same time, start a timer if your machine does not have one built-in; and place a vessel under the group head to collect the espresso. Turn off the water at the appropriate time. Most coffee shops pull shots between 22 and 32 seconds for regular espresso. Brewpoint ends their shots at 28 seconds. You can end your shots around 18 to 22 seconds for ristretto shots. (More on ristretto later in this chapter.)

9. Mix the espresso with any milks or syrups necessary for the drink, and serve immediately because espresso's flavor deteriorates quickly.

10. Remove the portafilter and knock out the espresso puck. (That's the used grounds, which should come out as one piece.) Wipe the interior of the brew basket with the dedicated portafilter towel, and purge the group head again.

Learning how to make espresso takes dedication, and no one gets it right the first, the fifth, or sometimes even the fiftieth time. Every employee will likely add his or her own personal twist to the brewing process, but first they—and you—must master the basics.

Counter *Talk*   Ever go to a coffee shop and get an amazing espresso drink, return the next day for another one, and it doesn't taste as good? It's probably because the staff hasn't been calibrating the grinder. This results in coffee particles that are a different size, which affects the flavor of the brewed coffee. The grinder calibration goes off bit by bit over time and with changes in the weather, so Brewpoint staff calibrate the grinders every couple hours.

Specialty Espressos

When is an espresso not an espresso? When it's one of these espresso variations:

* **Americano.** Espresso with water added to dilute the espresso so it's more similar to drip brew

* **Double (or *doppio*).** A double shot, for the ultimate pick-me-up

* **Espresso con panna.** Espresso topped with whipped cream

* **Espresso macchiato.** Espresso topped with a dollop of foamed milk

* **Espresso Romano.** A serving of espresso with a twist of lemon on the side

* **Lungo.** Espresso made using more water and a longer extraction time, resulting in a weaker drink

* **Ristretto.** About .75 ounce of espresso; the first, sweet burst of espresso that comes out of the machine

But wait, there's more! For many customers, espresso is merely the base into which everything else is mixed or added. Learning to pull is the first step; next you start mixing and matching, gaining more knowledge with every drink about what espresso can do.

Counter *Talk*   Melissa and Angelo planned to buy an espresso machine to practice with before opening their coffee shop. If you can find a machine that's in your budget, this is a great way to test your skills while you're working on the rest of your business plan.

How to Make Specialty Coffee Drinks

You've got the espresso (after enough measuring and timing to make you feel like a scientist), and you've got the steamed milk. Let's look at how to put them together to make delicious specialty coffee drinks.

Counter *Talk*   Keep in mind that each shop uses its own formulas, and you're free to experiment with different amounts of espresso, milk, and syrups. At Brewpoint, for example, a classic small vanilla latte has two shots of espresso and two pumps of vanilla and is topped with latte milk. Some other cafés may use only one shot of espresso.

CAPPUCCINO

1. Pour or pull espresso into a cup—12-ounce cup for small, 16-ounce cup for medium, or 20-ounce cup for large. (The amount of espresso varies by shop; Brewpoint puts two shots in a small, two in a medium, and three or four in a large.)

2. Fill the cup with cappuccino milk, and serve. (A "dry" cappuccino has more foamed milk and less hot steamed liquid milk.)

LATTE

1. Pour or pull espresso into a cup—12-ounce cup for small, 16-ounce cup for medium, or 20-ounce cup for large.

2. Fill the cup with latte milk, and serve.

CAFÉ AU LAIT

1. Fill a cup half full with coffee.

2. Top off with latte milk, and serve.

ESPRESSO CON PANNA

1. Pour a shot of espresso.

2. Top with whipped cream, and serve.

LUNGO

1. Make an espresso, but use 5 to 7 ounces water and run through for about 60 seconds.

2. Serve.

BREVE

1. Prepare a standard latte or cappuccino, but use half-and-half instead of regular milk.

2. Serve.

MOCHA

1. Cover the bottom of an 8-ounce cup with chocolate syrup. (For a large, use a 12- to 16-ounce cup and two shots of espresso.)

2. Pour or pull one shot of espresso into the cup.

3. Fill the cup seven-eighths full with latte milk, top with whipped cream, and serve.

HOT CHOCOLATE

1. Cover the bottom of a cup with chocolate syrup. Use about .75 ounce for an 8-ounce cup, 1 ounce for a 12-ounce cup, and 1.25 ounces for a 16-ounce cup.

2. Fill the cup seven-eighths full with latte milk, top with whipped cream, and serve.

FLAVORED STEAMED MILK

1. Pour flavored syrup and cold milk into a foaming container. Use about .5 ounce syrup and 6.5 ounces milk for an 8-ounce cup, .75 ounce syrup and 10.25 ounces milk for a 12-ounce cup, and 1 ounce syrup and 14 ounces milk for a 16-ounce cup.

2. Steam the mixture to a temperature of 160°F (71°C), and serve.

COLD BREW COFFEE

1. In a 2-quart pitcher, combine 1¾ cups coarsely ground coffee and 3½ cups cold water.

2. Cover the pitcher with plastic wrap, and set aside at room temperature for at least 12 hours.

3. Strain out coffee, and you have 2 cups coffee concentrate.

4. To serve, pour equal amounts coffee concentrate and water, milk, or half-and-half over ice.

Counter *Talk*   Cold brew coffee is known for its smooth taste and lower acidity. Unlike regular iced coffee, which is brewed hot and then chilled, cold brew coffee is brewed in cold or room-temperature water. It's easy to prepare, although a bit time-consuming because it needs to brew for at least 12 hours. Large-batch cold brew coffee systems are available; Brewpoint uses the Toddy Cold Brew System.

Syrups and Sauces

Many customers want more than the perfect shot of espresso, blended with the exact quantity of steamed milk—they also want it flavored. You can purchase syrups and sauces with flavors that go well in coffee drinks, hot chocolate, Italian and French sodas (more about these in Chapter 17), and steamed milk. Here are a few of the flavors available:

* Vanilla

* Almond

* Mint

* Hazelnut

* Raspberry

* Lime

* Orange

* Mango

* Boysenberry

If you have a half dozen or so different flavors to choose from, your customers should be very happy. Select half of your syrups from the nutty or sweet side of the spectrum for coffees, such as vanilla and almond, and half from the fruity side for Italian and French sodas, such as raspberry and boysenberry.

Getting Creative

If you want, get really experimental and develop your own drinks. Coffee shops these days are making surprisingly unique concoctions by mixing coffee or espresso with ingredients like these:

* Eggnog

* Rose water

* Coconut water

* Coffee jelly

* Beer

* Ice cream

* Tea

* Vanilla cola

* Sea salt

* Condensed milk

* Honey

* Chocolate hazelnut spread

You name it, and someone's probably putting it in coffee—and using it as a brand differentiator. Try mixing and matching new flavors, taste-testing the recipes, and even holding a contest for customers to create their own drinks or help name the ones you came up with.

The unique flavored syrups available today can help you come up with new taste sensations. Fig-vanilla, toasted marshmallow, brown butter, tiramisu, kiwi, smoked maple syrup, and cardamom rosewater are just a few of the more-unusual syrup flavors available.

Look to other countries for inspiration, too. For example, there's a Senegalese drink called café Touba made with African black pepper, and one called Portuguese mazagran that contains espresso, water, ice, and lemon juice.

Counter *Talk*

Two of Brewpoint's most popular drinks are a lavender chai, made with lavender, cardamom, and other unique flavors, and a salted prazelnut latte, which contains praline, hazelnut, and sea salt and is topped with whipped cream and sprinkled with more sea salt. Every season Melissa, Angelo, and the general managers taste-test new creations proposed by employees or even customers to decide which recipes will make it onto the menu.

This chapter is packed with enough information to keep you practicing your steaming and pulling, refining your technique, and testing new recipe ideas for weeks. In the meantime, let's move on to another key drink. Coffee is the basis of any good coffee shop, of course, but you'd be leaving out a large portion of the drinking public if you ignored another popular beverage: tea.

Tea for Two— or Two Hundred

Let's take a break from our immersion in all things coffee and spend a few pages talking about the world's other favorite hot drink: tea. Not everyone who walks into your store will be a coffee fan, after all, so to keep all your visitors happy, you'll want a variety of drinks on hand.

An obvious choice for a coffee alternative, tea can be served both hot and cold. Its preparation requires many of the same items as coffee (clean filtered water, insulated cups, sugar, milk), and it's best taken with a side order of cookies or biscuits—thus boosting food sales at the same time!

Tales of Tea

Tea, known by the scientific name *Camellia sinensis,* has been part of our culinary menu for anywhere from 1,800 to 4,700 years. The origins of tea are unclear, but Chinese legend credits Emperor Shen Nung, who ruled in the 2730s B.C.E., with the discovery.

Supposedly Emperor Nung was boiling a pot of water to drink (boiling sterilized the water) when a leaf from a nearby tea bush landed in the pot and infused the water with its flavor. The emperor tried the flavored water, found it invigorating, and added tea to his stock of herbal medicine. (Would you drink water that had been tainted and discolored by a random leaf? Probably not, but that boldness must be why Shen Nung was emperor in the first place.)

The Japanese offer a competing tale of tea's origin, which involves Bodhidharma, the man who brought Buddhism from India to China and Japan. Around 520 C.E., Bodhidharma started a 9-year course of meditation, during which he would do nothing but stare at a wall.

Five years into his mission, Bodhidharma grew weary for a moment and closed his eyes. When he awoke, he was so furious with himself for falling asleep that he ripped off his eyelids and threw them on the ground. A plant grew from the bits of his flesh, and he brewed its leaves into a drink that kept him alert through the remaining 4 years of his meditation.

Putting aside the myths, written records show that tea was part of daily life in China by the eighth century. Chinese merchants spread tea throughout Asia by trading goods with Turks, Japanese, and others.

The Dutch started importing tea from China in the early seventeenth century and made the drink a hit with aristocrats in England. By the 1650s, prices had dropped enough that British coffeehouses were serving tea as an alternative to coffee and hot chocolate. (The more things change ….)

European traders spread the love of tea to North America and throughout the rest of the world. Now it's a hugely popular drink. The global tea market was valued at more than $49 million in 2017, according to GlobeNewswire (globenewswire.com), and is expected to reach $73 million by 2024. Sri Lanka, the Indian Ocean island formerly known as Ceylon, is now the third-largest producer of tea in the world—and for an interesting reason. Sri Lanka once produced only coffee, but in 1869, disease wiped out the coffee bean plantations. Tea was introduced to replace the beans, and now Sri Lanka is a powerhouse of tea production.

Then we have iced tea, which we can't leave out of our history lesson. In the summer of 1904, Englishman Richard Blechynden was hired by Indian tea growers to promote tea at the World's Fair in St. Louis, Missouri. To no one's surprise but his, the hot tea was a sales failure in the steamy American Midwest. Desperate to make sales, Blechynden poured the tea over ice and created a cool treat that was a hit with hot fair-goers.

Tea Leaf Tutorial

As with coffee and its range of roasts, the flavor of a tea bush's leaves depends as much on how the leaves are processed as it does on the type of bush from which the leaves are picked.

In fact, you can take leaves from a single bush and process them in different ways to make green, black, and oolong tea. The processing methods mainly differ in how much fermentation—the chemical reaction between air and the leaf's natural enzymes—occurs inside the leaves.

The best-tasting teas are those made from a *fine picking,* or a harvest in which only the top two leaves and bud are plucked from the tea plant. A *coarse picking* grabs up to five leaves from the stem, and these inner leaves provide a harsher-tasting tea that usually ends up in CTC (crush, tear, curl) products, such as low-cost tea bags.

Processing Green Tea Leaves

To make green tea, the freshly picked leaves are steamed or pan-fried, destroying the enzymes and preventing fermentation. Without fermentation, the leaves' oils and antioxidants remain in their natural state, which is why green tea tastes most like the leaves themselves.

Steaming also softens the leaves, which makes it easier for handlers during the next step: rolling or twisting the leaves. This action, performed by machine for mass-production batches and by hand for specialty blends, breaks down the cells in the leaves so the flavorful oils and juices will infuse the water during brewing.

The leaves are then heated again to dry them out. The rolling/heating cycle might be repeated one or more times to slowly remove the moisture from the leaves.

Finally, the green tea is graded based on its age and shape. The best grade, gunpowder, is given to young leaves rolled into tiny BB-like pellets. Other grades include young hyson (rolled or twisted middle-aged leaves) and imperial (old leaves that resemble gunpowder), but the names might vary depending on the source of the leaves.

Want to grow your own tea? You can grow *Camellia sinensis* on your own—it's often grown as an ornamental plant—but be sure to keep a pair of pruning shears handy. In the wild, untended tea plants can grow up to 30 feet high!

Processing Black Tea Leaves

Black tea is everything green tea isn't. During processing, the leaves are laid out to dry, either in the sun or the shade, depending on the type of tea. After the leaves have started to shrivel, they're rolled by hand or machine to mix air with the natural juices, and this starts the fermentation process in earnest.

After only a few hours, the leaves have turned a coppery red and are dried a second time to stop fermentation from changing the leaves' taste any further. When they're dry, the whole leaves, broken bits, and dust are sifted so particles of the same size end up together. This creates a finished product with an even brewing time.

Grades for black tea correspond to the size of the leaves or pieces: *orange pekoe* (OP) refers to whole leaves, *broken orange pekoe* (BOP) is used for large pieces of leaves, *fannings* is used for small bits, and *dust* is exactly what it sounds like.

Fannings and dust grades typically end up being used in mass-market tea bags because the large amount of surface area causes the tea to infuse quickly and make a dark cup of tea. As with coffee, though, the large surface area also means that any unpleasant flavors in the leaves will find their way into the cup.

Oolong: Between Green and Black

Oolong tea falls between green and black in that the leaves are fermented, but not completely, so the leaves carry a mix of their natural flavor and the fermented juices. Whereas green tea is favored throughout Asia, and black tea far outsells everything else in the Western hemisphere, the "little bit of this, little bit of that" taste of oolong tea accounts for only 2 percent of all tea sold.

More specialized teas with even smaller market shares (and higher retail prices) include pouchong tea, which also falls between green and oolong on the processing scale, and white tea. White tea is processed like green tea—that is, not very much—but the leaves are harvested before they fully open, when the buds are covered with delicate white hairs.

Flavored Teas

As with coffee beans, tea leaves can have flavors and scents added to them to create tastes not found in nature. The Chinese have had flavored tea for at least a thousand years, and their methods still work today, although machines now give the process a bit more *oomph*.

To create jasmine tea, for example, harvesters gather jasmine blossoms at dawn before they've bloomed for the day. The blossoms are placed on or mixed with dry tea leaves destined to be either green or oolong, and when evening comes, the blossoms open their petals and the tea leaves absorb the jasmine aroma. This process is repeated anywhere from two to nine times to create the desired level of jasmine flavor.

In other cases, such as with vanilla, peach, and orange teas, the flavoring is sprayed on the tea leaves before they're heated. Earl Grey, for instance, is made with oil of bergamot, which is extracted from the peel of the bergamot orange, a sour pear-shaped fruit cultivated mostly in southern Italy. As the tea leaves dry, they absorb the flavor of the oil. Lapsang souchong, on the other hand, gets its intense smoky flavor by smoking the tea leaves over pine wood. Spiced teas often contain dried spices and pieces of fruit rinds to perk up the flavor and increase the visual appeal of the tea.

Chai Tea

In many parts of the world, *chai* is the word for "tea." In the United States, however, *chai* refers to a specific kind of milky spiced tea that originated in India, where it's known as *masala chai*.

Typically, chai is made using black tea leaves. A combination of cardamom, cinnamon, cloves, ginger, black pepper, fennel, and allspice is added, as are warm milk and a sweetener such as granulated sugar, honey, or a flavored syrup.

Making chai by hand is time-consuming because different ingredients must steep for different lengths of time and the spices must be strained from the drink prior to serving. Thankfully for busy coffee shops that can't afford to spend 10 minutes on a single drink, dry chai mixes are available that provide a taste nearly equal to homemade.

Chai latte, which is more popular than chai in many coffee shops, is similar to chai except it's made specifically with steamed milk instead of milk warmed any other way. (We talked about how to steam milk in Chapter 15, and that advice will serve you well with this popular drink.)

Herbal "Teas"

All teas are herbal because an herb is any plant with medicinal, savory, or aromatic qualities—the very definition of tea, in other words—but not all herbal teas are actually teas. Instead of using the leaves and buds from *Camellia sinensis,* most herbal teas use dried leaves, bark, roots, or flowers from other types of plants.

Rose petals, mint, ginseng, chamomile, and even catnip are all examples of plants that aren't actually tea that make a surprisingly tealike drink when they're infused in hot water.

New Tea on the Block: Rooibos

Speaking of herbal tea, one that's recently skyrocketed in popularity is rooibos (pronounced *ROY-bohs*), a caffeine-free red tea made from the leaves of the South African shrub *Aspalathus linearis.* Rooibos is known for its high antioxidant content and is hearty enough to drink like black tea, with milk and sweetener, and even as a tasty latte with cinnamon and honey. (Can't get the pronunciation right? Check YouTube for videos showing you how to say it.)

Antioxidant Matcha

Another popular antioxidant powerhouse of a tea is matcha, which is an earthy-tasting green tea powder from Japan that's used in tea ceremonies. In the United States, matcha has become popular on its own or in lattes with flavored syrups like rose, vanilla, or mint.

Key Tea Considerations

We've filled your head with a treasury of tea lore, but now you need to push aside the romance of tea and make a practical decision on how you should sell tea at your coffee bar. In no-name tea bags? In specialty tea bags? Loose in individual teapots? By the pot as well as by the cup?

To help you decide, consider the following questions:

How many customers will buy tea? Clearly you won't know the answer to this question before you open, but you can estimate the number by examining coffee shops and restaurants around town. How many types of tea do they offer compared to types of coffee? How do tea sales compare to coffee sales at the local doughnut shop? Does your town already support a tea shop?

What image are you trying to project in your coffee shop? If your image is homespun and down-to-earth, customers will welcome commonly known brands of tea bags. If you're aiming more for an upscale image, shy away from supermarket brands of teabags and sell only specialty brands or even loose tea.

With loose tea, you then have to decide whether to use tea balls (stainless-steel, wire-mesh strainers that allow water to circulate through the leaves), opt for filters that fit into teapots, or throw the leaves in loose.

What can you charge for tea, and how long will it take to make? Serving tea is akin to serving specialty coffee drinks—you make each order individually as the customer requests it. If you decide to carry loose tea, employees need to measure the tea as they make each cup or pot and heat the water to the right temperature. (More on that coming up.) They'll spend as much time preparing tea as they would making, say, a latte. Can you charge an equivalent price, or will customers reject the price tag?

Keep in mind that you can choose a combination of offerings—loose tea leaves for most drinks but a dry mix for chai, for example—and you can always change your store's offerings should tea prove to be more or less popular than your research originally showed.

Tea Brewing Basics

The title of this chapter could have been "Separated at Birth?" because coffee and tea share an amazing number of similarities: they're the two most popular hot drinks in the world, their taste depends largely on how the raw materials are roasted and cooked, and flavored versions are becoming increasingly popular.

With that in mind, let's look at what goes into brewing a cup or pot of tea and see what other similarities we can find between the two brews.

Water Essentials

As with coffee, brewed tea is 99 percent water and 1 percent solids and essences extracted from the raw materials. To ensure that the water doesn't distract the drinker from the taste of the tea, use only filtered, nonchlorinated water for brewing.

If you have a pour-over coffee brewing system (one in which you heat water and add it manually to the brewer) you're all set because you can use the same water source for tea that you use for coffee. If you own an in-line brewing system that heats the water internally, the machine most likely has a separate valve that dispenses hot water.

Unfortunately, "hot" water isn't specific enough for our purposes. Teas require water certain temperatures for optimum brewing results. (They also require certain steep times, which we discuss a little later in the chapter.)

* Green tea leaves are the most fragile, delivering their best flavor when steeped in water that's between 160°F and 175°F (71°C and 79°C).

* Oolongs are best when steeped in water that's heated to 203°F (95°C).

* Black teas are best when steeped in 203°F (95°C) water.

* Herbal teas are best when steeped in 203°F (95°C) water.

To take the water's temperature, you can use the milk thermometer you bought to help steam milk. With a bit of experience, though, you'll be able to judge the temperature solely by sight and sound. Between 160°F and 170°F (71°C and 77°C), the water will be on the verge of simmering, so it should appear somewhat restless. At 190°F (88°C), steam will rise from the water and bubbles will come to the surface. A rolling boil is exactly what it sounds like: bubbles tumbling all over each other like children in a ball pit.

> **Counter** *Talk*   Brewpoint baristas use electric tea kettles that can be set to different temperatures depending on the tea being made.

Measuring Cup Size

At home or in the office, most of us make a "cup" of tea in a standard 8-ounce mug. Tea experts, however, have a different size cup in mind—one that holds only 5.5 ounces.

You should feel free to ignore the experts and use whatever size cups you want in your business, but keep in mind that all references to cups in instructions for making tea refer to those holding 5.5 ounces.

Speaking of cups, consider the material of the vessel you're serving tea in. Tea cups and pots build up a brownish haze over time that can add a slight bitterness to each new cup. If you plan to use disposable cups in your coffee shop, this is a nonissue. But if you're using ceramic teapots and cups to satisfy an upscale clientele, be sure to clean all vessels thoroughly with a mild detergent or baking soda to remove the haze.

Measuring Tea

How much tea should you use? For each cup of water—5.5 ounce cups, mind you—a cup or teapot holds, add 1 teaspoon loose tea or 1 teabag. With loose tea, use an actual teaspoon when first measuring the leaves and then transfer the tea to the spoons you'll use every day in the shop so you can eyeball the measurement in the future.

Tea Times

Brewing time is really the key to tea. Brew it too long, and it gets bitter. Brew it too little, and you'll just have colored water with barely a hint of flavor.

In general, the smaller the leaf, the faster the brewing time. Tea bags, which use tiny bits of leaves and dust, should brew for no longer than 3 minutes for individual cups. Medium- and large-size black tea leaves should brew for up to 5 minutes. Green teas should steep between 2 and 3 minutes, while oolongs need from 4 to 7 minutes. Soft water infuses tea more easily than hard, so we recommend increasing brewing times a bit if your shop uses hard water. (Although do consider a filter if you have hard water because it can affect the flavor of your drinks.)

You'll likely hand the tea to customers right away, and that's both good and bad. Fast service is good because, like coffee, tea tastes best when it's consumed immediately after brewing—and you can start serving the next customer and keep the line moving! The bad part is that the customer doesn't know how long the tea has brewed. Color alone doesn't tell the whole story; a tea isn't ready to be sipped just because it's brown (or green). And once the tea is in the customer's hands, he might leave the tea bag or leaves in the cup long past the optimal brewing time, making the tea more bitter.

The best thing you can do—aside from waiting by the customer's table and yanking out the teabag at the proper time—is tell customers how long to wait for the brewing process to run its course. You can also hand out small sand timers for customers to use while in the store, which is a nice touch.

Milk and More

Like coffee, tea can be enjoyed black, or it can be jazzed up with skim, 2 percent, or full-fat milk and sweeteners such as granulated sugar, sugar cubes, honey, or (as the Russians sometimes like it) a dollop of raspberry jam. Some tea drinkers also like a touch of fresh lemon juice.

Whether you add these extras to the tea yourself or let customers customize their own tea depends on the layout of your coffee shop, a topic covered in detail in Chapter 11.

Counter Talk Don't limit your staff training to coffee topics. Melissa includes tea education in her staff training because customers often ask questions about the different tea varieties, too.

Iced Tea

So far we've talked only about the hot stuff, but when the summer months roll around, your customers will likely be far more interested in your selection of iced teas.

Iced tea, unlike its hot, fresh-today, stale-in-an-hour cousin, doesn't need to be made fresh for each customer. Equipment vendors have many styles of iced tea machines that create the drink with just a touch of a button, and iced tea typically retains its flavor for a full 24 hours.

If you like—and if you think your customers will appreciate the difference—you can make your own iced tea by hand.

ICED GREEN TEA

1. In a 2-quart pitcher, combine 20 grams green tea and 1 quart (160°F/71°C to 175°F/79°C) water.

2. Steep for 12 minutes.

3. Remove tea, add ice to fill the pitcher, and serve over more ice.

ICED BLACK TEA

1. In a 2-quart pitcher, combine 20 grams black tea and 1 quart (203°F/95°C) water.

2. Steep for 7 minutes.

3. Remove tea, add ice to fill the pitcher, and serve over more ice.

ICED HERBAL TEA

1. In a 2-quart pitcher, combine 35 grams herbal tea and 1 quart (203°F/95°C) water.

2. Steep for 20 minutes.

3. Remove tea, add ice to fill the pitcher, and serve over more ice.

When it comes to herbal tea, the steeping time may vary depending on the type of tea you use. This timing is for a fruity herbal. Experiment to discover the right steeping time for other types of herbal tea.

You might have noticed the steep times for iced tea are longer than for hot tea. That's because you'll be cutting the brewed tea with ice, and then it will go over more ice later, so you want to start with a stronger brew, which requires a longer brew time.

Sugar dissolves better in hot water than in cold, so if your market prefers the sweet stuff, dissolve the sugar in the tea before you add the room-temperature water and serve the tea presweetened. Feelings vary widely about how much sugar is enough—and how much is too much. You'd do best to add no more than ½ cup sugar and allow customers to sweeten the final brew to their own taste.

Another option for sweetening iced tea (and iced coffee, for that matter) is to offer simple syrup, which is made from two simple ingredients: sugar and water. You can buy it by the gallon from restaurant supply stores or make your own pretty easily.

SIMPLE SYRUP

1. In a pot, combine equal amounts of sugar and water. Bring to a boil.

2. Reduce heat to a simmer and cook for 3 to 5 minutes or until mixture is clear. Remove the pot from the heat and let cool to room temperature.

3. Transfer contents to a tightly lidded glass container and voilà! You have simple syrup. (If you prefer your simple syrup a bit thicker, add a little more sugar next time.) Store in the refrigerator for 2 or 3 weeks. Sugar acts as a preservative so simple syrup lasts quite a while.

You've got your coffee down pat, and in this chapter you learned about the different varieties of tea, how to choose the best ones for your shop, and ways to prepare them. Now let's get to work on the rest of your menu, from smoothies to paninis.

CHAPTER 17

The Rest of Your Menu

To run a coffee shop, you must sell coffee. These days, that usually means you offer cappuccinos, lattes, and other espresso-based drinks as well. And once you decide to sell these, you might as well add hot chocolate and tea to your menu to cover the rest of the hot beverage market.

This might seem like a lot—especially when you have to teach new employees how to make it all—but even so, you'll inevitably face customers who frown at the menu and say, "Is that all you got?" To satisfy your target market, and keep them from running to your competition, you might want to carry even more types of beverages, like juices and smoothies. We talk about these options and more in this chapter.

Then there's the food. Many customers like to enjoy a snack with their drinks, so it might be smart to offer an array of goodies and sweets, either freshly made at local bakeries or prepackaged from large manufacturers. If the market is right, you might even consider adding sandwiches, soups, or other hot foods to your menu. But before you put on your oven mitts, read on to discover the legal ins and outs that come with food preparation.

Cold Drinks, Hot Profits

As coffee-based drinks brew, they produce an inviting aroma that draws customers in off the streets and up to your counter. Cold drinks lack that enticing element, but what they lack in aroma, they make up for in profits.

Bottles and Cans

Thanks to decades of marketing muscle, soft drink giants Coke and Pepsi are known throughout the world, from the school down the block to villages in far-off lands. In addition to the cola itself, the parent companies of Coke and Pepsi sell a number of other soft drinks, like root beer, ginger ale, and orange soda. Selling multiple products from one of these companies makes perfect sense because your customers know and enjoy them. The real question for you is how to sell them: from a vending machine, in bottles, or from a fountain.

Offering canned sodas in vending machines requires the least effort from you, as a local distributor will likely provide the machine for free and visit your shop regularly to stock it. With little effort, though, comes little reward. The distributor will keep most of the money the machine collects, which means you're giving up space in your coffee shop to advertise and sell another company's product for a relatively small return.

Selling bottled soda from a cooler offers a better return because you buy the soda directly from a distributor and keep all the cash you collect. You need money up front to purchase the initial deliveries and storage space in the back room to hold stock (a subject we take stock of in Chapter 18), but after a while, you'll be able to use past profits to buy products for the future.

Counter *Talk*

With drinks come straws. Some coffee shops are now using biodegradable paper straws, an eco-friendly option many customers appreciate. However, they are expensive, and you need to do what's right for the environment *and* for your business. Melissa calculated that the cost of paper straws was too high to consider, but Brewpoint does its part for the environment by selling metal straws and offering reusable cups for water.

Bottled Juices, Seltzers, and More

Besides stocking the standard sodas, you can pack a cooler with fruit juices, plain and flavored seltzers, and other types of cold drinks. The only limitations on your product line are your budget and the size of your cooler.

With bottled beverages, you're never locked in with your offerings. If an intense ginger ale just doesn't catch on with customers, for example, clear it out and use the space for a new pomegranate fruit drink or carbonated raspberry soda instead.

Keep in mind, though, that extra stock of bottled beverages requires a lot of space in your store's back room. Also, the heavy bottles probably shouldn't sit on shelves, so you'll need plenty of floor space to house them.

Fresh-Squeezed Juices

Fresh-squeezed juices appeal to health-conscious consumers, but squeezing a load of oranges or grapefruits for each serving takes a lot of time. You can juice the fruit at the start of the day, but then you have to take great care storing it to prevent microorganisms from setting up house. Check with your local health department before offering fresh juice to see whether you can balance the demands of health and labor.

You can also purchase prebottled fresh juices, which last a little longer and have the seal of approval from the health department, but the price is often exorbitant. Be sure your target market is interested in $6 juices before you start stocking up on them!

Want to serve lemonade? Instead of offering the bottled kind, consider purchasing fresh lemon concentrate (an oxymoron, we admit) from a supplier and make lemonade to order for mere pennies.

Water

When it comes to water, you can sell bottled water or provide a water spout. Depending on your demographic, you might even offer a pitcher of iced water infused with fruit or melon slices so customers can help themselves. Customers will appreciate the access to free water and, because they don't have to pay for bottled water, might spring for a treat instead.

Counter *Talk*

They *will* come into your coffee shop: the folks who just want a cup of water and nothing else. Brewpoint employees charge 10¢ for a cup of water if the patron isn't buying anything else. They want to be accommodating, but cups and straws do cost money. This is a good compromise that keeps the customer happy and the coffee shop in business.

Italian Sodas and Granitas

In Chapter 15, we talked about flavor shots, such as fruity raspberry, orange, and mango. Some madcap customers might like lime-flavored syrup in their coffee, but most customers prefer fruit flavors in cold treats like Italian sodas and granitas.

You'll need either a soda maker machine or a stock of bottled seltzer water to make Italian sodas. If your customers aren't crazy about these drinks, this might not be a good investment, but if you think they'll be a hit in your shop, invest in either a machine or some fizzy water to make Italian sodas—and its creamy cousin, French sodas.

ITALIAN SODA

1. In a soda maker machine or a large glass filled with ice, mix 2 tablespoons flavored syrup with 1 cup fizzy water such as seltzer or sparkling water.

2. If using a machine, pour into a large glass filled with ice. Serve.

FRENCH SODA

1. In a soda maker machine or a large glass filled with ice, mix 1 tablespoon flavored syrup with ¾ cup fizzy water such as seltzer or sparkling water.

2. If using a machine, pour into a large glass filled with ice.

3. Add 2 tablespoons half-and-half, and serve.

Granitas are frozen, slushy drinks that combine fruity flavor shots with other flavors such as coffee. To make a decent granita, you need a granita machine, which tends to cost as much as an espresso machine. As always, research your market thoroughly before making this type of investment.

Egg Creams

You already have the flavored syrups close at hand, so you might consider adding egg creams to your list of liquid treats. Egg creams, which were invented in Brooklyn and aren't well known outside New York, are an easy-to-make treat that will delight your customers.

Despite the name, egg creams contain no eggs and no cream. The only ingredients are milk, seltzer, and flavored syrup. Chocolate syrup is most common, although other flavors work just as well. Think of it as an ice cream soda without the ice cream. As with Italian sodas, you'll need a source for the seltzer.

EGG CREAM

1. In a chilled 12-ounce glass, add ½ cup cold whole milk.

2. Squirt in about ½ cup seltzer until a nice, creamy head forms.

3. In a thin stream, pour 2 tablespoons chocolate syrup through foam.

4. Carefully insert a long, thin spoon through foam, stir syrup into milk without disturbing the head, and serve.

In addition to using milk and cream for drinks, you might consider stocking extra supplies of these dairy products for retail sale if your dairy source can't be found in a common supermarket. If you use creams from a local dairy farm, for example, you can be sure your customers will want to take some home for themselves.

Smoothies

We included a smoothie machine on Chapter 10's list of equipment you might consider purchasing for your coffee shop. Here's where we convince you that you want one.

Smoothies are sweet enough to satisfy a customer's sweet tooth, yet contain lighter ingredients that appeal to health-conscious customers who might pass on ice cream and chocolate cookies. You can make smoothies with fresh or frozen fruit, sherbets, sorbets, liquid concentrate mixes, or even vanilla-based powders, with each drink prepared fresh for each customer. A potential bonus: if you've already decided to sell fresh juices, the fruit you buy can do double-duty in smoothies.

Come coffee shops offer healthy add-ins as well, like protein powders, chia seeds, or greens powders. If you cater to a health-conscious clientele, you might want to consider including these trendy—and profitable—extras.

The range of smoothie flavors is wide, but keep in mind the potential for waste if certain ingredients can't be used for anything else. If an orange sherbet is used in smoothies only twice before it turns icy and frostbitten in the freezer, you're going to lose money on the wasted food. In addition, it can be difficult to find a supplier who can deliver fresh fruit often enough to keep up with your smoothie needs. Some suppliers do carry packaged purées for smoothies, which last longer.

Counter *Talk*

Melissa recommends working on your coffee menu until it's as close to perfect as you can get it before adding other drinks. When you're ready to expand, think of yourself as a curator: analyze what your customers like, and create a unique drink that will appeal to their taste buds. For example, Brewpoint is known for its lavender chai latte.

A Little Something on the Side

The appeal of adding food items to your menu is easy to understand. Many coffee drinkers—dare we say most—prefer to have something to nibble on while they drink their cuppa, and rather than sending them back to their office vending machine for a three-pack of powdered doughnuts, you can fill the void with goodies of your own.

Keep in mind, though, that you don't have to carry food to succeed. In the right location, sales of coffee drinks alone can support your shop. If you've set up in such an area, you might choose to avoid complicating your business by adding food distributors, buying new display cases, applying for additional licenses from the local government, and so on.

Not only that, but if you consider yourself a "third wave" coffee shop, where coffee is more of a gourmet drink like wine than a commodity, or even a "fourth wave" shop that elevates the process of sourcing and brewing coffee to an art, offering a lot of food items—or the wrong ones—can dilute the experience for your customers.

If, however, your sales need a boost to push you into profitability (a topic we cover in Chapter 25), or you want to draw in customers who might otherwise opt for chain coffee shops, read the following sections and learn how you can feature food for fun and profit.

Counter *Talk*

Keep your food menu simple, at least at first. Melissa has learned from experience that the more extensive your menu is, the more suppliers (and the more ordering, stocking, and invoices) you need to deal with. One supplier won't have fresh fruit, for example. Another will have sweets but not savory treats. And you'll need a third for those special panini you want to carry. Start with a few items, get to know your customer base, and add more high-quality items when you're ready to handle it.

Morning Munchies

For many businesspeople, the day begins with coffee, but that coffee rarely flies solo. It often travels arm-in-arm with a muffin, croissant, cinnamon roll, scone, bagel, or Danish—all handheld treats that can add a couple dollars to any coffee sale. If you want to carry these items in your coffee shop, find a local bakery or food supplier that can deliver these items fresh to your door each morning. (We talk about how to find and judge suppliers of all types in Chapter 18.)

Hot tip: if you do decide to carry breakfast treats, offer to warm them up for your customers. Many customers would prefer a warm, aromatic scone or a hot and gooey ham and cheese croissant over refrigerator-cold ones.

All-Day Treats

In addition to breakfast items, you can offer many other tempting, low-cost impulse foods that are perfect to accompany coffee throughout the day, such as cookies, brownies, candies, pastries, and slices of cakes and pies. Arrange these items in the display case customers pass on the way to place their order and on glass-covered plates near the register. After all, it's hard to sell impulse foods when customers don't have a chance to be impulsive!

What about baking these goodies yourself? You might make the best rocky road brownies in the world, but think twice before offering homemade treats in a retail establishment. Many state health departments require separate food permits for home bakeries and demand inspection of the premises. Some even insist that the bakers establish separate commercial kitchens in their homes.

Unless you're willing to jump through these hoops, stick to selling goodies from commercial suppliers—or offer treats made by local home bakers who *do* jump through the hoops. But be sure they're certified because if a customer becomes sick after eating one of the treats, it's *you* the authorities will come down on.

Counter *Talk*   A good rule of thumb is to offer some foods that are savory, some that are sweet, and some that appeal to people with dietary restrictions. For example, Brewpoint has a supplier that delivers gluten-free and dairy-free treats.

Full-Meal Deals

If you're feeling ambitious or want to distinguish yourself from the competition, you might go so far as to add complete, albeit small, meals to your menu, such as a sandwich and chips or hot soup with a side of bread.

The easy way to make such meals is to order them from food suppliers in nearly complete form. You can heat frozen or canned soups in a countertop electric holding unit, for example, and order bread from the bakery that supplies your morning pastries.

Food suppliers can also provide panini that you store in a refrigerated display case and grill in a panini press as they're ordered. Within minutes, you can serve lunchtime customers a hot sandwich far superior to whatever cold leftovers they would have brought from home.

Another possibility for ready-to-eat meals is a local deli willing to prepare and deliver fresh, pre-wrapped sandwiches at wholesale prices each day. You'll have to order enough sandwiches to make it worth the effort, so before jumping into such a deal, balance the profits against the potential for waste.

We do have to provide a few warnings if you go this route. First, before adding foods to your menu, be sure the food license granted to you by the local health department covers such sales. Prepackaged foods like candy and bagged cookies usually fall under a different licensing category from cookies and brownies, which themselves fall under a different category from refrigerated cakes and made-to-order foods like sandwiches and soup.

Second, even if your panini and soups are a hit with customers, don't fall into the trap of feeling you should do even more, like offering cold-cut sandwiches with a choice of toppings or freshly made salads. The purpose behind offering foods to complement your beverages is to provide customers with enough options to keep them coming to your establishment, thus boosting your bottom line. The last thing you want to do is overburden yourself and your staff with prep work and the cost of ovens, exhaust vents, and wasted food.

A final concern for some entrepreneurs is competing with neighboring businesses that already sell hot meals. If you expand into their turf by offering surf-and-turf dinners, they'll probably start magically finding room for coffee and cookies on their menu.

Food Without the Financing

If you want to offer customers food to go along with their drinks but don't want to prepare the food yourself, steal a page from the fast-food market and *dual-brand* with a local restaurant.

Dual-branding is when two businesses that sell separate product lines come together in one building to create a more attractive draw for customers. Pizza Hut and Taco Bell, both owned by Yum! Brands, commonly dual-brand with one another. Having both businesses in one location provides a greater variety of products for sale without the need for two buildings.

You probably won't convince a nationally known franchisee to split the costs of business with you, but you might able to find a locally owned business, such as an ice-cream parlor or deli, that will partner up with you. Doing so may lower the costs of rent and other utility bills without affecting your level of sales.

Even if this option doesn't appeal to you initially, keep it in mind when you start to consider expanding to a new location, something we cover more thoroughly in Chapter 25.

Should You Serve Alcohol?

If you plan to operate late at night in a busy downtown area or near a college campus, you might consider serving alcoholic coffee drinks. In addition to widening the scope of your menu, you'll also score a decent chunk of change with each sale because customers are often willing to shell out a premium for alcoholic beverages.

Before you go buying bottles of crème de menthe and Kahlúa to dress up your coffee drinks, we need to bring your attention to a few legal issues.

Landing a Liquor License

Sales of liquor, even for businesses like yours that won't be dishing out straight shots of whiskey, require special licenses from the local government, perhaps from a special alcohol control board.

Many towns are divided into districts that prohibit alcohol sales in certain zones. If you open in one of these "dry" parts of town—next door to an elementary school or a church, for example— you have no chance of garnering a liquor license. If this isn't the case, you might be out of luck simply because the town issues a limited number of licenses, all of which have been claimed.

If a license is available, you'll likely have to post a notice on the store window of your intent to sell alcoholic beverages so residents in the area can lobby against you, if they so choose.

Filling out the liquor license application is only the first step in some parts of the United States. In Arizona, for instance, first-time applicants must attend a management training course (which can be completed online) to learn about their responsibilities as sellers of alcohol in the state.

Staff Spirit

When you have a liquor license in hand, you need to train your employees on how to handle the hard stuff without running afoul of the law. Ignorance of the legal issues won't protect an employee from being prosecuted, or your liquor license from being pulled, if the offense is severe enough.

To begin with, aside from the usual regulations that apply to food and drink preparation, employees must now be wary of serving alcoholic drinks to intoxicated customers. If a drunk individual causes an accident after leaving your coffee shop, you or your employees could be held liable or named in a civil lawsuit—even if the drink contained only a trace of alcohol.

You could also be held responsible for alcohol-related crimes that occur in a parking lot adjacent to your shop, even though the lot might not be considered a part of your location.

Localities generally prohibit underage employees from serving alcohol, so you now must consider employee age when making work schedules to ensure an employee of the proper age is always on hand to prepare and serve certain drinks.

Inventory control also takes on a whole new meaning when you start serving alcohol. Keep these supplies under lock and key, and maintain a rigorous reorder policy, perhaps keeping the empty bottles as a check-and-balance system.

All these restrictions might deflate your enthusiasm for carrying alcohol-flavored hot drinks, but given the weight of the legal material you're already bearing—food establishment license, reseller's license, business license, business lease, vendor contracts, and so on—you might consider these limitations merely a few more pebbles on top of the mountain.

In the right market, alcoholic coffee beverages can really boost your sales volume, thanks to the high retail prices they bring—a boost that might reduce the drawbacks to an afterthought. As always, a mix of market research and trial and error is the key to knowing what will sell best in your business.

Beyond Coffee and Food

You'll spend a lot of money purchasing equipment for your shop and, assuming you learn how to use it all correctly, your customers will greatly appreciate the investment you make.

Some of them will appreciate it so much, in fact, that they'll want to purchase similar equipment for themselves. Oh, they might not spring for a $1,000 espresso machine, but they'll lay out a few hundred dollars for a smaller model. If espresso doesn't grab them, they might still buy a French press, a grinder, or even an old-fashioned percolator.

Where are they going to purchase these items? Why, from you, of course! That's right—in addition to selling the drinks themselves, you should also offer the equipment that makes these drinks. If you do your job right, your customer base will include dozens, if not hundreds, of discriminating coffee fans. There's no sense directing them elsewhere to purchase coffee-making equipment if you could be selling the items yourself.

Not ready to approach your equipment vendor about selling espresso machines on commission? Maybe you can focus your retail energies on hand-painted coffee mugs, souvenir spoons that memorialize your area, travel mugs, books on coffee, or milk thermometers. The list of retail items you could sell is far longer than you'll have room for on your shelves.

In any case, you should absolutely carry retail goods other than food and drinks. Install shelves in your seating area, and fill them with goods for sale. Otherwise, that space is going to waste because no sales will ever result from it.

Counter *Talk*

According to Melissa, 70 percent of Brewpoint's sales is in drinks, 20 percent is pastries, and 10 percent is merchandise. The coffee shop sells products like art prints, coffee-scented soaps, and candles made by local artisans, all on a commission basis. The creator gets 60 percent, and Brewpoint's cut is 40 percent. Because Brewpoint didn't purchase the items outright, there's no risk if the items don't sell.

In this chapter, you got the scoop on noncoffee beverages, treats and meals, and coffee-related equipment you could be selling in your shop. Where do you get these things? From suppliers, of course! In the next chapter, we talk all about how to choose the right suppliers for your business.

Working with Suppliers

We've covered a lot of ground in the preceding chapters in terms of the food and drinks you can offer your customers. After you decide what to include on your menu, it's time to figure out where those items will come from. You'll need to purchase every single item you plan to sell or use in your store from a supplier—or, more likely, from many different suppliers.

We covered big-ticket items like espresso machines and refrigerators in Chapter 10. Now let's review the smaller items you need to purchase to run your coffee shop. Depending on your product line, you won't necessarily need to purchase all these items, but if you ever decide to expand your offerings, you'll know where to look to find the goods.

Finding Suppliers

As a coffee shop owner, your first concern naturally will be hunting down the raw materials for the finished food and drinks you'll serve, with a main focus on coffee bean importers and roasters. (Appendix C contains a list of bean importers and roasters you can contact, as well as potential suppliers for most of the other items listed in this chapter.)

Whichever supplier, or suppliers, you choose will provide the base around which you build everything else.

The steps outlined in this section apply to almost all the types of suppliers you'll deal with, but to keep our focus, we'll stick to talking about coffee suppliers, as that's what's driving your business.

Meet, Greet, and Eat

Contact each coffee supplier you find and arrange to meet the salesperson who covers your area. Explain a bit about your business, and ask him to bring samples of his company's products to your meeting.

When you meet, offer more details about your shop-to-be, such as your target customer market and your theme and décor ideas. Share your logo and store design, if he's willing to look, and ask for feedback. He's likely seen hundreds of stores on the job, and he might spot trouble points that would otherwise go unnoticed.

Once the representative has absorbed the details of your coffee shop, pepper him with questions like these that will reveal all you need to know about the supplier:

* The frequency and flexibility of the delivery schedule

* Whether delivery is available on the weekend in case you run out of product

* The minimum dollar amount of each order

* The availability of discounts based on volume

* Whether the supplier offers special products for holidays

* What type of point-of-purchase promotional material is available to boost sales

* Whether free product is available if you want to run in-store tastings or other special promotions

* What makes their product stand out over those of their competitors

* Whether the supplier can provide references from current customers

* What terms they offer new clients—that is, how quickly they ask to be paid for deliveries

Treat the salesperson as a partner in your business, because in all likelihood he'll be able to suggest products that will fit your needs perfectly. He'll also be aware of your competition and be able to describe how his products differ from what they offer. Take notes during this part, because eventually you'll want to be able to describe that difference to your customers.

Don't just take his word, though. Let him offer product samples based on the market and goals you've described. Ask him to suggest markups for the product so you can gauge what percent of each sale will be profit and judge whether the product is right for your image. (We cover pricing in more detail in Chapter 19.)

Opening Lines of Credit with Suppliers

Once you've decided that a supplier's products fit your budget and match your target market's needs, it's time to ask for credit.

Yes, you'll be borrowing money again—many times, in fact, because you'll be starting relationships with a number of suppliers to get all the goods you need. Don't worry about sounding needy or cash-poor; suppliers are used to extending credit to their customers.

For each supplier, you'll complete a credit application to show that you'll be able to pay the bills if the supplier does issue you credit. Bills from suppliers are typically due 1 or 2 weeks after delivery, which gives you a bit of time to work some alchemical magic and turn those goods into gold. (The business shorthand for this type of arrangement is "net X days," which means that payment for a shipment is due X days after delivery.)

On the application, you'll note details about your coffee shop, let the supplier know how much credit you're asking for, and list prior credit references. If you have no business references, which is quite possible if this is your first business, you may be able to list personal references instead, such as credit card companies or the bank that holds your home mortgage. If you're in this situation, ask the supplier what's the best way to handle it.

If the supplier turns you down, ask why and see if you can address his concerns in the months ahead. He might just be nervous that you have no business experience, for example, and be willing to reconsider your application after you've been open a few months.

Even if the supplier does grant you a credit line, be aware that your orders for the first few months will still likely be cash on delivery (COD), so the supplier can see if you pay on time. Once you pass that hurdle, the credit program will kick in and you'll have a bit of breathing room between delivery and payment from then on.

Whether you have to place only those initial few COD orders or you have to do it each time (because you weren't granted credit), be sure to contact the supplier for the total amount due so you can have a check ready to hand to the driver. If you do cash payouts from the register, have the delivery person sign your receipt, showing that payment was received. This practice keeps you from having to search for your checkbook while the driver—and lines of customers—wait for you.

Deciding How Much to Order

If you haven't run a coffee shop before, you probably aren't sure what an appropriate opening order would be. Should you order three types of coffee or ten? Two bags of beans or two hundred?

Rather than guessing how much to order, ask the salesperson for advice on how he would stock a location of your size in your area. Admittedly, some sales reps will be quite, shall we say, *optimistic* with their figures because large orders from you equal bonuses or pats on the back for them from their bosses. If you have qualms about his suggested figures, reduce the numbers slightly or ask about arranging a second order to follow soon after the first.

After you make it past your first few orders, you'll have an inventory to work with and the start of a sales record, both of which will make later orders align more closely with your immediate needs. (Sales records, ranging from daily to yearly, are covered in Chapter 20.) Although we don't recommend trying this with your initial order, once you have a handle on what you need, you can solicit prices from multiple suppliers and see who can provide the goods at the lowest cost. You don't necessarily want to jump back and forth from one supplier to another—this eliminates any loyalty you've established—but shopping by price can lead you to amazing deals sometimes.

Maintain a file for all your orders so you know what's coming in and don't accidentally duplicate an order with another supplier. You also need to keep the order sheets close at hand to refer to when the goods arrive.

Deciding Who Can Order

Be sure your suppliers know which of your employees, if any, are authorized to place orders. In the early days, that's you and nobody else but you, but after you grow enough to hire other managers—a subject covered in Chapter 25—you'll need to give them ordering authority as well.

This setup prevents employees from calling suppliers on their own and placing rush orders for items that are nearly out of stock. Allowing employees to place orders is fraught with all kinds of risks:

* You might already have an order on the way, which means you'll now have twice as much stock.

* You may have discontinued that product and switched to something else but haven't yet told your employees.

* You may have to pay the supplier a rush charge.

* You might not be out of the product after all, and the employee just missed seeing a box in the stockroom.

You want your employees to be smart enough and confident enough to take charge in difficult situations, but you don't want their "charges" to end up hurting your business financially.

Checking Deliveries

When the supply truck pulls up behind your coffee shop, have the order sheet available to compare what you asked for with what's on the truck. Did you ask for a case and receive only a box, or vice versa? Make a note of it on the shipping receipt. Inspect boxes and bags quickly for tears and water damage. Again, note any problems on the shipping receipt. If something is completely wrong or unusable, refuse it, note the reason, and have the delivery person take it back.

Have the delivery person initial all the notes you've taken so you can later request a credit for damaged, missing, and unordered items.

> **Counter** *Talk*
>
> Every so often, do an audit of your suppliers to see if you should consolidate to fewer suppliers, find better or less-expensive ones, or revamp your menu. Melissa realized she was wasting tons of money because she had too many items on the menu. She also discovered that because Brewpoint now had enough buying power, she could save at least $10,000 by overhauling her ordering system.

Taking Stock of the Stockroom

All the action in your shop might happen out in front of the customers, but if you don't do the prep work behind the scenes, there won't be any out-front action.

So let's go to where the magic begins: the stockroom. As we explained in Chapter 11, the stockroom is a functioning work area where practicality always trumps prettiness. You need plenty of shelves and open storage units to start with, and in the months ahead, you'll probably build in even more as you get a better handle on the size of each box and bundle you order.

Organize your storage areas, whether the back room or shelving underneath the front counters, so similar items are stored together—all the cups in one location, with the lids next to them, and so on. Don't cram goods into every available space; you want to be able to reach everything in stock with minimum effort.

Making Room for Deliveries

When you're expecting an order, clear the backroom floor of broken-down cardboard boxes and anything else that might impede a delivery. Make room on shelves by consolidating items and restacking supplies on the floor. If you've labeled the storage areas, a quick look at the order sheet lets you know exactly where you need to make room. After you've received a few orders and are familiar with the box sizes, you'll have a better handle on how much room you'll need.

As you move boxes around, be sure to place the oldest goods in front to be used first. Even with disposable goods such as plastic wrap that have a long shelf life, rotating goods keeps them from getting dirty or damaged through repeated handling, or getting lost behind other types of supplies.

What about cleaning supplies? Storage of these items is a potential safety issue, and they must be kept separate from food and anything used to serve food. They also should be stored as close to the floor as possible to reduce the damage caused by any spills.

Putting Away Deliveries, from Cold to Hot

After you receive an order, put away any frozen items first and then any refrigerated goods, with the expiration date facing out so employees can be sure to grab the oldest item first. Lastly, put away the dry goods that are okay spending time on the backroom floor.

If you have bug or rodent issues, or even a fear of attracting bugs or rodents, store vermin-attracting items like sugar in sealed containers. Label the containers clearly on the outside so employees can find what they need quickly without having to open anything. You can even put plastic labels on the container and mark the expiration date on the label with an erasable pen.

Taking Inventory

For ordering purposes, it's enough to survey your storeroom once a week to see what's turning over, what's not, and what needs to be ordered for the coming week. But every 6 to 12 months, it's important to inventory every item you have for sale in the shop. You'll need this information for your taxes; you also should keep an inventory list of every single item you've ever ordered.

On your inventory sheet, include space for 6 or 12 months of inventory as well as the cost of each item so you can figure out the total cost of goods on hand. (We include a sample inventory sheet in Appendix B.)

Include waste items in the inventory, too. One or two cups isn't an issue, but if an employee accidentally dumps a 10-pound bag of sugar into a bucket of mop water, note that unexpected cost on the monthly summary. These notes might remove the need for detective work at the end of the month to figure out why the numbers don't add up.

Counter *Talk*   Many apps are available to help manage inventory, but Melissa finds that they have too many complicated bells and whistles for a simple inventory—and are too expensive for a small business. Instead, she uses an Excel worksheet customized to her shops, including the equations that automatically tally the numbers she needs.

Ask your employees to participate in the inventory count. This not only educates them on where everything is but also provides variety in their workday.

Counting Your Cash in Storage

Don't think of taking inventory as only counting cup lids and pounds of sugar. Think of taking inventory as counting money—*your* money. You spent money on all these items with the intention of selling them, either directly or indirectly, to make a profit. The only way to know whether you're achieving this goal is to track what's on hand, what's missing, and what's never moving.

Ideally, you'll have exactly the right amount of product on hand to last from one delivery to the next. If you can manage this, you'll avoid having money tied up in excess product that never leaves the shelves. The longer goods stay in storage, the more likely they are to be damaged, which means you'll never get back the money you invested.

Counter *Talk*   You may be surprised at how much cash is sitting in your stockroom. In the beginning, Melissa would calculate that there was $5,000 to $8,000 worth of goods in storage at the end of the year. Now that Brewpoint has a wholesale roastery, that number is as high as $15,000 to $20,000. Cash flow is king in your business. If you don't have the money to pay your staff or suppliers, it may not be that your coffee shop isn't succeeding, it may be that too much of your money is tied up in stock.

Additionally, be sure to update your inventory sheets to reflect the current cost of replacing goods. Prices fluctuate frequently due to market and weather conditions, and calculating the value of your inventory using an outdated rate doesn't yield valid information.

Managing Inventory and Ordering

Inventory and ordering go hand in hand, with each constantly affecting the other. If you avoid taking inventory, you might constantly order twice as many small cups as large because you seem to recall selling twice as many small drinks. What a surprise you'll have months later when you find yourself with boxes and boxes of small cups and nowhere to put them.

By taking inventory, you don't rely on your memory, and you avoid ordering by intuition. Instead, you have the definite numbers on hand to show exactly what's being used and what needs to be replaced.

Tracking Your Inventory Turnover Rate

Beyond a mere inventory count is the idea of tracking your inventory turnover rate—that is, how quickly inventory moves through your coffee shop and is converted back into money. To determine your inventory turnover rate, use the formula shown in the following table.

Inventory Turnover Rate	
Step 1: Calculate the cost of goods used during a month:	
Inventory cost at the start of the month	$3,500
Add: purchases made during the month	$11,400
Total cost of goods	$14,900
Subtract: inventory at end of month	$3,800
Cost of goods consumed	$11,100
Step 2: Calculate the average cost of goods on hand:	
Beginning inventory	$3,500
Add: end inventory	$3,800
Total amount	$7,300
Average inventory (total amount divided by 2)	$3,650
Step 3: Calculate the inventory turnover rate:	
Cost of goods consumed ÷ average inventory = inventory turnover rate	
11,100 ÷ 3,650 = 3.04 times	

In our example, inventory is turning over slightly more often than three times per month, or roughly every 9 or 10 days. Ideally, you would like to have as high a turnover rate as possible. That would mean goods are being instantly converted to cash with little money tied up in the stockroom.

This ideal is, alas, impossible to reach because if you cut inventory to the bare bones, you risk running out of drinks and supplies. Sure, the turnover rate will be in the double digits, but if you're sending away customers empty-handed, you're losing money and damaging the long-term health of your coffee shop.

Using your inventory sheets, you can break down your inventory into smaller categories—baked goods, hot drinks, disposable goods, and so on—and examine the inventory turnover rate for each category. Baked goods, for example, should have an incredibly high turnover because their shelf life is limited to a few days at most.

By examining the turnover rate on select goods, you might discover avenues for potential growth. If, say, you're using twice as much half-and-half as skim milk, that tells you your customers want richer, creamier drinks. What can you add to your menu to satisfy this desire?

Counter *Talk*

It's smart to group like items together in the stockroom, but when you have a lot of suppliers, this can make ordering more difficult. Brewpoint is reorganizing its stockroom so every supplier has its own shelf or area. That way, when the owners or managers are preparing an order, they can see at a glance what they need to order from each supplier.

Beyond Beans: The Rest of Your Shopping List

The equipment list in Chapter 10 warmed up your credit card, but you might find hundreds of other items that might come in handy for your business, too. Appendix B includes a thorough list of possible purchases—many of which might seem impractical, useless, or baffling at first glance.

Before you go out shopping, though, let's look at a few of the items in more detail.

Investing in Coffee-Related Supplies

Your shop is all about selling coffee, which means you need plenty of supplies that will make this happen. Typical coffee sizes are 8, 12, and 16 ounces, so when you're purchasing mugs and cups, search for these sizes. To cut down on inventory, look for a vendor who carries different sizes of paper cups that can be covered by the same size lid.

You can investigate the cost of imprinting your store's logo on these items, but you usually need to order massive quantities to make such a purchase cost effective. We recommend holding off on branding anything until the business has proved itself so you don't wind up with a garage full of unused mugs.

In addition to standard coffee mugs, you need demitasse cups and saucers for espresso beverages. With all these items, your best bet is to stick with plain white ceramic. Basic white is the cheapest option available, and any fancy designs on cups and saucers tend to give them legs—that is, they go walking out of the shop with customers.

As with your tables and chairs, purchase only those coffee cups, demitasse cups, and so on that can be easily replaced for many years to come. You'll break more of these than you'll care to think about in the months ahead.

Counter *Talk*

Should you invest in reusable plates, mugs, and so on? It depends on the vibe of your shop. If most of your customers grab their drink and head out the door, you'll be fine with paper products. If you have more of a sit-down atmosphere where people linger for hours, reusable items are a nice touch. Brewpoint serves espresso in demitasse cups with saucers and also has reusable mugs and plates for customers who want to enjoy their coffee and treat at a table.

Getting the Most for Your Money

Low-end paper cups probably suit your wallet and the needs of your coffee shop, but sometimes you're better off spending a little bit more.

Take a simple item like a hand tamper, which you use to tamp espresso grounds into a portafilter. Plastic tampers are cheap, but they tend to chip when dropped or mishandled, which means you have to buy another one, which makes them not so cheap after all. Spring for a hard wood or anodized aluminum tamper, and you'll be set for a few decades.

A steaming pitcher is another purchase to splurge on because you'll use it dozens of times each day. Look for a high-grade stainless-steel pitcher with a welded-on handle because screws loosen over time. Pick one that holds at least 32 ounces—remember, milk increases in size when it's steamed. Search for one with a rolled pouring edge; this allows you to develop your skill of pouring off foam, milk, or a mix of both.

Search for condiment shakers that balance the needs of function and form. You want ones that won't clog because the holes are too small but still have small-enough holes that customers don't shake out a pound of sugar or cinnamon with each tilt of the hand. The shakers you choose should be easy to clean and refill, too.

Buying with an Eye on the Law

Some purchases you make will be driven by style or cost, but others will come because the government tells you what to buy. Some health departments insist that napkins be available only in dispensers, for example, instead of loose in baskets or other holders. In your case, this restriction is good: customers won't just grab a handful as they pass and then throw away all but one.

Another health issue concerns loose versus wrapped straws. Some communities insist on individually wrapped straws; others are fine with a dispenser that releases one loose straw at a time.

Cream and milk containers are another source of concern. Your health department might insist that milk be stored on ice or that you use a particular type of storage container. (You also want milk containers that reduce drips and are easy to use. Customers want to make their drinks and move on, not solve a puzzle to access the milk.)

The health department might also have a few words to say about the type of soap and hand towels in your washrooms. Bar soap, for example, is verboten in many areas due to fears that they spread germs through hand-to-hand contact.

To find out about all the kitchen, bathroom, and other regulations in your area, contact your local health department and ask if they have any resources that will help you abide by the rules. You'll learn more during the health department's preopening walk-through and still more during subsequent check-ins.

You've contracted with suppliers who deliver your beans and other products, and you know how to store and track it all in your stockroom. Next, let's talk about how to price all these items to bring in a profit.

Pricing to Sell—and Selling Those Prices

We're sure you hold your customers so dear that you would give them all the free drinks they want, but that's not really how business works. If you don't cover costs, not to mention make a bit extra to pay for your salary, the business will go bust and no one will get anything.

Setting prices is relatively straightforward. Ensuring those prices will sustain the business is another matter. We take you through the pricing process in this chapter, as well as point out what to do when the system falls out of balance.

Determining What to Charge

For most food establishments, the cost of the food sold equals 30 to 35 percent of the total sales volume. Using this figure as a general target, you can determine the retail price of any food by tripling its cost. If, for example, a bakery charges your coffee shop 50¢ for a bagel, you should charge your customer $1.50 or somewhere thereabouts.

By charging three times the cost of an item, you are working into the price all the intangibles the customer purchases with that bagel, whether he's thought about them or not. This price includes, for instance, the napkin that accompanies the plate, a small portion of the cost of the toaster, the knife that cut the bagel, the cutting board on which the bagel was cut, and the mortgage for the building that houses all these items. This price also covers the cost of cleaning the knife and plate as well as the labor to wipe down the cutting board. Finally, we have the labor cost of clearing and wiping the table after the customer leaves and the miniscule cost of garbage service to remove the butter wrapper and wadded-up napkin.

Whew! All that from $1 over the cost of the bagel? Yes, indeed, when you add up the sales of everything in the store. Every drink and every treat adds its share to the kitty to cover the costs of everything else.

Counter *Talk* — One item that goes against the "multiply by three" rule is drip coffee. Brewpoint brews new coffee every 2 hours to be sure it's fresh—a good practice to follow in your shop, too—which creates a lot of waste. For that reason, Brewpoint charges *six* times the cost for drip coffee.

Understanding What the Market Will Bear

We suggest using this pricing method almost across the board—and we say *almost* because in some cases you'd be wise to aim the figure a bit higher or lower.

Back in Chapter 4, we sent you on a research mission to competing coffee shops to see what they offered and how much they charged. Now's the time to pull out that research and see if it says anything about your business.

Examine your competitors' prices, looking for prices that are either much higher or much lower than yours. Multiple reasons exist for these differences, and because you don't have access to your competitors' brains to find out the exact reasons why, we'll venture a few guesses.

Peaks and Valleys

The simplest explanation could be that the cost of a competitor's goods might differ from yours. If he pays a quarter more for an item than you do, that translates to a 75¢ difference on the retail price. A similarly low price probably means that his cost is lower than yours.

If you're contacting multiple suppliers to compare costs of goods before placing an order—a practice we recommended in Chapter 18—you might be able to determine which supplier handles your competitor's account. By setting up an account with this supplier and cherry-picking the low-cost goods, you can lower your own costs and, therefore, your retail prices.

Sometimes cost differences result from package deals offered by suppliers. If you take A, B, C, and D, they say, we'll knock 10 percent off the total. Don't rush into such deals unless you normally stock all these items or feel you can use them in your business. Otherwise, any cost savings you achieve will be eaten by unused goods that sit in your back room forever.

Leading by Losing

Another explanation for why a competitor charges less than you is that he's using the item as a loss leader—that is, a ridiculously low-priced item that's meant to draw in customers.

Supermarkets advertise loss leaders all the time: milk at half price, fruit in the winter at summer prices, a deep discount on turkeys at Thanksgiving. Supermarkets don't push loss leaders because they're nice and want to give customers something for next to nothing. They push loss leaders to get customers to choose their store over a competitor's.

A supermarket gains nothing on the sale of loss leaders—it might even lose money—but shoppers rarely visit a store for just one item. Once they're in the store grabbing the cheap turkey or milk, they'll load up their carts with all sorts of other items, too. In the end, the supermarket will make a profit anyway.

Coffee shops use this practice of loss leaders, but on a smaller scale, perhaps along the lines of "Buy two cookies, get one free" or "Free biscotti with the purchase of any espresso." With a smart sales program, you'll make back the costs through sales of other items.

Practicing Premium Pricing

If a competitor charges significantly more for an item than you do, he may be doing so for a very simple reason: customers will pay the price.

When you sell dark chocolates or premium organic coffee beans, customers often expect to pay a premium. The rich taste of the good is worth paying more, and they don't think twice about whether the good actually costs more to make than milk chocolate or nonorganic coffee. Not to mention, dark chocolate or organic coffee that's too cheap may make customers suspicious. After all, they *expect* to pay more for these items.

You can experiment with this type of pricing when you introduce new items on your menu, especially if no one else in your area sells a similar item. Price the item at three and a half or even four times the cost, and see if customers are interested. If sales are slow, you can either drop the price or transform brownies into loss leaders and offer a free brownie with the purchase of said item. If customers learn to like the product, they might keep buying it after the promotion ends.

No Reason at All

A final possibility for widely diverging prices is that your competitor made a mistake—or you did. Examine your order receipts to be sure the problem isn't on your end. If you're not careful, you could miss a cost change and not realize it for months, barely breaking even on an item that should carry a higher price.

Speaking of cost changes, don't apologize to customers when you raise the price of an item to account for higher costs. Let the prices stand on their own. Quick, quality service is the only support they need.

How Not to Sell Yourself Short

Let's return for a moment to our $1.50 bagel that costs 50¢ from a local bakery. Now, a customer could visit that same bakery and purchase a bagel for far less than the $1.50 you charge. The same situation likely applies to your coffee and soda. A customer could buy either at the supermarket for less—sometimes much less—than they can buy the same item from you.

Does this mean you're ripping off your customers? Should you charge less for your bagels, coffee, and soda? No, for at least two reasons.

First, if you did lower prices to compete with those of the primary supplier (the bakery) or the discount seller (the supermarket), you would go out of business. No question about it. Your costs are not the same as their costs because they either make the goods themselves or order in volumes that dwarf the quantities you order. You can't compete against them in terms of price, and this brings us to the second reason.

In your coffee bar, you offer customers an environment and a selection of goods they can't find anywhere else. Your coffee tastes better than any available on supermarket shelves, and you can offer a glass with ice to complement the already chilled soda. You provide comfortable seating, pleasant music, probably Wi-Fi, and a desirable social atmosphere so the bagel-eater can relax and enjoy his snack. Creating an environment costs money, and that cost must be worked into the retail price of the bagel. Customers know—or they should know—that part of the price they pay is for the surroundings.

In short, don't ever engage in a price war. Even if you win, you'll still lose because you won't make any money on the now-discounted goods. Stick to providing quality and atmosphere, and your business will be far better off.

At some point, however, you will encounter a customer who demands to know why you're ripping off customers by charging such high prices. Don't let him bait you into an argument. Simply explain that based on your costs, you must charge the amounts you do to stay above water and leave it at that. You can't win this argument against cheap customers, so don't knock yourself out trying.

Counter *Talk*

Speaking of not selling yourself short: always check invoices thoroughly when receiving orders because incorrect invoices can be the cause of a lot of loss. Sometimes Brewpoint doesn't receive a product Melissa ordered because the distributor ran out. If she doesn't track this, she might accidentally pay for something she didn't get.

Boosting Your Bottom Line

Raising your prices is one way to boost sales volume, assuming customers aren't chased away by the higher prices. Another way to increase sales is to raise the average amount customers spend at each sale.

Offering food is an obvious way to do this and one we've already discussed. When a customer picks up a croissant to accompany his morning latte, he's doubled the amount of his bill and added a couple bucks to your bottom line. If you offer the right array of goods so every customer does this, you'll double your gross income. Pretty sweet!

Suggestive Selling

Unfortunately, not every customer will automatically reach for a sweet on the side. Many customers order on autopilot and don't really realize the true extent of your menu.

Your mission—and you've already chosen to accept it—is to make them aware of other food and drink items in your coffee shop. Not the whole menu, mind you, because customers can only absorb so much at once, but mention one item on the menu that would nicely accompany his current order—a chocolate-covered cookie spoon for a young person ordering coffee or a scone for a tea-drinker, for example.

The practice of asking customers if they want to order something else is known as *suggestive selling,* and every successful restaurant uses it. Go into any fast-food establishment to order a hamburger, and the cashier will automatically ask if you want fries as well. If you did order fries with the burger, the cashier will ask if you want large fries. If you ordered large fries, she'll ask if you'd like an ice-cream sundae to finish your meal.

Suggestive selling isn't badgering. You can't ask a customer more than once if he'd like something else because he'll probably get annoyed and leave. The idea is to mention an item he might not see otherwise and leave it at that. If he doesn't order it now, maybe he will next time. You lose nothing by asking and have the potential for huge financial gains if this and other customers take you up on the offer.

Your suggestive selling can also be as simple as a sign near the register that features new items. Feature seasonal items, special offers, and other short-term promotions in this location so customers always know where to look to see what's new in your coffee shop.

Truffles Aren't Trifles

Suggestive selling works wonders in terms of boosting sales, but you have to use it on the right items. If you focus your energy on promoting the French presses you have for sale in the seating area, don't be surprised if they're all still on the shelf at the end of the day.

A better idea is to surround your register with low-cost items, typically under $2, that require little from the customer in the way of investment. Individually wrapped truffles, for example, might retail for around $1 apiece. That low price means you make only around 60¢ for each one you sell, but it also inspires dozens upon dozens of customers to add one—or more—to their purchase. At the end of the day, those small gains add up to big bucks.

Feature the Future

In addition to using suggestive selling on the actual product, you can promote upcoming events at your coffee shop, such as an open-mic night, a poetry reading, or a writers' group. If you encourage customers to return on a night when they'd normally stay at home, that's just as good as having them spend more—maybe better if they bring a friend or two with them.

We gave you details on how to price your food and drink items—and how to sell those prices, including using loss leaders and suggestive selling. Next, let's take a look at some more financial matters that help you determine if your shop is earning money.

Running a Successful Coffee Shop

As a business owner, turning a profit is what it's all about. That's why it's crucial to learn business skills like counting inventory, tracking sales, and creating business goals. Another big part of your job is keeping customers happy, so in Part 5 you also get the scoop on conducting customer surveys, handling difficult customers, and knowing what to do in an emergency.

A well-run coffee shop and happy customers are a good start, but you have to get the word out about your shop, too, so we share some marketing and publicity tips. Finally, we look to the future and give you some ideas on reassessing your menu, hiring managers, and even expanding your empire with more shops.

Money Matters

How can you tell if your coffee shop is a success? The number of customers served or the amount of goods sold per customer might sound like a good measuring bar, but finding out where you really stand financially requires a far more concrete number: your *net income,* or the amount of money coming in minus the amount going out.

Nailing down your net income comes only after you've tracked a lot of other numbers, such as employee hours worked, utility expenses, and the cost of new goods and inventory on hand.

Tracking these numbers doesn't require a PhD in math—only an eye for detail and the patience to record everything that enters and leaves your store. Sound tedious? It may be at first, but once you have a system going, tracking sales figures becomes more like a game, where you do everything you can to push the numbers higher.

Tracking Sales Numbers

To keep your coffee shop's financial figure in fine shape, track sales on a daily, weekly, monthly, and yearly basis. Don't think you're making busy work for yourself or duplicating numbers for no reason. Each of these income and expense statements serves a different purpose.

At first the sales numbers will seem like random throws of the dice. They go up; they go down. They seem out of your control. As the days and weeks pass, though, you'll start to see patterns in the numbers. Rain will drop (or raise) sales by X percent. Snow affects sales X much. And 3-day weekends push down Fridays and raise Saturdays.

Over time, this knowledge will help you order goods and supplies more accurately and create more efficient work schedules. Knowledge is power, as the saying goes—but more importantly for business, knowledge is money!

Choosing a Point-of-Sale System

In Chapter 11, we talked about the importance of having a cash register. Unless you enjoy recording sales, expenses, and so on the old-school way with a pen and paper—and there's nothing wrong with that!—you'll also want to adopt a digital point-of-sale (POS) system.

A POS system is a digital network that's linked to your checkout terminals. The software can process everything from cash and credit cards to gift cards and coupons. The best restaurant-specific POS systems also do the following:

* Help you manage your menu

* Maintain a customer loyalty program

* Track tips

* Work for counter, table, take-out, and delivery service as well as online and phone orders

* Track sales data so you can easily analyze it

Cloud-based POS systems work with any internet-enabled device. If you've ever swiped your credit card through a device attached to a tablet, you've seen a cloud-based POS system in action.

Here are some of the more popular POS system options for coffee shops:

* Square for Restaurants (squareup.com)

* Lightspeed (lightspeedhq.com/pos)

* ShopKeep (shopkeep.com)

* Toast (pos.toasttab.com)

* Loyverse (loyverse.com)

* CAKE (trycake.com)

Costs for POS systems can range from free to $79 per month and up, not including the hardware required to run the POS system, like tablets or countertop terminals. Many POS companies offer a free trial so you can decide if the system is right for you before you buy.

To help you decide which system might be best for your coffee shop, check out the software review site Capterra (capterra.com) to read user-based rankings of the aforementioned and other POS systems. If you can't find exactly what you want, keep in mind that some POS companies will customize their software to meet your needs.

Counter *Talk*   When you're choosing a POS system, compare the cost of the hardware, the software, and the installation plus the cost per transaction for credit card processing. That last one can add up. Melissa calculated how much Brewpoint would pay in credit card fees using different processing companies, and the number ranged from $22,000 to $38,000 for $650,000 in credit card transactions.

Counting Your Cash

Now let's talk about what to do with your digital POS system—or your old-school paper-based system. The processes we outline here work no matter how you choose to record and analyze your sales, expenses, employee hours, and other data, so if you prefer paper records, go for it.

Your Daily Bread

At the end of each sales day, reconcile what's in the cash drawer with the sales tracked by the cash register, computer, or POS. (If you prefer a paper-based system, turn to Appendix B for sample income and expense statements.)

You can count the drawer yourself or have the employee who manned the register do the count. After you've tallied the amount of cash in the drawer, subtract the *float* from this total. The float is the amount of cash in the register drawer at the start of each day. The exact amount of the float is up to you, but be sure the drawer holds enough $1s and $5s that employees won't need to ask for change after only a few sales.

This gives you a figure for *net cash,* also known as the deposit. This is the actual amount of money that was added to the register during the day.

Ideally, employees should complete the drawer count without seeing the amount shown in your payment app or sales tape. You don't want to give them a target to shoot for; you just want to know how much is in the drawer and then determine for yourself if that amount is correct or not. This practice avoids possible funny business by employees who will add (or remove!) funds to make the totals match.

Subtract the sales total from the net cash. If the sum is negative, the drawer is *short,* meaning it has too little money; a positive sum means the drawer is *over.* If the figures match, the count in the drawer is exactly right, and you should give your employee a high five.

Remove enough cash from the drawer so what remains is exactly equal to the float. At the beginning of the day, or any time any employee uses a fresh register till, he should count the cash first to be sure what's there matches the float.

Finally, note the weather or any unusual happenings in your records so you can use that information in your weekly summary.

Counter *Talk*   Brewpoint increased the accuracy of the cash drawers by 300 percent by incentivizing perfect drawers. For every perfect drawer, the team accrues points that get them free shift drinks or bags of coffee.

Weekly Write-Ups

The purpose of a weekly summary is to look for sales trends. Do certain days of the week bring in more sales than others? Are you using your employees wisely, or do you have too many in the store during slow times?

To create your weekly write-up, every 7 days you'll carry over the daily sales totals onto a weekly summary sheet (also available in Appendix B). Ignore dates and pay attention only to the days. For example, adopt a Monday-to-Sunday or Sunday-to-Saturday schedule and stick with it, even when the week crosses over the end of one month or year into the next. Sales on particular days of the week tend to be regular from week to week, and weekends draw different crowds than weekdays. You'll miss this distinction if you compare June 6 with July 6 instead of the actual days of the week.

In addition to sales figures, record the total number of hours worked by all employees. Divide the day's sales figures by the number of labor hours to determine the sales per person hour (SPPH). This measure is one way of looking at the value of each employee's labor. If SPPH varies widely over the course of a week, you might consider reworking your schedule to have employees start work an hour later or leave an hour earlier. In some cases, such as opening and closing the store, this might not be practical, but throwing money away on unused labor is hardly practical either.

Carry over the weather information you recorded in the daily summaries, and note any other relevant events, such as national holidays or local happenings.

Counter *Talk*	Take note of everything you can, from local transportation schedules to school holidays, and over time you'll start spotting patterns. For example, Melissa discovered that Brewpoint gets a surge of high schoolers on late-start Wednesdays, when juniors and seniors start an hour late. Another revelation: retail sales are slower in June and July thanks to family vacations.

Monthly Recaps

Whereas the weekly summary looks for sales trends, the monthly summary takes a snapshot of the financial health of your entire business, allowing you to compare income and expenses from month to month. You should keep records from the very first day you open, but don't rely too heavily on those initial numbers. During your first month, for example, your expenses will be much higher than in any other month because you'll be spending money to build up an inventory from nothing.

To start creating the monthly summary, add sales figures from a month's worth of daily cash sheets. For the monthly summary, we *do* care about the days of the month (rather than the days of the week), so work with daily cash sheets from the first of the month to the thirtieth or thirty-first, or however many days the month has.

Subtract the cost of all goods sold from the total month's worth of daily cash sheets you tallied in the preceding paragraph to get your gross income for the month. To determine the cost of all goods sold, start with the value of your inventory at the beginning of the month, add the cost of all purchases received during the month, and subtract the value of inventory on hand at month's end. (We talk about taking inventory in more detail in Chapter 18.)

Next, list all expenses (except for loan payments) for the month in their appropriate places on the sheet, and tally these figures. Subtract the total expenses from your gross income to determine your monthly income prior to the cost of the money borrowed. Subtract your loan payment from this number to determine your actual monthly income.

Why not include loan payments? These payments are different from other expenses because they're eventually going to disappear. Raw materials, labor, insurance, and so on are all operating expenses that will be consistent every month as long as the business is open. If you ever try to sell the business (a topic we discuss in Chapter 25), you want to be able to show prospective buyers income *prior* to the cost of borrowed money because their borrowing costs will differ from yours.

Now, divide each expense by the monthly sales figure you calculated earlier to determine what percent of sales each expense represents. For example, if the cost of goods sold during a month is $8,500 while sales equal $28,000, then food costs equal 30 percent of your sales. (Keep in mind, of course, that the total for "food costs" includes expenses for napkins, cleaning fluids, and all other consumables.)

New Year, New Records

Each January 1 closes one financial year and opens another. Compile the monthly totals on one sheet, and see what 365 days of labor have brought you.

This summary is similar to the monthly sheets in terms of creating a financial snapshot, but its primary purpose is to help you prepare for filing taxes. You need to know the numbers, both income and expenses, for the entire year so your accountant can have everything she needs in one place.

Speaking of your accountant, if you can hand over a digital file as well as paper printouts at year's end, she will love you. Using a POS system along with accounting software like QuickBooks can make your daily, weekly, monthly, and yearly reporting and analysis easier. As you plug in daily numbers and pay your bills, you can create profit-and-loss statements as well as balance sheets with the click of a button.

Making the Most of Your Money

We already explained how you can use the SPPH figure in your weekly summary to adjust employee work schedules. The monthly summaries, with expenses listed as a percentage of sales, will point out where you should attempt similar cost-cutting measures.

Has electricity doubled from 1 to 2 percent of your monthly expenses? Contact the electric company and ask a representative to visit your business to point out what might have caused such an increase. Have office expenses jumped unexpectedly? If so, what's the cause, and what can you do to bring that expense back in line?

Whatever spending cuts you make, don't slash your marketing budget to save money. Advertising and promotions, topics we cover in Chapters 23 and 24, bring new customers through the door. Cutting these costs is like cutting off the roots to make a tree grow stronger—it just doesn't work that way.

Setting Sales Goals

In addition to lowering costs, you can use your sales records to set sales goals for any time period of your choosing: daily, weekly, biennially, and so on. At first glance, sales goals seem rather ridiculous. *If I'm going to set a goal,* you might be thinking, *why not make it a million dollars a minute? It's not like I can control whether or not customers come in and spend money.*

You have far more control over your sales volume than you might think. Don't clean the counters for a few days, cut down your open hours, and take a customer favorite off the menu, and we're sure you'll soon discover how much control you actually have over your sales.

As for *positively* influencing your sales, that's one reason we insisted in the previous section that you shouldn't reduce your marketing budget to cut costs. Every business loses customers over time—they move away due to marriage or work, their doctor tells them to cut down on sweets, or they start new hobbies that take up their time … and sometimes they migrate to the competition.

Customer attrition threatens the long-term survival of every business, large and small. The smart entrepreneur knows that marketing is an essential tool just to keep the customer base from shrinking, never mind expanding it and boosting profits.

Sales goals help give your marketing efforts direction. Instead of simply saying, "I'm going to make twice as much money next month," you can use the sales records to create specific sales targets: "I'm going to sell twice as many iced coffees this summer" or "This month, 50 percent more customers who buy cappuccino will buy a sweet to go with the drink."

With goals like these, you can narrow your marketing efforts to make the goals a reality. For example, for the goal of increasing the purchase of sweets with your cappuccinos, you might try the following:

* Hand out coupons that promise half-price sweets with the purchase of a hot drink.

* Distribute fliers with a similar offer.

* Teach employees to practice better suggestive selling.

* Create a special offer for your social media followers.

* Place signs and pictures near the register that make the cappuccino/sweet combination look so tasty customers won't be able to resist.

Set sales goals so they're challenging yet still attainable. Trying to earn twice as much in a month is hopeless; trying to boost sales on a particular item or add-on isn't.

Even if you don't achieve your goal, you're sure to see higher numbers than in the previous sales period, which means you just have to try a little harder next time. As coaches like to say, *making the goal isn't what's important—trying is.*

Practicing Responsible Accounting

You may have hired an accountant to double-check your sales figures and file tax returns, but the bulk of the record-keeping load still falls on your shoulders. If you want to keep Uncle Sam happy and out of your hair, you'll take this responsibility seriously every business day.

In addition to tracking sales, you need to keep receipts for every business expense you plan to deduct, no matter how small. Divide receipts into categories such as these:

* Rent

* Utilities, with subdivisions for phone, gas, electricity, water, and internet access

* Advertising

* Payroll costs

* Auto expenses

* Professional fees

* Travel and entertainment

It might go without saying, but we'll say it anyway: these expenses must be made with the intent of increasing your business income. Driving to the bank to discuss a business loan counts as a reasonable mileage deduction; driving to a restaurant to talk with your spouse about starting a business is borderline—especially if you order a whole lobster for your meal.

If you do decide to classify questionable expenses as business related, be ready to explain to the Internal Revenue Service (IRS) why they were necessary and reasonable. Contrary to the American legal system, in the eyes of the IRS, you are guilty until you prove yourself innocent.

If you can't convince them an expense was justified, you must recalculate your business income and pay any taxes owed. If the IRS feels you deliberately tried to game the system, you could be charged a penalty as well.

As for sales taxes, these must be turned over to the state on a regular basis, with the exact time period—monthly, quarterly, or otherwise—determined by the state and your sales volume. Good record-keeping helps you avoid the stiff penalties that fall on those who pay less than what's due.

Counter *Talk*

Doing the books can be a pain, but it's crucial to get it right from the very start. That means hiring not only an accountant, but also someone who can manage your accounts in QuickBooks or another financial program. Melissa didn't do this in the beginning, and it cost so much to clean up the mess, it would have been cheaper to have hired someone to handle it in the first place.

Managing Shrinkage

Shrinkage is business-speak for "theft," whether it's a loss of inventory, a con man scamming the counterperson, or an employee dipping into the till. Opportunities for shrinkage abound in any business. We examine the most common ones you might encounter here, along with ways to rein in a robbery before it leads to ruin.

Quick-Change Artists

A quick-change artist works like a magician, misdirecting your attention so you don't even realize you're being tricked.

One possible misdirection is that someone shows you a large bill when paying but then actually gives you a smaller denomination bill. If you didn't notice the switch, you'll hand over more change than you should, and the drawer will come up short at the end of the day.

Another possibility is someone who purchases an inexpensive item but presents a large bill, say $100, for payment. But then, as you're handing over the change, he finds a $5 bill and offers to pay with that instead. You take the change back and return his $100—just as he realizes he *does* need to break the C-note to pay back $20 to his Uncle Joe. The money flies back and forth so quickly, you realize only later you gave change for the $100 but only received the $5!

To prevent this type of con artist from tricking you, lay the bill he gives you horizontally across the till. Pull out the proper amount of change and count out the transaction as you place the change and then the bills in the customer's hand: "The total came to $3.28, and you paid $10, which means you receive $6.72 in change. Here's 72¢, a $5, and a $1."

If he protests that you're giving the wrong amount of change, you can point to the bill on the register to show what he paid. If he tries to pay with a different bill, stop him and make him accept the change, place the bill in the register, and close it. Then you can ask him if he'd like you to make change separately.

In general, keep the bill the customer offers in view and finish the transaction before doing anything else. Con artists rely on confusion and intimidation, so by sticking to one task at a time, you can foil their plans.

Some thieves rely on sneaky cons, but others will just reach over and grab what they can while you turn around to find a stirrer for them. Thievery takes less time than you think! To thwart these bad guys, whenever you handle money, close the register as soon as possible, and *never* step away while the till is open.

Employee Register Theft

You'd like to think register shortfalls are always the work of con artists, but unfortunately, that's not always the case. Employees occasionally dip their hands in the till as well—in fact, employee theft costs U.S. businesses $50 billion each year, according to CNBC (cnbc.com). And unless you know what to look for, you might not even realize funds are missing.

Some common problems are undercharging (not entering a sale and pocketing the customer's money), overcharging (charging a customer a higher price and keeping the difference), and skimming (simply keeping money and having the drawer come up short).

To avoid these problems, start by having only one employee on a register at a time. If, for example, all three employees on a shift use a register and the drawer comes up $20 short, you have three people to question about what might have happened. When only one person is responsible for the cash drawer, the investigation is much quicker.

When you have a single person handling a register, you can also detect patterns over time. If the drawer is short each time Madison handles it, for example, you might need to have a talk with her. If Jacob has twice as many "no sales" as other employees, you need to find out why. (An employee who undercharges might hit "no sale" to open the drawer and give the customer change for his purchase without attracting suspicion.)

If an employee's drawer comes up short time and time again, despite her being warned about past errors, you might be better off letting her go. Don't imply she's done anything illegal. Merely point out the section of the job description in the employee manual that says, "Must be able to make change correctly." No accusations—just a failure to perform a key job function.

Next, insist that every employee offer the customer a receipt with their purchase. This can lessen the temptation to under- or overcharge customers because the customers will have a printout or email of their order.

You can conduct surprise register counts in the middle of an employee's shift, too. This might catch someone who undercharged a customer but didn't yet remove the booty. At a minimum, this practice lets potentially shady employees know you're keeping a constant eye on the money.

Finally, keep in mind that the security system we discussed in Chapter 10 can help deter employee theft, especially if you have one of the cameras trained on the counter area.

One important note if you suspect an employee is helping himself to the till: never accuse an employee of theft unless you are absolutely sure of the claim. Seeing him pocket money is proof. A register drawer that's constantly short is not; he might just be incompetent. If you accuse an employee of theft, that's sure to sour the relationship should he be exonerated later—not to mention you might be sued for slander.

Counter *Talk*   At Brewpoint, an employee is written up if their drawer comes up $5 over or under. Three writeups, and the employee is subject to a 1-week suspension.

Employee Product Theft

Another way employee wrongdoing can cost you money is through giveaways and a generous "self-serve" policy. Friends naturally like to treat friends, and a young employee might not feel like he's harming your business if he offers a free bagel or coffee to a friend. Another employee might pay for a cookie when she leaves her shift but actually take two because she worked extra hard that day.

A free cookie might seem like small potatoes, so to speak, but magnify this practice to 10 friends or 10 free cookies a week, and your profit margin will take a serious hit.

You can usually spot such giveaways through inventory records, but to pinpoint the real cause of the shortfall, you might need to take a daily inventory of certain items before and after an employee's shift. If the count comes up one cookie short each time Nicole works a shift, you need to have someone else pack Nicole's order before she leaves.

In fact, this practice is a good idea for all employees—even you! Set an example by never ringing up your own orders, and don't serve your own drinks. If you plant yourself in line with other employees, they'll never question this practice. Plus, you'll get to experience a transaction from the customer's viewpoint and see where it might need improvement.

Inventory records can also spot employees' gifts to friends, but this practice is harder to keep in line unless you want to watch employees every minute of the day. If you're sure you've pinpointed the employee who's giving away certain items, you might convince him to mend his ways by casually mentioning the discrepancy in inventory. He'll pass the word along to his friends, and they'll stop looking for a handout.

Finally, make room behind the counter for a special trash container for waste products such as cracked cookies, mashed muffins, and so on. Track these items on the inventory so employees can't take something for themselves but then claim it was waste. Some coffee shops, including Brewpoint, let the staff eat pastries that would otherwise go to waste. Just be careful if you do this because it can become an incentive for some to "accidentally" drop a cookie or two.

Burglaries

We hope a robbery never happens to you and your coffee shop, but be aware that it could happen. Most burglaries occur at night, so insist that employees follow security procedures when closing the shop to protect both themselves and the business.

After the doors are locked for the night, for example, they shouldn't be opened for any reason until the next morning. If a customer comes to the door and asks to use the bathroom, direct him to another local business that's still open.

In addition, you (and your managers and staff) should …

  * Keep the back doors locked at all times except during deliveries.

  * Double-check the back door and office locks as well as the safe before you leave in the evening.

  * Leave the register drawer open with an empty till inside so thieves know there's nothing worth grabbing within easy reach.

  * Check windows and door locks periodically for signs of tampering. A burglar may need more than one try to break in, and you might notice foul play before any real harm is done.

  * Never exit the shop by the back door in the evening; instead, leave by the front entrance. If this entrance isn't lit by streetlights or other lighting, install timer lights in the building's front (after asking the landlord) so you and your employees can see the environment around you at night.

  * Leave the store in pairs whenever possible so no one is left on his or her own.

  * Install a peephole in the back door so you can verify that a delivery person is waiting, or insist that all drivers enter through the front of the store before you open the back door.

  * Take out all garbage during daylight hours.

  * If you encounter a burglar, or if someone attempts to rob your store during the day, have employees hand over the money. Don't put anyone at risk by trying to be a hero.

Despite all these precautions, you might still be hit by burglars at some point. Insurance might cover lost product, depending on the size of your deductible, but the cash is gone for good. If this ever happens, learn what you can from the experience and change your security to prevent another hit in the future.

In this chapter, you learned how to track, analyze, and protect your coffee shop's money. Next, we discuss the people who actually bring that money into your shop: your customers.

Customer Relations

You might have the most beautiful coffee shop in history, with the freshest coffee, the finest selection of treats, and the best atmosphere. Without customers, however, you have nothing.

A business needs products and services to sell, yes. But equally important are customers to purchase those items. When customers enter your store, your job (and your staff's job) is to welcome them, find out what they want, and go the extra mile to satisfy their needs. They're in your store to satisfy their thirst or hunger, or both, but you can provide a deeper level of satisfaction through a positive customer experience.

Some customer-winning tactics are easy—like actually getting their orders right, for example—but you can do much more to ensure you win their loyalty and repeat business. In this chapter, we tell you how, as well as cover what to do in those rare situations when things go awry.

Making Your Customers Happy

Customers have many choices of where to shop for coffee. They can purchase drinks from a chain store, or fill up with coffee at a convenience store when they fill up their car with gas. They can order coffee while dining out at a restaurant. They can purchase grounds from the supermarket and make their own at home.

Or they can buy from you.

Which one they choose depends on many factors—price, convenience, and selection, for starters—but the important thing for you to remember is that they do have a choice. No matter why they chose your coffee shop initially, if you don't treat your customers well, they'll go spend their money somewhere else.

This means you can never rely on any customer for sales over the long term. They're not tenants under contract; they're guests in your home. By treating them well, you encourage them to get into the habit of returning to the same place at the same time to order the same thing—and enjoy the same great service.

Smile and Say "Hi"

What's the first thing you do when a guest arrives at your home? You make eye contact, smile, and greet her. The same principle applies for customers. By saying hello, you do many things:

* You acknowledge her presence so she feels welcome.

* You let her know who to turn to if she has questions.

* You tell her that employees are paying attention, in case she intends any funny business. (Guests don't normally steal from your home, but you *are* inviting lots of people you don't know into your coffee shop.)

It's important to warmly greet every single person who enters, whether they're daily drinkers or complete strangers. It doesn't matter what kind of mood you're in or how lousy sales have been that day; treat every customer as if she might be the last, and win her over. After all, if you greet some guests and not others, members of the latter group might feel slighted and take their business somewhere they do feel welcome.

Employees follow your lead, so if you're an enthusiastic greeter, they will be, too. Don't feel that you have to come up with lots of different ways to greet people. A simple, sincere—that is, nonrobotic—smile and "Hello" is all you need.

Give Them a Tour

When a guest comes to your house for the first time, what do you do? You show them around your home, pointing out the bathroom, the location of the hors d'oeuvres, and where they can have a seat and get comfortable. You ensure they can easily find what they need to enjoy their visit.

Do the same in your coffee shop. Provide a quick tour to new "guests" so they know what's interesting and special about your home away from home. Start by asking if they've been in your shop before. If they haven't, offer a brief description of your business or mention something that might be new to them: "We're glad you could stop by. We offer six types of organically grown coffee, ground fresh every hour, along with a new line of flavorings in case you want a cup with a little something extra. Want to give one a try?"

You also can tailor your talk around the individual's order while he waits for it. If he ordered an espresso, whoever's minding the machine can talk about how you choose the beans. If he ordered an herbal tea, you can ask whether he thinks you should carry iced herbal teas in the summer.

Try to engage customers while simultaneously educating them about your shop. Keep it short and relevant so you don't take up your customer's time if he's in a hurry. (If he sticks around to continue the conversation after receiving his drink, that's great—just be sure not to ignore the next customer who's waiting in line.)

Above all, be sincere. If you feel like a recording playing the same spiel over and over, customers will definitely hear it in your voice. Love your work, and let that love come through in your voice every time you talk about coffee.

Counter *Talk*

At Brewpoint, staff members are expected to greet customers within 10 seconds and are encouraged to find some connection, like complimenting the customer on something they like about them, or remembering something about them they can mention the next time the customer comes in. On the other hand, employees should be able to read the subtle signals that show when a customer isn't interested in chit-chatting. Your staff needs to be kind and helpful to everyone, but they don't have to force customers to talk.

Get to Know Your Customers

When you're taking an order, do what you can to satisfy the guest's needs. Offer suggestions if he's staring at the menu without a clue. Find out whether he wants whipped cream or a dash of nutmeg in his drink.

Most importantly, ask for his name. If you need to, write it on the cup so whoever makes his drink—whether you or another employee—can let him know when his order is ready. After all, if you yell out "Hot chocolate," you might have several customers who are ready to claim the drink. Call out "James, I have your hot chocolate ready," and you'll avoid any confusion. James, along with everyone else, will appreciate this.

Before too long, you'll be able to place names, faces, and orders together and converse freely with customers when they approach you. You can offer suggestions based on previous orders or even start making their drink as soon as you see them walk in.

If you're not making a customer's drink yourself, don't yell the order down the length of the counter. Either write the order on a cup or walk over to the drink-maker and tell her in person. These approaches show more care for the order than the "loud" approach.

Counter *Talk*   Brewpoint baristas don't write customers' names on drink cups. Instead, they try to remember what each customer ordered by engaging with customers from behind the counter. This becomes much easier once your staff members get to know the regulars.

Don't forget about customers as soon as they've given you their money and received their order. Instead, walk around the seating area and see if you can bring them anything else. Ask how they're enjoying a newly introduced flavored coffee or baked good.

Thank Them Again on Their Way Out

When customers head for the door, don't just let them slip out unnoticed. Thank them for stopping by and wish them well. You'd do the same with guests in your home when they leave, wouldn't you?

Keeping 'Em Coming Back

The key to a successful coffee shop is a stable of repeat customers who provide a steady stream of business. Treating customers like guests is a good first step in building customer loyalty because everyone appreciates a good host or hostess.

Beyond that, recognize that customers are *shoppers* and that they appreciate receiving a financial incentive to return to your coffee shop. The following sections offer some suggestions on perks you can offer your customers to ensure their repeat business.

Free Samples

Cut a cookie or muffin into eight pieces, walk around the seating area, and offer samples to everyone. If one customer buys just one item in response, you've broken even. What's more likely to happen, though, is that a customer (or two) will buy one or two items that day and then continue to buy the item on future visits.

Samples give customers a taste—a tiny, tantalizing taste—of a treat they might have found visually appealing but not compelling enough to spend money on. When the customer finally gets that taste, however, resistance is futile.

Loyalty Cards

How many loyalty cards do you have in your wallet? Probably several, if you're like most people. You can offer one for your coffee shop, too.

Present a frequent buyer card to each customer with the offer of a free drink after they purchase a set number of drinks. Ask each customer at the register if he has a frequent buyer card. If he does, stamp it or run it through your point-of-sale (POS) system; if not, tell him why he should have one.

Discount Coupons

Another way to attract repeat business is to offer coupons buyers can use during their next visit. Walk through the seating area and hand out coupons for, say, a free drink with the purchase of any bakery item or a free cookie with the purchase of any drink.

These coupons make customers aware of aspects of your product line they might otherwise have overlooked. More importantly, they may draw customers back to your shop earlier than they otherwise would have visited.

Counter *Talk*

Brewpoint offers coupons at outside events the shop is involved in and whenever a new item is introduced. During the launch of new springtime drinks, for example, employees hand out coupons for 25 percent off a spring drink that last through the weekend.

Volume Discounts

Just as some movie theaters sell passes good for 10 movies at the price of 8, you can offer a $20 card that's worth a certain number of drinks. By buying the card up front, the customer gives you money before you provide any service, which improves your cash flow. On future sales, you can serve the customer his drink faster because you don't have to exchange funds.

One final benefit of discount cards: customers tend to spend a bit more and buy more frequently when they're getting a discount. The coffee costs less, they figure, so why not add a cookie as well because the total order is only a few cents over the price of a nondiscounted coffee—not to mention the money is already spent anyway.

Branded Mugs

If you're more ambitious, you can have your coffee shop logo imprinted on mugs and offer a discount to anyone who buys a mug and brings it in for a refill. Sure, you're making less per drink, but you're also lowering your cleaning and labor costs—plus profiting from the sale price of the mug itself. Many customers also appreciate the eco-friendliness of a reusable mug over paper cups.

Gift Cards

Of course you'd prefer to *sell* gift cards, but you can also give one to current customers and ask them to pass it on to a friend or family member. By giving them something of value they can pass along to someone else, you help them look good to others. The advantage to you, of course, is that the customer might bring new customers into your shop.

Receipt Recommendations

If your register or POS system allows you to add messages at the bottom of each receipt, include pitches for new products or a discount on a future sale to encourage customers to return in the future—or perhaps even make a second purchase right away.

Be sure to include your store's address and phone number on your receipts, and on everything else you give away, like coupons or loyalty cards. Don't make them hunt you down, or they might find somebody else instead.

Finally, whenever you hand over coupons and other sales incentives to customers, express your appreciation for their support, but avoid communicating that gratitude in terms of dollars and cents. No customer wants to be thought of solely as a wallet that transfers money into your register.

Counter *Talk*   Brewpoint has punch cards that reward customers with a free drink for every 10 they buy. The punch cards, which are the same size and shape as business cards, come from a website that prints the latter.

Seeking Feedback

The only way to know if customers are satisfied is to *ask them*. You can walk around the dining room and ask for comments, but you're unlikely to get more than a "Fine" or "Great!" from most customers. In most cases, they're talking with friends, reading, or doing something that requires more attention than the drink in front of them.

To get more detailed comments, make it easy for customers to reply in their own time. Even more important, let them do so anonymously. Many people will write what they'd never say in person, especially if given the option to remain unknown.

The following sections offer some ways to solicit—and use—feedback from your customers.

Asking the Right Questions

Before you go all out with surveys and so on, learn how to create a feedback form people will actually want to fill out. Here are some suggestions:

* **Keep it short.** Everyone's busy, so the shorter your survey or comment card, the better.

* **Mix up the format.** Instead of all multiple-choice or yes/no questions, use a combination of both plus rankings, text boxes, and other question formats as appropriate.

* **Make them choose.** If you offer only checkbox-style questions, many customers will check off everything. Yes, they want longer open hours, Fair Trade coffee, more syrup flavors, *and* better music! Instead, ask them to pick their top few or rank items according to importance.

* **Give them a voice.** Be sure to include an "other" option with a text box below each question so customers can elaborate on what their "other" is, and also include some essay-style questions where the customer has space to let it all out. On some online survey platforms, you can limit the number of characters in these fields so customers have enough space to be heard, but not enough to write an entire novel.

Now that you know what types of questions to ask, let's talk about how to create that survey and get it to customers.

Choosing Your Survey

Depending on your needs, your budget, and your brand, you can solicit feedback from customers in a number of ways, such as comment cards, online surveys, and even POS surveys.

Paper comment cards are quick, easy, and inexpensive to put together. Make them available throughout the store by handing them out with to-go orders, leaving a supply near the restroom, and tucking them into a display near the cream station. Also place a locked box nearby where customers can drop their completed feedback.

Later, you could post the comment-card questions, and your answers, on a bulletin board near the bathroom or somewhere else in the store. A customer might ask, for example, why you don't carry a certain type of coffee, and by posting your answer, you can explain the reasons to him and everyone else at the same time—or you can announce for all to see that you'll start carrying it next month.

If you have an email newsletter or social media accounts for your coffee shop (more on these in Chapter 24), send your fans and followers a link to an online survey. These are easy to create using platforms such as the following:

* SurveyMonkey (surveymonkey.com)

* Survey Anyplace (surveyanyplace.com)

* Crowdsignal (crowdsignal.com)

Many of these platforms offer a free trial or are free up to a certain number of surveys or responses.

Ever pay for your drink at a café and instantly get an emailed receipt with a survey that asks you how satisfied you were with the service on a scale of 1 to 10? Some POS systems offer this capability, and it's such a quick survey, it's almost impossible not to take it. When you do take the survey, it sends you to a page where you can offer more feedback if you like, although it's not a requirement.

Counter *Talk*

One caveat about online and POS surveys: they hit only those customers who are comfortable taking surveys online or who request emailed receipts. Melissa has found that also offering a paper comment card ensures you get feedback from a wider range of customers.

Enticing Customers to Play Along

There's no point coming up with a survey if your customers won't fill it out. Try these ideas to encourage them to participate—and make them feel appreciated afterward:

* **Promote brevity.** If your survey is short, let people know: "Take our two-question survey!" for example, or, "This survey should take only 2 minutes of your time."

* **Offer a goodie.** Giving a coupon or a free drink in exchange for feedback may lead to more responses to your survey or comment card.

* **Add it to the receipt.** If your register or POS system allows it, include a note about the survey, and a link to it, at the bottom of the receipt.

* **Give a prize.** Some businesses enter survey or comment card respondents into a prize drawing for a month of free drinks or a complimentary cake, for example. Certain laws govern giveaways and sweepstakes, so run the idea by your lawyer to ensure your prize drawing is on the up-and-up.

* **Respond to comments.** Let customers know you're paying attention to them. If customers leave their email or mailing address, write to them and answer their questions. For customers who don't ask questions, send a simple thank you note and a coupon. You can even give a shout-out to commenters on social media, in your newsletter, or on your website, assuming you have their permission to do so.

* **Keep in touch.** Don't treat feedback as a one-time communication. Assemble a mailing list of customers' addresses and send them thank you cards once a year, perhaps right before the winter holidays or on your shop's anniversary. Use a marketing newsletter— a topic we cover in Chapter 24—to stay in touch with past customers and introduce new products.

* **Actually use their feedback.** Examine the survey results to look for common themes in customer compliments and complaints, and take action. For example, if 75 percent of respondents complain that your coffee shop is too loud, look for ways to change the layout to solve the problem. Then promote the changes you've made based on customer feedback, and customers will be even more likely to offer it in the future.

You've got a survey set up, and the feedback is flowing in. But what happens when that feedback happens on a platform you don't control, like review sites, and the feedback isn't so great?

Turning Haters into Fans

With review sites like Yelp, Google Reviews, and TripAdvisor, it takes unhappy customers only a few clicks and keystrokes to leave negative comments about your shop, your coffee, and anything else that might irk them. Handle these negative reviews the wrong way, and visitors to those review sites will be warned away from your shop.

Here's how to deal with not-so-great reviews in a way that turns the unhappy customers into happier ones and shows other readers that you do everything you can to provide a positive customer experience.

Monitor the Sites

Make it a habit to regularly check the review sites where your customers are most likely to leave comments so you can quickly act on bad reviews. (And good ones! More on that in a bit.)

Ask Happy Customers to Leave Reviews

Does your coffee shop have just one review, and it's a negative one? That's not good. Have 100, and 1 is negative? That's okay. If a complaint is surrounded by a sea of praise, it won't have as much of an impact on review site visitors.

When a customer offers a compliment in person, or you can see they're enjoying your products and your service, ask them to leave a review on whatever site impacts your business most, such as Yelp or Google Reviews. You can do the same via email when you receive positive comments on a survey or in an email. Be sure to include a link to the review site to make it as easy as possible for the customer to follow through.

Act on Negative Reviews

Respond to bad reviews as quickly as you can, apologizing for the situation and explaining how you plan to fix it. For example, if the customer complained that your coffee tasted like acid, offer them a coupon for a free coffee—and if you get this complaint frequently, consider a new coffee supplier and retrain your staff on proper grinding and brewing techniques.

Many negative reviews are legit, but some are from people who harshly criticize your shop without offering any details on why they're unhappy. Some of these are even from competitors looking to scare customers away from your shop! If you get any of these types of reviews, don't sink to their level by engaging in a virtual shouting match. Instead, respond in the same even tone you do with the others, apologizing and asking for more details.

Love the Lovers

Letting your fans fall through the cracks on review sites shows that you're more concerned with assuaging the feelings of complainers than appreciating the customers who love your shop. Be sure to thank your happy customers who leave positive comments for the kind review.

And speaking of bad stuff, it's time to dive into the topic of safety issues, real-life unhappy customers, and other emergencies large and small.

What to Do When Bad Stuff Happens

Despite any precautions you might take, accidents and other undesirable incidents might happen in your coffee shop. Let's run through some possible common scenarios so you're better prepared to act when circumstances warrant it.

> **Counter** *Talk*
>
> Safety is everything. Brewpoint has a three-step safety policy. If a customer is doing something that makes other customers uncomfortable, an employee asks them to stop. If the customer doesn't stop, the employee asks them to leave. No luck? As a last resort, the employee calls the regional manager, Melissa, or the police. (Of course, in higher-stakes situations, the employee would call these people right away.)

Dealing with Spills

Working in a coffee shop, you and your employees will handle hundreds of drinks in any given day, and you're bound to spill a few of them. If anyone is splashed with hot liquid, immediately apply an ice pack to the affected part of the body to reduce the pain and swelling. (More on first-aid kits coming up later in this section.) If the burn is serious, send the employee home and let them know their injury will be covered by workers' compensation.

Customers spill things, too, so give them the same emergency treatment if necessary. If the spill is merely embarrassing, clean up the mess as quickly as possible and replace the customer's order without charge. By treating the customer as a guest and not as a nuisance, you'll leave a better impression and help her forget about the spill.

Dealing with Unsatisfied (and Unsatisfiable) Customers

No matter how friendly and speedy you are, some customers will never be satisfied. They'll complain about the length of the line, the size of their Danish, or the lack of a particular flavored syrup.

Don't become defensive or try to explain why they're mistaken. You cannot win this argument, and if you insist on trying to, you will only look worse in the eyes of other customers. Your goal with these customers, as with any customer, is to satisfy them the best you can, apologize for what you can't fix immediately, and promise to work on eliminating the problem in the future.

Keep that promise, too, because in some cases difficult customers do have valid complaints. Perhaps you *should* hire another employee to keep lines moving faster or reassess your baked goods supplier. If you dismiss the complaint solely due to the manner in which it was presented, you'll miss opportunities to improve your business.

A common belief about customers is that a happy customer might tell 1 person about his experience while an unhappy customer will spread the word to 10 people. If you do whatever you can to satisfy a customer before he storms out, not only do you save that customer, you also potentially save 10 others who might have been turned away.

Counter *Talk*	Complaints you have to deal with, but abusive or impossibly demanding customers you don't. Brewpoint staff will remake a drink a couple times, but if the customer still isn't satisfied, they'll suggest he might be happier getting coffee elsewhere. If a customer is berating a staff member, the staff is empowered to ask him to leave.

Dealing with Medical Emergencies

Part of your employee training should cover how to handle medical emergencies in the coffee shop, from customers who are choking to those suffering from cardiac arrest or seizure.

Before you open, for example, you might ask a medical intern to visit the store and speak to the entire staff about what they should do in an emergency. You can practice doing the Heimlich maneuver on one another and be sure everyone knows where the landline is in case they need to call 911.

With each new hire, you or a senior employee can run through this safety training, again both to teach it and to reinforce the material for your current staff.

Place a medical kit behind the counter in case employees need to apply an ice pack to a spill, wrap a wound, or treat other injuries. The American National Standards Institute, in conjunction with the International Safety Equipment Association, offers a list of what you should include in your first-aid kit, including a cold pack, adhesive bandages, and burn treatment. Find the current list by searching for "first-aid kit" on the Industrial Safety and Hygiene News site at ishn.com. Or instead of assembling your own first-aid kit, purchase a restaurant-specific kit that follows these suggested guidelines from businesses like MFASCO Health and Safety (mfasco.com).

Dealing with Robberies

If you are ever confronted by a robber or group of robbers, your goal is simple: give them whatever they want, and urge them to leave.

Keeping everyone safe, both employees and customers, is far more important than whatever amount of money you'll lose. Respond to a robber's demands in a slow, nonthreatening manner, while at the same time mentally noting characteristics that might help the police catch them later such as height, hair color, facial hair, and so on.

Counter *Talk*

Brewpoint has never been robbed (thank goodness), but a customer once tried to trick the staff into walking away from the tip jar in order to steal it. Fortunately, another customer noticed what was happening and called it out, and the would-be thief scurried out the door empty-handed.

Dealing with Fires, Tornadoes, and Other Acts of God

Every airplane flight begins with a reminder of safety procedures, even though the number of air accidents is extremely small. Use the same amount of caution with your business, and your employees will be ready to tackle fires, storms, and other surprises that might arise.

Be sure all employees know where to find the fire extinguishers, and keep them charged and up to date. Practice evacuating the shop through both the front and rear doors in case you need to leave in a hurry.

Stay up to date on weather readiness by reading the advice at Ready.gov's Severe Weather page at ready.gov/severe-weather. You'll read about how to prepare your shop for severe weather events, spot signs of tornadoes and floods, and keep your staff and customers safe.

In any emergency, you're automatically the one in charge because you own the business, but proper training helps every employee learn how to react automatically so they can lead customers to safety.

Counter *Talk*

Brewpoint has dealt with all kinds of crazy incidents, including a bomb scare, tornado warnings, power outages, and a missing person report where the child was last seen at Brewpoint. (She was later found safe and sound, thank goodness.)

With luck, you'll experience nothing other than sunshine and friendly, nonspilling, nonrobbing customers. But just in case, the customer service best practices, pointers for handling unhappy customers, and tips on preparing for serious events covered in this chapter should help you deal with any issues you might face. Be sure to work with your lawyer to ensure you're legally covered against all these eventualities as well.

In the next chapter, we get into the nitty-gritty of cleaning and maintaining your coffee shop.

Cleaning and Maintaining Your Shop

Every coffee shop owner wishes his or her shop worked like a self-cleaning oven. You'd lock the door at the end of the day; press a button; and magically, all the dirt, dust, and grime that comes with food preparation would be eliminated and every surface would be sanitized, ready for the next day.

Alas, the only way to clean your coffee shop is to use old-fashioned tools like clean water, linen cloths, and elbow grease.

Cleaning is essential both to creating a welcoming environment that customers want to come back to again and again and to maintaining good standing with the local health department. If you fall behind on cleaning, you face an uphill battle to get your shop back in shape. You probably know this from experience in your house or apartment. If you let the cleaning go for a couple days, when the weekend comes, you have a huge mess to clean before your mother arrives.

Maintain a regular cleaning schedule, though—something along the lines of what we describe in this chapter—and cleaning will be relatively easy on a day-to-day basis.

Ideally, your shop will be so sparkling clean each customer will feel like she's the first person to order from you, which means she'll receive the most delectable drinks and the freshest food possible. Clean with this mind-set, and you can make it happen.

Creating a Cleaning Schedule

Creating an effective cleaning schedule takes only two steps. First, make a list of every single element in your shop: the lights, the doormat, the utensils, the inside of the portafilters on the espresso machine, and so on. If you don't list it on the cleaning schedule, it probably won't get cleaned—and even if it does, you won't clean it as often as you should.

Counter *Talk*	As you look around your shop and make your list of what needs cleaning, really think about *everything* that might ever need cleaning. At Brewpoint, staff members have to make it a point to remember to dust the ceilings, clean the janitor's closet, and deep clean the upholstery.

Next, after you've listed everything, decide how often each item needs to be cleaned: monthly, weekly, daily, hourly, or after each use. Manufacturer guidelines will help you out in some cases; other times, you must rely on observation. If, for instance, you notice the shelf that displays French presses for sale is dusty each time you pass it, you know to move that area up a notch on the cleaning schedule.

In general, your coffee shop can never be too clean. You're preparing items that people eat, after all, and cleanliness is one important way to avoid food contamination.

What's more, if your store gets a reputation as being unclean, you'll see customers trickle away as they decide to take their business elsewhere. You can hardly advertise that you're now cleaning on a regular basis ("Now featuring 75 percent less dirt and spider webs!"), so once you lose dirt-phobic customers, they're unlikely to come back.

The followings sections offer some guidelines on what to clean when.

After Each Use

Of prime concern in the clean-after-each-use category is the espresso machine, which baristas should wipe down after each and every use. The steam wands must be cleared, and the grounds from the previous shot should be dumped. Rinse the portafilters regularly as well. All this ensures that each espresso product is uncontaminated by the residue of drinks past.

Counters fall under this category, too. Employees should wipe them down immediately after finishing whatever task they're doing. The same directive applies for the front counters as well. If crumbs drop from a plate when you hand over a piece of cake or lint falls from a customer's hand when he gives you money, run a barely damp cloth over the counter after the customer moves on so you can present the next customer with an unblemished surface.

If the cloth leaves the counter damp, follow up with a dry cloth to remove the water. Customers tend to get disturbed when they touch something wet that shouldn't be. If you keep the counter dry, they won't worry.

At Least Once an Hour

When you consider what might need to be cleaned hourly, you'll find yourself returning again and again to the customers' point of view—what they expect to see when they visit your coffee shop.

Number one on the list, to the surprise of many, is clean bathrooms. The bathroom serves as shorthand for the entirety of your business. In the customer's mind, if the bathroom isn't clean, there's little hope for anything else.

This means employees must service the bathroom on at least an hourly basis, picking up paper towels, wiping fingerprints off mirrors and water off the sink, cleaning toilet bowls and urinals, and so forth. Backup rolls of toilet paper need to be restocked and soap dispensers refilled. Post a cleaning schedule on the back of the bathroom door, and have employees mark and sign or initial it each hour after they tidy the bathroom.

In addition to bathroom maintenance, survey the exterior of your shop every hour to be sure your doorway is unobstructed, the street or walkway is free of debris, and your windows are unblemished. Employees should use a broom and handled dustpan to clean up cigarette butts and food wrappers. (If customers do see debris outside your shop when they enter, with luck your staff will have it cleaned up before they leave, thus proving you're on the ball and concerned about how things look.)

Another spot that needs attention at least once an hour is the sugar, cream, and milk station. Customers tend to make a mess when they prepare drinks, so you want to clean up their spills frequently and leave the station fresh for the next person. Staying on top of this area also helps avoid the dreaded, "Do you have any more skim milk?" question, which interrupts service to both that customer and the one you're waiting on now.

Employees should pass through the sitting area to clean off tables and remove trash customers leave behind. Use a damp white cloth to wipe down tables, and follow that with a dry cloth. Store both cloths out of customers' sight.

Also examine trash levels on these hourly rounds, replacing full bags with empties when appropriate. Hauling trash in front of customers is never pretty, but when the alternative is to risk trash falling out of the can and onto the floor, the choice is clear.

Don't slip and start pushing your hourly cleaning tasks to every 70 minutes or even longer apart. Stick to your schedule. If necessary, set your phone alarm to go off every hour, or purchase an electronic timer that serves solely as a cleaning alarm. When the timer goes off, start making the rounds.

Think an hourly cleaning is too much? Consider the broken windows theory, conceived by criminologists James Q. Wilson and George Kelling, which states that crime results from disorder. If a window in a house breaks and isn't fixed, people assume no one watches over the house. In short order, the house will be covered with graffiti and have more broken windows. In the same way, if your coffee shop has messy tables and a dirty milk station, customers won't feel guilty about adding to the mess. If you keep everything spotless, however, customers will tend to clean up after themselves. Cleanliness breeds cleanliness.

Several Times Each Day

Espresso machines are delicate beasts and need regular care. In addition to cleaning the steam wands and wiping down the machine, employees need to *backflush* the groups a few times each day to be sure the old grounds are removed. During the backflushing process, extremely hot water might be ejected from the group in unusual ways. Be sure to wear long sleeves to protect yourself from being burned.

To backflush, place a *blind* filter (a filter without holes) in a portafilter, attach it to a group, and run the water for up to 1 minute. Then run the water in short bursts while simultaneously loosening and tightening the portafilter in the group. This loosens residue in the group's sealing gasket. Replace the blind filter with a regular one, run the water a few seconds more, and you're good to go.

In slow moments after a rush period ends, employees also should inspect counter displays and the pastry case for spills. Remove all uncovered foods before spraying any cleaner inside the case, and replace the serving utensils as often as needed.

Inspect these cases from the customer's side of the counter, too, so you can see exactly what they see. In fact, it's a good idea to look at *everything* in the store from the customer's point of view.

Throughout the Day

Some simple cleaning chores are easy to overlook … until a customer points out you haven't done them. Such tasks include refilling napkin holders and sugar dispensers, dusting displays of retail goods, and wiping down table and chair legs. Restocking cups, lids, stirrers, receipt tape, and other consumables also falls into this category. Train employees to use free moments to refill supplies so you'll always have everything you need during busy periods.

Another all-day job is cleaning used dishes and putting them away. If you have a dishwasher, this means scraping off plates, scrubbing off lipstick marks (which persist far longer than you might imagine), and loading the machine. When the load ends, inspect the dishes as you unload and store them in their proper locations—mugs near the coffee carafes, plates by the display case, and so on. Look for chips and cracks and, if you find any, discard that item immediately. It can no longer be cleaned properly and, therefore, poses a health risk to customers. Keep a tally of items you throw out so when it comes time to reorder, you know how many replacements to purchase.

If you're washing items by hand, set up your triple sink so you wash in one sink, rinse in the second, and sanitize in the third. Fill the wash compartment with a detergent solution, and wash lightly soiled items first to give dirtier pieces time to soak. Use clean hot water in the rinse compartment, and drain and refill it whenever the water becomes dirty. Fill the sanitizer compartment with a warm sanitizing solution, and let items soak in the solution for at least 2 minutes. (Ask your health department for details on the proper triple-sink procedure in your area.)

Counter *Talk* Brewpoint's staff have additional opening, midday, and closing tasks to take care of. Turn to Appendix B to see their task checklists.

After Closing

Because you and your staff use much of your coffee shop's equipment throughout the day to make food and drinks, you often have to wait until after hours to clean these items. Again, let's start with the espresso machine:

* Pour hot water down the drain box to unclog any residue.

* Take off all removable parts (ask the supplier for a list if you're unsure what qualifies), clean them, and set them aside to dry.

* Remove the filters from the portafilters, soak them in hot water for 15 minutes, and brush them free of any remaining grounds.

* Soak the steam wands overnight by placing each wand in a pitcher of hot water. Give them a quick rinse in the morning before using them for the first time.

As for other equipment, brush the coffee and espresso grinder dosing chambers free from all grounds, remove the hoppers, wash them in soapy water, and let them dry overnight. Scrub the insides of the coffee carafes and the milk frothing pitchers. Drain clean water through the spout of each carafe to ensure no soap remains behind.

Dump the cream and milk that remain in the containers at the serving station. Break down the containers and clean them thoroughly, taking special care with rubber parts that could trap milk inside. (Again, your local health department will have details on how you should handle dairy products in your state or county. Depending on their guidelines and your storage techniques, you might be able to store the cream and milk in separate containers and reuse them the next day. If so, label the dairy products so the next morning's employees know which supplies to use first.)

Many baked goods are at their best for only one day. Wrap these items and place them in a half-price basket for sale the next day, or mark them as waste on your inventory sheets and discard them. If you know of a local homeless shelter that accepts them—not all do—you could share your day-old pastries with them.

Wipe out the bakery display case to help prevent pests such as ants and rodents from being wooed by crumbs. Clean food labels in the display case, and replace those that are dirty. A greasy croissant label doesn't say "Fresh! Clean!" to your customers. (And speaking of pests: if you're located in an old building or a city environment, bugs and rodents *will* be scampering around your coffee shop. Consider hiring a pest control service on a monthly basis. Better to be proactive than wait until a mouse scampers across a customer's feet!)

Empty the garbage cans and then hose them out in the mop sink in the back room so no odors linger the following day. Sweep and mop the floor, no matter how clean it might look. (If you do mop while the store is open, place a "Wet Floor" sign out so customers know to watch their footing.)

Counter *Talk*

In Chapter 20, we mentioned Brewpoint's employee incentive program, in which staff members can earn points by having a perfectly balanced till or, say, arriving on time every day for a week. The points can be traded in for free drinks or coffee beans. Another way employees can earn points is to sell out of pastries, which helps keep waste low. The morning staff or the evening staff earn double points if they sell out before the shift is over.

Once a Week

In addition to the items that require daily cleaning, your shop has other hard-to-reach spots that require the occasional wipe-down. Light fixtures and air circulation vents are good examples. Customers are hardly likely to examine such items up close, but the last thing you want is dust bunnies falling into someone's drink from above so make the effort to clean them.

Other overlooked spots include the kick guards underneath the front counters, curtains/blinds, window ledges (especially if you have curtains or blinds), and foot mats (not to mention the floor underneath those mats).

You can purchase a squeegee and a bucket to clean the windows yourself or hire someone to do this job for you. A once- or twice-a-week cleaning, both inside and out, should be enough to keep the front of your shop looking good.

Hiring a linen service also might be appropriate because you'll use a *lot* of white cloths each day to wipe down equipment. In fact, it's key to replace dirty cloths with clean ones at every opportunity. In general, if you look at a cloth and can't tell whether it's clean or dirty, replace it with one you *know* is clean. You can choose to use disposable cloths, but be sure to weigh the environmental and replacement costs before deciding which type of cleaning material suits your shop best.

In addition to regular backflushing each day, your espresso machine requires a weekly backflushing with special cleaner that foams in hot water to reach spaces that would otherwise go untouched. Repeat the final step of backflushing—where you loosen and tighten the portafilter to clean the group's gasket—at least a dozen times to rinse all the cleaner from the machine.

Long-Term Maintenance

On top of the day-to-day chores, you'll need to track maintenance schedules for the larger pieces of equipment. Either ask the suppliers to send you service and maintenance reminders, or mark a yearly calendar with service dates. Notes on this calendar might include the following:

* When to change the filter on the water treatment or water softening device.

* A reminder to change the burr on the grinder after every 1,000 pounds of coffee processed.

* A replacement schedule for portafilter inserts because the holes grow larger over time, which affects the taste of the espresso.

* A monthly reminder to vacuum the refrigerator coils.

* A regular schedule for checking tables and chairs for wobbly legs, loose tops, and torn fabric.

Marking these less-frequent cleaning chores on a calendar also helps you properly schedule staffing for the day, even if all you need to do is add a couple hours to one employee's shift so he can handle these tasks.

Keeping Your Staff Tidy

We shouldn't have to say it but we will: on top of all the cleaning you expect your staff to handle, they must also clean *themselves*. Naturally they should arrive for work each day in clean clothes, having showered and groomed themselves so they present a fresh face to customers. We suggest you ask them to avoid wearing perfumes and colognes as company policy because such odors can overpower the aroma of the drinks and foods on sale.

You might even consider keeping a spare shirt and pair of pants in your office or in a spare locker just in case an employee (or you) suffers a spill or other accident and suddenly looks unpresentable. Even if they don't fit perfectly, it's better to wear ill-fitting clothes for the remainder of a shift than be dirty in front of customers.

Beyond these expectations, train the staff on how to handle food safely. They must wash their hands before touching food or preparing drinks, whether they just returned from the restroom, took out the trash, or merely rearranged their hair. Even time spent at the register handling bills that have passed through dozens of hands necessitates a wash. Employees should wear rubber gloves when they use cleaning fluids, both for their own protection and for the well-being of customers.

> **Counter** *Talk*
>
> Melissa shares Brewpoint's employee dress code in Appendix B. Check it out for more pointers on what to require of your staff in terms of cleanliness and appearance.

What Customers Should (and Shouldn't) See

Customers appreciate a clean business environment. If they have a choice between a neat coffee shop and a so-so one, they'll gravitate toward the clean shop every time.

This doesn't mean they necessarily want to *see* every cleaning effort you make, however. If you walk out of the restroom with a toilet brush held high and proudly exclaim, "A beautiful bowl awaits you all," they will not be impressed.

Some cleaning chores must obviously wait until after hours, but it's also a good idea to push some tasks, such as cleaning the lights and circulation vents, to times when the shop is empty or nearly so. These tasks could be done during normal working hours, but no one wants to see dust falling from the ceiling and imagine this is a common occurrence.

Along the same lines, employees should remove boxes and paperwork from public view so customers aren't reminded of the less-appealing aspects of running a coffee shop. If, for instance, you mop the floor while customers are still in the store, they might inadvertently associate your products with dirty water instead of the pure image you'd prefer they have.

Despite all these cautions, customers will be pleased to see some cleaning going on. By clearing and wiping down tables while customers are in the shop, you make the seating area more inviting. By picking up debris in front of the store, you're beautifying the community. By posting a cleaning schedule inside the bathroom for employees to mark, you demonstrate a commitment to cleanliness. Just don't do it all in front of your customers!

Now that you have a clean and sparkling store (and staff), it's time to brag about it. In the next chapter, we explain how to get the word out about your coffee shop and position yourself as *the* local coffee expert.

The Power of Publicity

Want to get people talking about you and your coffee shop? Then prepare to become a publicity professional, pronto. Getting your name into the public eye doesn't have to cost a lot. By issuing press releases, responding to journalists online, and positioning yourself as a coffee expert, you can have reporters calling you for stories. When an unbiased media source like a reporter or TV news anchor puts you on stage, your credibility jumps a lot higher than it does from a paid advertisement that says, "Hey, I'm great!"

You might be wondering, *Why do I need to worry about seeing* my *name in the press? Shouldn't I focus on marketing my coffee shop over myself?* By promoting yourself, you're promoting your coffee shop. Think about it this way: there are lots of coffee shops owned by people you've never heard about and probably won't ever hear about. Then there are coffee shops you read about in newspapers or watch spots about on your local news. Chances are, the owners of the featured coffee shops promoted themselves to the local media outlets as coffee experts to earn that coverage. You should, too.

In this chapter, we show you how to get your name in print, garner positive word-of-mouth for your café, and turn your customers into advocates for your business.

Writing a Press Release

The key to promoting yourself—and your coffee shop—is a press release. A press release, sometimes called a news release or a media release, is a quick description of what's going on at your business. You send press releases to media outlets like newspapers, magazines, websites, and radio and TV stations in the hope that someone there will find your coffee shop's happenings interesting enough to cover.

Don't worry if members of the media don't pick up your press release and run a breaking news story on the live events your shop offers or the new Himalayan coffee you sell. If your press release hits them right, they'll keep your contact information on file as an expert to call for future stories, which can be just as good.

By keeping a few considerations in mind as you write your press release, you can increase the chances of it piquing someone's interest enough that they'll give you a call.

Ensuring It's Newsworthy

Press releases are not the same as advertising. If you want something in print that says you rock the house, you should buy an ad that says just that.

To be successful, a press release has to present a reporter with some real news and information that will matter to his readers. A press release that's nothing more than a self-serving piece of fluff will be trashed quicker than a used coffee cup. Here are some examples of real news:

* A business opening—like yours!

* News such as a study linking caffeine to better grades in college students, or a new report on how many cups the average American drinks per day, with quotes from a coffee expert—namely, you!

* A special happening in your shop such as a networking event or a book signing (which we discussed in Chapter 13)

* A summary of your shop's community service efforts, such as a donation of free coffee to a local sporting event or a percentage of a day's receipts given to charity

* A contest, such as an essay contest or a ticket drawing

* A move to a new location

* A new product or service—but *only* if it's truly new, such as, say, being the first to offer coffee catering to preschoolers (no, preschoolers shouldn't drink coffee, but this should give you an idea of how unique your idea has to be) or something of equal *wow* value to the local news

If you're not sure what qualifies as newsworthy, spend some time reading the publications in which you hope to appear. Not only will you discover which news is new, you'll also find charities you can sponsor, info about competing businesses, and much more. If nothing else, you can respond to news stories with a letter to the editor, which will naturally include your business name should it appear in print.

Drafting Your Release

When a member of the media opens a press release, she expects to see certain things in certain places with a format that makes it easy for her to digest this information. If you design some wild-looking press release to stand out from the crowd, she will most likely toss your sheet without a second glance simply because she won't be able to find the information she needs quickly.

Most people send their press releases via email, so that's the format we focus on. However, some businesses have good luck dropping off their releases in person if it's feasible. That could be a good way to stand out.

Here's how to format your press release:

* Start with a snappy subject line for your email, not something dull like "Press Release from Coffee Express Shop." Come up with a subject line that gives the journalist the info they need in a few words and entices them to open the email to read more. For example, "Local Coffee Shop Donates 1,000 Cups of Joe to Keep Students Awake During Midterms."

* Do not send your press release as an attachment. Many journalists don't open attachments from people they don't know.

* At the top of the email, write out a quick note like, "Hi, Mary! I hope you can use this press release about a fun new event we're introducing." Then you'll paste in your press release, which will look like the following example.

* If the release has limited time value, start with "Hold Until XX/XX/XX" or "For Release During the Christmas Season."

* Write out a few paragraphs describing your news, including quotes from the relevant person in your business. (That might be you!)

* End with a short paragraph on your company and more detailed contact information. For example, you can write, "Coffee Express Shop offers coffee, pastries, coffee-related gifts, and catering from its convenient location in downtown Boston."

* Include all your contact information, like so: "For more information, visit coffeeexpressshop.com, email owner@coffeeexpressshop.com, or call 617-555-1212."

Again, don't worry if your press release looks boring; it's supposed to look boring. Worry instead about making the *information* special, not the style in which it's presented. Check out the following press release for an example of how it's done.

Don't Roast Yourself! Learn How to Play with Fire at Bertha's Bodacious Beans

Want to learn to play with fire? Come to Bertha's Bodacious Beans at 123 Main Street in Chance, Maryland, on April 1 for a free lesson in juggling flaming batons from veteran circus performer Lotta Burns.

Burns ran away and joined the circus after her parents punished her at age eight for playing with matches. She quickly became the favorite student of the world-renowned fire juggler Smoky Tuckis, who taught her all his secrets. After the circus burnt down in 2010, Burns took her one-woman show on the road, giving fire juggling lessons to children and adults across the country and even overseas in cities such as Bern, Switzerland—and now, she's bringing her talents to Bertha's Bodacious Beans!

"We're so excited to be able to bring Burns to our store," says store owner Bertha Bean. "Learning to juggle fire can help our customers meet new people, get into Harvard, win the Pulitzer Prize, and get rid of unsightly warts."

Lotta Burns's workshop is just one in a lineup of exciting classes offered at Bertha's Bodacious Beans, including sword swallowing, monster truck driving, shark hunting, and knitting. "We always take chances with our workshops," says Bean. "For example, knitting can be very dangerous, what with those sharp needles and all. But we're committed to bringing only the best and most interesting workshops to our valued customers."

Bertha's Bodacious Beans sells organic, free-trade, free-range coffee beans that are grown by elves in the Black Forest without the use of herbicides, fungicides, or pesticides. Bertha's Bodacious Beans boasts the biggest disaster insurance policy on the East Coast.

For more information, call 212-555-1212, email bertha@berthasbodaciousbeans.com, or visit the store's website at berthasbodaciousbeans.com.

###

The body of your press release, or everything between the headline and the closing paragraph, should take the format of an inverted pyramid. Critical information—the who, what, where, why, and when—goes in the first paragraph, information of next highest importance in the second paragraph, and so on.

Sometimes a harried editor prints press releases as is, and the inverted pyramid format allows her to slice off paragraphs from the bottom of the release, as space requires, without sacrificing important information.

Sending It Out

You've written and refined your press release and are sure it'll get picked up. But who should you send it to? Here are some ideas for the types of local media outlets that may be interested in sharing your news:

* Print magazines

* Online magazines

* Print newspapers

* Podcasts

* Blogs

* TV programs

* Radio programs

* Streaming radio shows

Even though it costs nothing to email a press release, don't throw yours at every editor, journalist, and producer from here to Timbuktu. Target your release at appropriate markets. If you want coverage for a new catering service, for example, you wouldn't send a release to *Wastewater Quarterly* magazine. (Or even want your business associated with *Wastewater Quarterly*.)

Luckily, lots of nice people have compiled online lists of just about every type of publication, blog, podcast, TV show, and radio show you can think of—and if they haven't, a search engine like Google will make it happen. Simply search for, say, "Boston area magazines," "newspapers in Boise" or "Los Angeles food bloggers," and you'll find your targets. Just be sure that whatever media outlets you choose are specific to your local area (unless you also happen to distribute products nationwide).

Here are some other ways to find media outlets in your area:

* Radio-Locator.com lets you search for radio stations by zip code, city, and format (such as talk radio or classic hits).

* The Federal Communications Commission website (fcc.gov/media/engineering/dtvmaps) lets you enter your zip code to see all the TV stations that broadcast in your area.

* To find local affiliates for national stations like NBC and CBS, search online with key phrases like "NBC local stations." Most stations offer a list.

* Visit The Business Journals (bizjournals.com) to find the business journal website for your closest large city. These sites run news on local events, businesses, and more.

From there, do some digging to find out who at your chosen news outlet is the best person to send to. This can be a laborious process, but if you add the info to a database as you go, you can use it over and over. Luckily, many news outlets have an email address dedicated to press releases, which will be easy to find.

For magazines and newspapers, you want either journalists who write for the most relevant section in the publication or the editor who edits that section. For blogs and podcasts, send to the owner or producer. And for TV and radio stations, find the producer of the program you want to pitch.

LinkedIn and Google can help you find the email address of the correct person if it's not easily available on the outlet's website or in the publication's masthead (that's where editors and contributing writers are listed). You can also try a free service like Hunter (hunter.io) that digs up all the email addresses related to a particular website.

Counter *Talk*

When you land in the press, more potential customers will be visiting your coffee shop and your shop's website. While you're working on garnering more press, be sure your website is up-to-date and your shop operations are at 100 percent. Also, be sure to spread the word about your press appearance in your shop, on social media, on your website—everywhere. When Brewpoint is mentioned in *Forbes* or the coffee trade Sprudge, the mention is highlighted front and center on the website, which further elevates Brewpoint's brand.

Meeting the Press

If you're persistent, the day will come when you send out a press release and a journalist or radio producer calls soon after to schedule an interview. That might initially make you a bundle of nerves, but you've got this.

Publicity has a big benefit over advertising with its low, low cost of $0, but unfortunately, you have no control over newspaper reviews, TV interviews, or articles about your business. Unlike with ads, you can't control what people write or say about you in the media. Have no fear, though. Unless you've been scamming seniors or watering down the milk at your coffee shop, your media debut will be a piece of cake. The journalist won't (intentionally) try to trick you with tough questions. She merely wants information, and your press releases have demonstrated that you have all the answers.

You might still be nervous about appearing in the public eye, but with the right preparation, you can transform yourself into a well-known media personality in your area.

Preparing for Your Interview

Remember how you prepared for oral exams in high school and college? Preparing for a media interview requires similar work and dedication.

Brainstorm questions, with friends and family if you can, the interviewer might ask you, and prepare interesting and concise answers to these questions. Hone your answers by having a friend grill you as if he were Anderson Cooper on *360°*. If you're stumped for an answer, smile and say, "That's a very good question," to buy yourself some time.

Be prepared for a curveball or two. For example, a reporter might ask, "What do you think about the way coffee growers are treated and paid?" Rack your brain for difficult questions you might be asked, and study hard to become an expert on all things coffee. If you know your stuff and make the reporter's job easy, she's sure to come back to you in the future.

Making Yourself at Home

Invite interviewers to visit you at your coffee shop to talk. You'll be more comfortable in a familiar setting.

Even more importantly, getting an interviewer into your coffee shop allows her to see—and drink and eat—what you do firsthand and dress up her article with details about your store and what you serve.

Try to arrange for the journalist to arrive during a busy time of day. If she's going to describe your location, which would you rather see in print: "Devoid of customers and smelling of failure" or "Packed with happy faces enjoying drinks of all varieties"?

Acing the Interview

You'll probably be a little nervous during the interview, but do try to relax and enjoy the experience as much as you can. Remember, you know your stuff, so answer the reporter's questions, be pleasant (smile!), and keep your answers succinct, and you'll be in good shape.

Be sure to strike a balance between answering the journalist's questions and promoting yourself and your coffee shop. There's nothing interviewers hate more than an interviewee who turns every question into an opportunity to spout off about how great his business is. Answer the question that's asked to the best of your abilities, and your professionalism and expertise will be the best possible advertisement for your coffee shop. Answer the question with a lot of self-promotion, and the journalist might leave you out of the article altogether, replacing you with someone who sticks to the topic at hand.

Sometimes an interviewer will ask a question you simply can't answer. The best thing you can say in this situation is, "I'm sorry. I don't know the answer to that, but maybe I can suggest someone who does."

Don't fake an answer because you can be sure someone in the audience does know the answer, and if your "creativity" is uncovered, you'll lose credibility as an expert. Simply apologize for not knowing, and offer to get back to the reporter later with the information.

Remember, too, that although you could talk about coffee all day, the reporter probably doesn't want to, nor have time to. If you take 20 minutes to get your point across, the interviewer—not to mention her viewers, listeners, and readers—may be fast asleep before you've finished. Distill your message into a sound bite, or a few memorable words that get to the heart of your message.

One final thought on the interview: the reporter might give you some pointers on what to wear if your interview is on camera (no pure white shirts or suits with stripes, checks, or small patterns that can "jump" off the screen), but otherwise, dress in what you're most comfortable wearing. Don't think you have to spring for an Armani suit if that's not what you usually wear. Dress the way you normally do for work so you'll feel comfortable and give the interviewer an idea of who you really are.

Working with Source-Finding Services

These days you can find anything online, including sites where journalists post requests for sources for their articles and blog posts. Sometimes they even ask for free products to go into goodie bags for events, which could be a good opportunity for you to get coffee samples or discount cards into many people's hands. Examples of source-seeking platforms include the following:

* Help a Reporter Out (HARO; helpareporter.com)

* SourceBottle (sourcebottle.com)

* ProfNet (profnet.com)

All you have to do is sign up, get on the right mailing lists, and respond to the requests that are relevant to you and your coffee shop.

Keep in mind that there are right ways and wrong ways to respond to journalists' requests on these services, and sometimes journalists get dozens of responses, so the competition is stiff. Use these tips to increase your chances of getting your name, and your coffee shop's name, in the press.

Follow Instructions

Many people are tempted to respond to a journalist's request even if they're not the right fit in hopes that they'll somehow squeak into the story.

Journalists usually include guidelines as to the kind of sources they need—women over 40, businesses with 50+ employees, vendors in particular industries, and so on—because the media outlet they're writing for targets those communities. Responding when you're not a fit is a waste of your time and resources.

Write It Up

The journalists who use these services most often just want a quick quote or tip via email and skip the interview process. For example, they might ask sources to "write 200 words on the topic" or "send along two tips at no more than 100 words each."

So when you write your response, keep in mind that what you write is likely to be exactly what ends up in print. Be thorough in your response while sticking to the word count guidelines, get quotes from someone else in your coffee shop if you're not the right source for the topic (for example, if the journalist is looking for quotes from male baristas and you're not one), and do a careful proofread of your draft before submitting it.

Be Unique

When you see a request on one of these source-finding services, you can often guess at what kinds of responses the journalist will get. Your job is to not be like those. The more unique and surprising your response is, the more likely you are to get press.

For example, if a journalist at a food publication is looking for tips on business owners' morning routines, skip the usual tips on exercise, meditation, and journaling, and think about what you do that's really different—like practicing on the trapeze or gargling with whiskey.

Counter Talk   Melissa met coauthor Linda when her PR rep responded to one of Linda's HARO requests.

Paying for PR

No, we don't mean you should bribe journalists. But you should consider outsourcing your public relations to help you get the word out about your coffee shop while you focus on growing your business.

You can either go for the big guns and hire an actual PR firm, or sign up for a press release distribution service like eReleases (ereleases.com), which is a lot more wallet friendly.

Whichever you choose, do the same due diligence you'd use for hiring a lawyer or accountant, which we discussed in Chapter 5.

Positioning Yourself as an Expert

You want to be the person the media come to when they have a question about coffee. This won't happen on its own, of course. Putting your name in the public spotlight and winning people over requires constant effort on your part. Writing press releases about coffee-related news and holding seminars on brewing are good steps that require little from you but time.

To take this promotion a step further, write "behind-the-scenes" articles for consumers on how blends are created, ways grinding methods differ, how to "cup" properly, or any of a hundred other facts you've learned, and submit them to blogs, local magazines, and local newspapers. When you turn in the article, also include a brief, one- or two-paragraph bio of yourself and mention your coffee shop. (Some blogs and online magazines have submission guidelines that state how long your bio can be, as well as what topics they're looking for and how to submit, so be sure to follow those instructions.)

Many of these media outlets rely on contributions by business owners, and your contributions can likely spur sales, depending on your topic. If you describe how to roast your own beans, you can mention your store as a source of green beans. Or you can discuss the different ways coffee is brewed around the world and mention your stock of French presses in the closing bio.

In examples like this, don't worry that your tips on creating the perfect cup at home or roasting your own beans will steal business from you as customers turn to DIY. Consider instead that you're promoting the growth of coffee consumption in your area—and with you as the expert on all things coffee, this will only increase your standing in the media.

Turning Buyers into Sellers

No one can give your business more publicity and better word-of-mouth than a happy customer. Your role in this process? Make your customers happy.

Beyond mere happiness, however, you should aim for bliss, nirvana, and satori all rolled into one. You want to satisfy the customer's needs, while at the same time encouraging him to spread the word about how much he loves your coffee shop. Customers who tell their friends about your shop, leave positive reviews, and talk up your shop on social media are called *advocates,* and you want lots of them.

The first step is the most important and obvious, yet one that can be missed in the day-to-day grind of business: give every customer 100 percent of your effort, and be sure your staff members do the same.

Ask customers what they need, and either fulfill their needs immediately or do what you have to do so you can satisfy them the next time they come in. Don't do this quietly, either. Speak up and let them know what you've done to fulfill their needs. They'll be impressed that you remembered them, never mind that you're actually satisfying their demands.

As we suggested in Chapter 21, leave surveys on tables that customers can fill out to tell you where you can improve your products and services. If they provide contact information, write or call them with the answer; if not, post their question and your answer on a bulletin board in the store, in your newsletter, on your website, or on your social media platforms. Customers love to know that business owners listen to their requests.

Make your business card and copies of your menu available at all times so customers don't have to ask for them. Let them take cards and menus and pass them on to others.

Hand coupons to repeat customers to thank them for their continued business. Again, these coupons might end up in the hands of others, which is all to the good. Be sure the coupons include your coffee shop's name, address, and phone number.

You also could sell T-shirts and mugs that boast your coffee shop's name and logo. They probably won't be quick sellers, but you could give them away as prizes during seminars and events to help spread the word about your shop. What's more, customers do like being able to take home a piece of a beloved environment. And if you've done everything else right, they'll be happy to call your shop home—and bring their friends into the fold as well.

We hope you're not tired of tips on how to get the word out about your coffee shop for free or inexpensively because in the next chapter, we give you the scoop on how to market your coffee shop on a shoestring. Get ready to learn about leveraging social media, garnering community goodwill, taking advantage of printed marketing materials, and much more.

Marketing Your Coffee Shop

If you want to make money in the coffee business and not keep all those great beans to yourself, you need to tell potential customers you exist. In addition to the publicity you sought for yourself and your coffee shop in Chapter 23, marketing is another way to make this happen. Perhaps an even more effective one.

Before you turn to the next chapter, thinking marketing is way out of your league, know that most small business owners do their own marketing, and they manage to do it even without a big marketing budget.

The key to successfully marketing your coffee shop is to remember that you don't need to make a name for yourself across the nation. All you need to do is create a presence in your local community. With that aim in mind, in this chapter, we give you all the information you need to get the word out about your business without breaking the bank.

Targeting Your Market

Who do you want to tell about your fine establishment? Everyone in town? Only those who can afford to buy your limited-edition diamond-encrusted bagels? The entire world?

Telling 7.5+ billion people they can buy coffee at your store would take a long time, so you need to develop what marketers call a *target market*. A target market is any group of people you feel would visit your coffee shop if they knew it existed.

Nailing down your target market before you blanket the universe with marketing promotions will save you bundles of money. If, for example, you feel that office workers in the nearby corporate park make up your target market, placing ads in college newspapers would be a waste of money. If your target market consists of college students, you shouldn't drop a load of cash handing out discount cards at the local retirement home.

Naming Your Niche

In Chapter 6, while developing your coffee shop's name and logo, you investigated ways to position your shop in the market. Maybe you wanted to be known as the coffee shop that caters to refined tastes with gourmet beans and gifts, or the shop that packs in a hipper-than-thou crowd with live music, or the shop with quiet study areas that's a haven for local students. If you've done your job well, your coffee shop's name, logo, décor, and product line all project your chosen image to the world.

Marketing provides yet another way to present this entire package to potential customers and help you stand out in their minds. But to do so, you need to delve deep into the psyches of the people who comprise your target market, figure out what makes them tick, and find ways you can interest them in your services. Ask yourself these questions about your ideal customers:

* **How old are they?** What age groups will feel most comfortable in the retail environment you've created: mid-career execs, students, young families, older adults, or a mix of these?

* **How much do they earn, and where do they live?** In what type of environment do the members of your target market spend most of their time? Do they live in the city, suburbs, or country? Do they live in houses, apartments, or dorms? Do they commute long distances, or work close to home? Does their style of living allow them to spend freely on gourmet items, or would coupons be more likely to catch their eye?

* **How do they spend their free time?** Do they focus on earning money and working, spending time at home, or donating time and money to social issues like the environment? How can your business complement their causes and become an important part of their lives?

* **Why will they visit you?** Are your customers interested in grabbing a quick pick-me-up for work, visiting with friends, studying or reading in a quiet place, shopping for gifts, or stopping in for a quick bite while shopping?

This final question is the one you need to spend the most time answering. Unless they live on a remote mountain peak, your customers will have multiple opportunities throughout the day to purchase coffee and other hot drinks. For your business to survive, they must choose *your café*. Really think about what makes your shop special. When you know the answer, share it with the public so they'll come in and experience it for themselves.

If for some reason you decide your shop really isn't that special, it's not too late to revisit earlier chapters for inspiration—and an image overhaul.

Defining Your Ideal Customer(s)

Now that you have a clearer idea of your target market, open your laptop or break out a pen and describe the kind of client you want to attract. A sample description might read, "I want to attract young families. They're concerned with balancing work and family life, and they'll stop in to have a nice bite together while shopping in the local stores." Another possibility: "My ideal customers are students from the local college, who will want to study during the day and hear live music at night. They're interested in inexpensive but tasty coffee and unusual coffee gifts."

Don't feel you have to limit your marketing efforts to only one target market. Your coffee shop might attract commuters in the morning, mothers at midday, teenagers in the after-school hours, and families at night. Each of these groups is a separate target market you can try to appeal to in different ways.

Your description helps you determine who your target markets are and how you can best reach them. Refer to your descriptions as you read through this chapter and develop a marketing plan.

Should You Pay for Advertising?

You may be tempted to shell out money to place ads in newspapers, on the radio, or even on TV. These types of ads are still common ways to introduce your business to thousands of potential customers—and just think about how cool it would be for your mom and all your friends to see you on the small screen!

But you know what? We say no.

Placing ads like these is expensive—mortgage-your-house and sell-your-firstborn-child expensive—yet you still can't accurately hit your target market in a meaningful way that will lead to a long-term boost in sales.

Let's say, for example, you pay to run an ad on your favorite radio station. Most of the people who hear the ad won't even live in your area, so most of the money you spent to hit their ears is wasted.

In addition to this problem, what really works with paid advertising is repetition: running an ad over and over again until the radio or TV audience sings the jingle in their dreams. To make this happen, you'd have to lay out a huge pile of cash up front—and then cross your fingers and hope. For the small business owner, Vegas casinos offer better odds for success than radio and television advertising.

Online advertising, on the other hand, can be an inexpensive and effective way to attract local people to your coffee shop. Local search ads on Google and ads on social media platforms such as Facebook let you aim your message at people in your target market.

But why pay if you can get the word out for nothing? You can always keep these paid methods in mind for when you're more flush with cash. In the meantime, let's talk about how to market your business for free.

Counter *Talk*
Melissa chooses one big advertising platform every year. For example, one year Brewpoint created a commercial that ran at the local movie theater before screenings. It's difficult to measure the return on investment on many forms of advertising, though, so Brewpoint prefers to get the word out via sponsorships. (More on that coming up.)

Marketing on a Shoestring

If your marketing budget consists of pocket change and lint, don't let it bring you down! Lint has a really good exchange value on the open market.

Seriously, smart business owners know how to market without spending a lot of money. The publicity tips covered in Chapter 23 are a good start, but you have plenty more options for getting the word out on the cheap.

You and Your Employees

The cheapest marketing medium is also the one you have the most control over: you. Your dress, the way you speak, your manner behind the counter, and everything you do can make a customer either want to buy from you or run the other way.

Without coming across like a cheesy salesperson, you want to project confidence and enthusiasm about your coffee shop and the products you sell. Try everything on the menu and develop a favorite hot drink and a favorite snack to accompany that drink. When a customer asks for your opinion on an item, you can then ask questions about her tastes to guide her to the perfect treat.

Needless to say, you should look the part of a successful business owner and leave the sweats for your off hours. Customers won't expect you to wear a suit or formal dress in your coffee shop, but they do appreciate a professional appearance.

Your employees are also walking billboards for your business, but you have much less control over them than you might like. Do your best to ensure they're presentable and happy so that spirit carries over to their interactions with customers. (More on working with employees in Chapter 12.)

Counter *Talk*

Simply knowing what you're all about can be a big part of your marketing. When the owner of a local art marketing business approached Melissa after Brewpoint first opened, Melissa's description of the shop's mission and values was so compelling, the art marketer asked Brewpoint to sponsor all her events, getting the shop's name in front of tens of thousands of people in exchange for nothing but free coffee and pastries. Not only that, thanks to their alignment in values, the art marketer made sure the sponsorship opportunities fit Melissa's budget. Brewpoint's sales spiked after each one of these events.

Social Media

If you're like millions of Americans, you spend countless hours every week on social media platforms like Facebook, Twitter, Instagram, Pinterest, and even LinkedIn. Luckily for you, social media is an excellent—and free—way to build buzz about your coffee shop.

Unluckily, though, it's not as easy as posting motivational quotes and photos of coffee. So many businesses are vying for views on social media, you need to work to stand out.

The first step is to pick your platform. If you're doing this on your own, attempting to master every social media platform out there will spread you too thin. Pick the one or two you're best at or enjoy most—and that will work with your message—and focus on them. You can always add more platforms later, but for now, commit to really doing well on just a couple.

Wondering which platforms will work best for you? Here are some details on the most popular social media, all from Hootsuite (blog.hootsuite.com):

Facebook lets you post text, images, and videos. As of this writing, Facebook boasts 2.2 billion monthly active users, including half of all Americans in every age group except the over-65 demographic, and is most popular with millennials. The platform's users span income ranges, making it a good pick for both budget and luxury shops. More women than men use Facebook.

Twitter gives you 280 characters to say what you want to say, plus post images and videos. Twitter has 69 million users in the United States. Millennials are the biggest audience, and usage drops as age increases. Twitter users have a higher-than-average income; more than a quarter earn between

$50,000 and $74,999. The same percentage of men and women use the platform. Twitter is great for small businesses, and the vast majority of Twitter users who follow small businesses either buy from that business or plan to do so.

Instagram is all about images and videos, which could be a good fit for you if you're a pro at snapping scrumptious shots of your coffee drinks and snacks—in fact, 60 percent of users say they find new products on the platform. Instagram has 120 million users in the United States, and active users are split between male and female. Like Facebook, Instagram's users come from almost every income level. Like Facebook and Twitter, the biggest user group is millennials, but more of the older demographics are coming on board every year; for example, 10 percent of the 65+ group are using Instagram, up from 8 percent in 2016.

Pinterest lets you "pin" images and create "boards" of pins in various categories that others can follow. Again, millennials are the biggest users, with usage dropping as age increases. Three-quarters of American pinners are women, and Pinterest users tend to be well educated and earn above-average income. Many people use the platform to find new products, come up with creative ideas, and make plans. One of the most popular categories? Food and Drink!

LinkedIn is the place for thought leadership, industry news, and job hunting. The platform may not be the most obvious one for a coffee shop, but it could be a good choice if your shop's image centers around your coffee expertise, your target market is businesspeople, or you cater to coffee lovers who are super serious about their beans. Sixty-one percent of users are in the 30 to 64 age bracket, which also happens to be the group that buys the most consumer goods. LinkedIn users tend to be well educated and have a higher-than-average income.

Now that you've chosen your platform it's time to learn how to use it, because there's more to social media success than tossing whatever thoughts you're having at the moment onto Facebook. You need to plan your posts and curate worthwhile content. Savvy coffee shop owners create a content calendar that works for their business, their target market, and the platform they're using. You can find social media content calendars for free on sites like Hootsuite and Hubspot. (See Appendix C for links.)

Once you have a calendar, fill it with an assortment of information that's of interest to your audience. Only a small percentage of posts should be selling your business, so also try the following:

* Curating interesting posts, videos, and articles about coffee from other experts.

* Sharing tips like how to brew the best pot of coffee or secrets to ordering a drink so it comes out just the way you want it.

* Creating infographics like the top latte flavors at your shop versus the rest of the country, for example.

* Running contests.

* Promoting people, charities, and events in the community.

* Asking your audience for their opinions on what to name a new drink you've concocted, their least favorite type of sweetener, or whether they vote for plastic straws or paper ones.

You don't have to sit there every day posting to each one of your platforms of choice. Social media scheduling apps like Hootsuite or Buffer (buffer.com) let you line up weeks' worth of posts at one time and then post them for you as scheduled. Some social scheduling apps also let you read your feed, respond to people, and analyze your post activity.

Search Engine Optimization

Getting your coffee shop to the top of search engine results when someone local is looking for a caffeine fix is an effective way to get people in the door. Search engine optimization (SEO) is the art and science of using keywords on your website that signal to search engines that your business should pop up when someone types in, for example, "coffee shop near me."

SEO is even more important now that voice search is becoming so prevalent. Many people using voice search are in their cars (which is why they can't type in their search) and have a high purchase intent. Because voice search assistants only offer the top result, only the one at the top will win.

SEO is such a huge topic, entire books and websites are devoted to it. Making things more complicated, the rules change all the time as search engines update their algorithms. If you're interested in boosting your ranking in the search engines, you can hire an SEO specialist or learn the ropes for free by reading SEO blogs such as these:

* Neil Patel's blog (neilpatel.com/blog)

* Search Engine Land (searchengineland.com)

* The Moz Blog (moz.com/blog)

Counter *Talk*   If you're tech savvy, or know someone who is, set up a system where customers go directly to your website when they log on to your coffee shop's Wi-Fi, or where customers have to "check in" on Facebook to access the internet, which increases your coffee shop's likes and views on the platform. Brewpoint did this, and by the time Melissa opened the third shop, Brewpoint had a massive Facebook following.

Local Searches

Want to get your coffee shop in front of local searchers? Sign up for a free Google My Business profile (google.com/business), which lets you control what people see about your shop when they look for coffee shops on Google Search or Google Maps. For example, you can share your address, a link to your menu, your hours, and photos. This is also the space where your customers can see your business's Google reviews and message you questions.

Bing Places for Businesses (bingplaces.com) is a similar service, catering to searchers who use Bing.

Finally, you can do the same on the popular review sites by, for example, setting up a Yelp business page (biz.yelp.com) or TripAdvisor listing (tripadvisor.com/GetListedNew). Sites like these walk you through the process, making it an easy way to boost your ranking in local searches. (We offer information about dealing with negative reviews on review sites in Chapter 21.)

Email Newsletter Lists

Many coffee shops offer email newsletters to their customers and customers-to-be that might include special offers, interesting articles, news, and information about the business such as a change in opening hours, for example. A lot of content that goes in your press releases or on social media is good fodder for a newsletter.

If your list is small, you can find email marketing platforms that will let you send for free. Mailchimp (mailchimp.com), for example, is free for up to 2,000 subscribers, and Mailjet (mailjet.com) lets you send 6,000 emails to an unlimited number of subscribers per month, gratis. This means, for example, if you have 6,000 subscribers, you can send one newsletter per month.

To convince people to join your email list, offer a small freebie when they sign up, like a downloadable recipe for one of your coffee shop's top drinks or a discount coupon. You also can gather subscriber information in your shop on a paper list, or some email marketing platforms offer a mobile app that lets customers sign up for your list on your POS tablet.

Email newsletters can be tricky. Be clear about what subscribers get when they sign up, such as how many emails you'll send monthly. Customers might trash your emails without reading them, or they can get caught in spam filters, so learn how to write subject lines that entice people to open your email, and adhere to email best practices, like requiring subscribers to opt in so you don't end up in the junk folder.

Finally, analyze your results to figure out what kinds of subject lines, content, and offers garner the most opens—and which are less successful.

Bartering

Long, long ago, before Visa and MasterCard, people traded for goods and services: chickens for baskets or a new axe in exchange for babysitting little Glog.

In these modern times, instead of trading chickens for baskets, you can exchange coffee products for marketing services, graphic design, copywriting, web design, and printing. In addition to saving you money right away, bartering could lead to the people you trade with becoming lifelong customers or referring their friends and business associates to your shop.

People might be more open to bartering than you think. Just approach a professional with whom you'd like to barter, and offer to trade *X* for *Y*. Explain how the trade will benefit him. If you trade coffee coupons for the printing of 1,000 menus, for example, the printer can pass the coupons on to his customers as a goodwill gesture.

In a barter, you know the cost of what you're giving away (because you calculated all those costs back in Chapter 19). Ideally, you've researched the market enough to know the retail value of what you're asking for, too. You need to trade items of roughly equal value to make each side feel comfortable with the deal, but bartering lets you lay out less cash for the same end product.

Warning: bartering will not get you out of paying taxes. Products and services you obtain through bartering are considered income, so you must include their fair market value in your earnings at tax time. Check with your accountant or search for the keyword *barter* on the Internal Revenue Service's website (irs.gov) for more information.

Counter *Talk*

You truly can bootstrap your way to success. For the first year or two of business, Melissa relied solely on free forms of marketing, from bartering for services to creating her own coupons and handing piles of them to local business owners. (More on coupons coming up.)

Charitable Donations

Want to do good for the community and generate positive word-of-mouth for your coffee shop at the same time? Then donate your products and services to charity.

Many charities auction off goods and give the proceeds to their cause, and you can easily provide a set of products or a gift certificate for such an auction. Charities might approach you about participating in such auctions, but if you want to be proactive, research local charity organizations, contact them, and offer your coffee products and services for their next fund-raiser. You can serve coffee to the auction volunteers, donate gift cards or pounds of beans for the auction itself, or both.

Auction organizers typically include your company's information in their catalog of goods being auctioned, so even if bidders don't win your wares, they'll see your shop's name and know that you're involved.

Another idea: donate a percentage of a day's (or a week's, or whatever) take to a local charity, and send a press release about the offer to the local papers both before and after the event. (See Chapter 23 for more information on how to write a press release.)

The possibilities for community service are limited only by your imagination. You can donate coffee to organizers of a church fair, cold drinks to officials in a marathon, or day-old pastries to a homeless shelter.

Naturally, you'd like to pick up regular customers and positive press coverage as a result of your generosity, but if you push too hard, you might come off as an opportunist instead. Never insist on press coverage as payment for your good deeds. Be satisfied with your generosity, and let karma pay you back in the long run.

Counter *Talk*

Melissa has found that knowing your values and standing up for them in your business has the lucky side effect of attracting customers. One of her favorite campaigns was called Not Afraid to Love, which encouraged the community to care for their neighbors—particularly Syrian refugees, for whom $3,000 was raised. The campaign spurred numerous newspaper articles, and a video Brewpoint commissioned for the project garnered more than 250 reposts.

Promotional Partnerships

The best thing about publicity is that it's someone else who says you're great. This praise is more believable because it comes from an unbiased source.

You can mimic this kind of endorsement in your marketing by teaming up with partners who are willing to spread the word about your café. The best way to do this is to provide these partners with free items they can pass on to their customers. Coupons for, say, free hot drinks or a free muffin with any purchase are naturals for this type of promotion.

To find a promotional partner, search for local shops that appeal to the same target market as your coffee shop. Approach the owners of these shops and ask if they'd be willing to hand out your coupons to their customers. Bring samples of your wares so they can see that your food and drinks are something their customers will enjoy. Acknowledge that you're asking the owner to commit his employees' time to an outside cause, but stress the benefits for him: a gift for each of his customers that costs him almost nothing.

Whichever shops you partner with, try to arrange the giveaway campaign so it reaches each customer at least once. For example, if customers at gas stations fill up roughly once a week, be sure the coupon giveaway lasts 10 days; if you team up with a flower shop, time the giveaway to occur during a holiday like Valentine's Day or Mother's Day. Even better, tie the coupon to the needs of the customers or the time of year. Offer Valentine's Day shoppers a free heart-shaped cookie or gym-goers a free flavored water, for example.

Ask the shop owner how many coupons he'll need, print out that many, and hand-deliver them along with instructions for handing them out. Good rules of thumb are that employees should hand a coupon directly to the customer, not set them in a stack on the counter, and each customer should receive only one coupon per visit.

If you run promotional offers with more than one local business—and there's no reason why you shouldn't—be sure to label each store's coupon in a different way so you can judge which set of customers responds better to your offer. If you find, for example, that customers of dog grooming salons rarely cash in the coupon, spend your time cultivating other partners for your next promotion.

Drop by the store on the second or third day of the promotion to ensure that the coupons are being handed out and to see whether the owner has any questions. Follow up regularly to be sure the store doesn't run out of coupons, and pass along any kind words about the gift you hear from customers.

Counter *Talk*   Melissa discovered that coupons for 25 percent off any drink were much more popular in their promotional partnerships than coupons for a free 12-ounce coffee. She guesses it's because many customers prefer specialized drinks such as flavored lattes over regular coffee.

Putting It in Print

Handing out product is all well and good, and internet marketing is easy and cheap, but sometimes you can achieve a much greater return with an investment of nothing more than a bit of paper and an hour of labor. Printed newsletters, brochures, and flyers give customers-to-be something they can hold onto, something that expresses the pure wonderfulness of your shop, something that—most importantly of all—has your shop's address and phone number on it.

Printing has changed a lot in the 500+ years since Gutenberg did his thing, but the permanence and impact of the written word remains the same. In fact, all the doomsayers who declared that print is dead are changing their tune as millennials flock to the medium because they like to hold and experience printed materials.

Print Newsletters

We already talked about email newsletters, but print newsletters are another great way to get the word out about your business, offerings, and events.

Newsletters won't do you any good if the recipients toss them into the trash unopened, though. To start with, send your newsletter to folks who might care to read it, namely those in your target market. Collect mailing addresses from customers who fill out survey cards and from anyone else who shows an interest in your business, and compile these into a mailing list. Compatible businesses such as gourmet food stores may exchange or rent lists of their own.

Decide how often you want to send out your newsletter, and stick with that schedule. A weekly newsletter might be tempting to begin with when you're trying to drum up business, but don't saddle yourself permanently with such a high frequency. Sales will inevitably pick up in the months ahead and take up more of your time. Monthly, bimonthly, and quarterly are all better choices.

Come up with an attention-grabbing title that makes customers want to read on. Instead of the rather drab "Perfect Brew Newsletter," choose something more creative like "News on Brews," which might inspire potential readers to look further.

Make your newsletter worth a reader's time by tossing out the hard sell and instead offering lots of take-home knowledge: the health benefits of caffeine, for instance, or advice on how to brew coffee in a stovetop pot. Include coupons and contests to keep your shop's name in the reader's mind after he closes the newsletter and sets it down.

Also be sure to include contact information—physical address, phone number, email address, and website URL—so potential clients know where you're located and can call or write with questions.

To look professional, adopt a clean, attractive layout, and use a traditional serif typeface such as Times, Palatino, or Courier to improve readability. For headlines, make the type two or three times larger than the text, and use subheads to break up long articles and keep the reader moving through the newsletter.

To find news stories you can include in your newsletter, check out PR Newswire (prnewswire .com), a media site that posts press releases on all sorts of topics, from business to health. You also can scan food-related blogs and food magazines at bookstores. These can provide topics you'd like to include in your newsletter, but don't use the articles word-for-word without getting the writer's permission first.

Sidebars or pull quotes—that is, quotes copied from the text and set in larger type elsewhere on the page—attract your reader's attention and break up large blocks of text. Use plenty of white space to set off graphics, headlines, and pull quotes. Too little white space will create a cluttered, confused look.

Brochures

Brochures are printed sales pieces that tell potential customers what your coffee shop offers and how it benefits them. They can include a menu of your products and prices as well as any information on catering or delivery.

Give away brochures like there's no tomorrow. Hand them out to customers, hang them on bulletin boards, and leave stacks of them in office buildings and on college campuses. Don't just pass through an area once and consider it covered. If a brochure is effective, customers will take it home so they don't forget your name and address. Revisit bulletin boards and other drop-off points on a regular basis so you can restock them.

Don't think that to be effective, brochures must be full-color, glossy, fold-out pieces with perforated coupons ripe for the tearing. You can create brochures that will entice customers into your coffee shop—but not empty your wallet—with nothing but word processing software or a free graphic design platform like Canva (canva.com), paper, a printer, and some time.

First, decide on the size. A brochure can be one piece of paper folded in thirds (which gives you six panels), two pieces of paper folded in half and stapled in the middle (which gives you eight pages), or any other size and shape you want. The less paper, the cheaper the brochure is to produce, but always make room for your address, hours of operation, and contact information.

Then choose your paper. You can find nice-quality paper at your local copy shop or office supply store. Alternatively, a specialty paper company like Paper Direct (paperdirect.com) offers papers with decorative and professional borders, and other graphics perfect for creating your own brochures.

When writing your flyer text, push your coffee shop's benefits. Stress *benefits,* not *features.* A feature is a new type of coffee; a benefit is the fact that your new coffee will be a hit at the buyer's next business meeting, ensuring that she gets a big promotion and a raise. You still get to mention your new coffee, but stressing benefits over features gives the reader a reason to care.

Be careful not to date yourself. Instead of writing "Doing business in the community for 4 years," write "Doing business in the community since [*year*]." That way, your brochure never goes out of date and you won't have to reprint it every year.

If you have testimonials from happy customers, especially those that talk about results, include them on your brochure: "My party was a huge success thanks to The Perfect Brew's catering!" or "Everyone at the meeting loved The Perfect Brew's new chocolate raspberry coffee." Customers are usually happy to be quoted, and you can be sure they'll show off their starring role to others.

Finally, make it stylish. Follow the style tips listed in the newsletters section earlier in this chapter to design an attractive brochure.

Flyers

A flyer is a single sheet of paper printed on one or both sides. It naturally contains less information than a brochure, but it's also less pricey. The point of a flyer is to produce it as cheaply as possible and spread it far and wide.

Don't be shy about flinging your flyers—or hiring others to do the flinging—on car windshields; in office lobbies; in supermarket flyer racks; and on bulletin boards in libraries, supermarkets, and university buildings. Just be sure to check with your city hall because in some cities, it's illegal to put flyers on cars.

Your flyers should include a catchy headline, the name of your coffee shop, a list of the benefits of visiting your shop, any special offers you want to make such as half-price espresso, and your location and phone number. Much of this info, and even the design work, can often be lifted straight from your brochure.

Coupons

Coupons have been a staple savings tool of supermarket shoppers for decades. Why do coupons work? For shoppers, it's the idea that they're getting a special deal available only to a limited number of people. Other people can buy the same thing, but the coupon holder pays much less.

For supermarkets, coupons either bring in customers who wouldn't have shopped at that store in the first place or pull in regular customers outside of their normal shopping patterns. Whichever category the shopper falls under, the supermarket wins because the shopper spends money she normally would have spent elsewhere. Even when coupons promote loss leaders (a practice we explained in Chapter 19), shoppers often add other items to their carts, so the supermarket ends up ahead of the game.

When used effectively, coupons will work just as well for your coffee shop as they do for gigantic chain stores. One option is to participate in a coupon deck—that is, an envelope full of coupons that local residents receive in the mail—like those from Valpak (valpak.com). The advantage of using a coupon deck is that you can choose which ZIP codes receive your coupon, thus allowing you to blanket an entire area, and by default, your target market, with your sales pitch.

Coupon decks do suffer from the same faults as other direct-mail efforts, however: namely that a large percentage of those who receive the coupon will toss it without even looking at it.

A more effective way to use coupons is to find a business partner (as described earlier in this chapter) or team up with other shops to create a coupon booklet particular to your location. If your coffee shop is in a strip mall, for instance, talk with other businesses in the strip about creating a coupon booklet every store can distribute to its customers. You might pick up customers from the dry cleaner, the dog grooming salon, the tailor, and other businesses that previously had no effect on your sales.

Again, label each type of coupon in a unique way so you can track which promotional efforts bring the biggest results. Don't just focus on the number of coupons returned, either; use special codes in your payment system to track every sale that involves a coupon. You may find that you merely broke even on one promotion, while another sale encouraged customers to add lots of other goodies. If you track the stats, you'll be able to build more effective marketing campaigns in the future.

Banners

You don't have to stick to paper to get your printed message across. You also could print banners that advertise special offers and place them above the entrance to your coffee shop. Check with your city hall and your landlord, though; city code requirements might prohibit large banners, and some landlords have rules about where you can place them.

If you want to try this high-impact ad medium, the most important thing is to keep it simple. People will be passing by your sign with lots of other things on their minds—what time they're meeting a girlfriend, the cop that just pulled out in traffic behind them, and so on. If your banner is going to catch their eye, the message on it has to be short and to the point.

Use bright colors, too. The reasons for this are the same as in the previous point, but if your store colors are brown and cream, don't opt for a neon green banner. There's a difference between bright attractive and bright "Ow, my eyes!"

Don't add dates or other restrictive limitations on the sign. If your banner touts sweets "Two for the price of one," it's timeless and you can use it anytime you'd like. Throw a time limit on the offer, however, and you've doomed yourself to using that banner only once a year.

Remember that *timeless* doesn't mean "all the time." Banners should be used sparingly. Their size and bright colors attract a lot of attention, but if you keep one on your store all year, potential customers will dismiss the promotion as a sham. We've seen mattress stores, for example, that have displayed "half-price sale" banners for 6 straight years. Such a phony promotion makes us wary of spending our money there.

You can let a banner stand on its own, but you also can use it as the entry point for an entire in-store promotion. Carry the colors of the banner onto signs inside the store, and repeat the message on display cases and at the register.

Counter *Talk*

Consider holding a grand opening as a way to bring customers into your new coffee shop. Grand openings are always newsworthy events. With each new store, Brewpoint does a "soft opening" for a month and then holds the grand opening—including a $1 12-ounce coffee deal for the entire month—after processes have been perfected at the new location. The grand opening of the most recent location resulted in 750 transactions in one day, with a line of people out the door for hours.

Don't Forget to Have Fun

Many business owners feel that marketing and promotion are the most tedious, time-wasting parts of their business—and if you approach the topic with that attitude, they might well be.

If, however, you approach marketing from a different angle, you can really enjoy yourself. After all, you've created a great café that relies on the efforts of skilled, friendly employees to deliver tasty and appealing drinks and eats to everyone in your community. If some of your neighbors haven't visited the shop yet, you should feel sorry that they're missing out on a good thing and think of it as your duty to convince them to stop by and try your wares.

Running a business is indeed a lot of work, but if you believe in yourself and the coffee shop you've created, you should do all you can to share your creation with the world.

You're now up to speed on writing your business plan, finding the perfect location, laying out and decorating your shop, deciding on what food and drinks to sell, handling money, pricing your products, keeping everything neat and clean, and getting the word out about your shop. In the next, final chapter, we talk about growing your business. You learn how to hire managers, open new locations, expand your shop—and even make an exit plan if you decide you'd like to sell your business.

Looking Ahead

When you're focused on the everyday challenge of serving lines of customers, cleaning the seating area, and ordering supplies, it's easy to forget that you started this business with larger goals in mind: being your own boss, for example, or providing food, drinks, and atmosphere that weren't available anywhere else.

It's important to take a break from the daily grind to reassess the future of your business—both the products you offer and the way you manage. If sales are so-so, this self-examination can help you determine what to change or adjust to make the business more profitable.

What if sales are constantly rising? Examining how you do business is even more important. You might be better off hiring managers to handle the hourly needs of the shop while you focus on what to do next, whether it's tweaking the menu or planning for store number two. Determining which skills bring in the most dollars—and hiring staff to take over the other roles essential for business—brings you the most success in the long run.

Adjusting Your Menu

No matter how much research you put into your initial menu, you're still going to have a few clunkers. The low-carb craze might have tanked brownie sales, for instance, or you discover that no one appreciates cinnamon-flavored coffee as much as you do.

Stick with your initial menu for at least a month to give newcomers—and they're all newcomers at this point—time to experiment and develop favorites. After this trial period, review the sales record and re-examine the menu with an eye toward replacing duds with new drinks and dishes that might get customers' taste buds a bit more excited. Let's look at some ways you can change up your menu.

Think Seasonally

Follow a seasonal menu. If you're headed into summer, think about adding iced coffees, granitas, or milkshakes. As winter approaches, consider a special hot chocolate blend you've never tried before or new flavorings that tie in with the season.

Keep an Eye on Trends

Stop at restaurants and other competitors to see how they've adjusted their menus. You might discover new items you can personalize to fit your establishment, or realize that everyone but you has moved away from an item you still have faith in. Have they spotted a trend away from this item, or are they trying to create a trend of their own?

Simplify Your Offerings

Do you really need to offer an ultimate chocolate chunk brownie *and* a double chocolate fudge brownie? Customers who buy one would undoubtedly switch to the other, and eliminating one type of brownie would leave room on the menu for a new product—or at least simplify your ordering process and reduce waste.

Just don't change your entire menu in one go. Once customers are used to your offerings, they expect certain items to be available each time they visit. Changing only one or two items gives you a talking point at the register while still allowing (most) customers to find their old favorites.

Expect resistance from some customers—and possibly even some employees!—when you remove slow-selling items from the menu. You'll quickly discover that every item is someone's favorite, no matter how much it's hated or ignored by the rest of the public. Consider whether you can special order items for regulars or whether it's better in the long run to try to turn them on to something else.

Play with Pricing

Don't feel that every drink has to cost no more than $X or every sweet should be priced between $Y and $Y.99. Experiment with your offerings and let customers tell you with their dollars whether you're out of line.

You may discover, for instance, that the market will support $5 per slice of chocolate turtle cheesecake even though you used to offer nothing more expensive than a $2 cannoli. You might also find that selling individually wrapped gourmet chocolates at two for $1 nets you far more money than you ever imagined possible from such an inexpensive item.

Upping Your Game

Maybe you don't want to merely change your menu, but instead seek to bring your coffee shop to a whole new level.

For example, maybe you're currently billed as a *second wave* coffee shop (many chain coffee shops today are), which serves pricier specialty coffee. If your demographic would support it, you could work to become more of a *third wave* shop, where your coffees are considered a fine food like wine and your customers appreciate the nuances of flavor, aroma, and body. (Check out the glossary in Appendix A for definitions of *first wave, second wave, third wave,* and *fourth wave.*)

This is how Perfect Daily Grind defines third wave:

> Increasing coffee quality, more direct trade, a greater emphasis on sustainability, lighter roast profiles, innovative brew methods—these are all intrinsic to third wave coffee. We chase sweetness, complexity, and distinctiveness in our brews. And we're happy to pay more to receive this.

Another key aspect of the third wave coffee shop is a higher level of customer service, where your staff can actually explain the origins of your beans, the differences between the roasts, and the grinding and brewing process—in other words, the story behind the beans.

You might also consider encouraging your baristas to learn to create latte art, or designs in the foam on top of a latte. This sounds easy, but it truly is an art and a hard-earned skill. In fact, there's a latte art world championship! (Visit the World Latte Art Championship's website at worldlatteart.org for more information.)

Finally, some higher-end shops offer *coffee cupping* events, during which participants can compare coffees from different regions, learn about the beans, and ask the shop owner questions.

Counter *Talk*

A good way to take your business to the next level is to examine and improve your processes. For example, after 4 years of being in business, Brewpoint did a complete inventory overhaul. Melissa analyzed the company's vendors, compared prices, and consolidated to the best vendors. In doing so, she discovered she could save a whopping $7,000 a year simply by switching to a new vendor for cup sleeves. That's pure money in the business's pocket.

Managing Managers

When you first open for business, you're likely to work every hour of the day for weeks on end. From morning to night, you'll be on hand to receive goods, keep employees on the right track, and match receipts to the sales tape at the end of the day.

Being involved in your business is a good thing, but you can't maintain this schedule forever. At some point, you'll burn out and potentially harm both yourself and your business, not to mention your family relationships. The only solution is to hire other managers, or at least train employees to open and close the shop.

Sharing Your Knowledge

When searching for a supervisor, promoting an employee who's currently on staff is probably the best bet because she already has a handle on what it takes to run the shop. She has seen you in action as you place orders or take inventory. She knows how to handle every station in your shop and can train new hires with ease.

Keep your eyes open for an employee who has a self-starter mentality—completing tasks on her own as she discovers them, for example—to complement an ability to follow the rules you've laid down. (Business owners need to be humble and open to learning from their staff, but a manager also shouldn't insist she knows how to do everything better than you.)

The key to preparing an employee for a management position is to offer her more responsibility over time and see how she responds. Teach her how to take inventory, for instance, or explain how to read the sales records and balance the till. See if she takes on these tasks herself in the future, whether she waits for you to tell her what to do—or whether she goes on to learn other duties on her own. Some employees thrive when asked to do more while others prefer to stick with what they already know.

Counter *Talk*

Looking to grow your sales? Grow your marketing. Melissa points out that the more content you have on social media, for example, the more people will get to know your business. Educate your customers, help them solve their coffee-related problems, and share helpful ideas with your community. You could even speak at industry conventions so other coffee shop owners can learn from your experience. It may seem counterintuitive to help your competitors, but the stronger the industry is, the better for everyone involved.

Handing Over the Keys

Once you find an employee who seems like a good candidate, take her aside and tell her you'd like to offer her a managerial position. Go over the duties such a position involves—many of which she already knows, thanks to your training—and the hours she'll be required to work. Explain her new rate of pay and her responsibilities over those who used to be her coworkers.

Don't be surprised if an employee turns you down. Some are happy to stay where they are, close to the customers with little responsibility beyond serving and smiling. If she does accept your proposal, work out a start date for her position. Make the date far enough in the future that you have time to cover everything she needs to know to run the shop on her own.

Make it clear that the position is only a trial run, and give her checks and balances so both of you can assess whether she's living up to the standards you've set. If she can't cut it initially, you both have choices: you can offer more training if you think she still has potential, or she can decide to return to her old position if she disagrees. If you had just given her the position without the trial run, you'd both be stuck if she didn't work out.

When you make the position permanent, you still need to monitor her performance during the first few months. If you're double-checking inventory dollars spent or labor dollars used, she'll naturally push herself to do the best possible job to show she can do everything she needs to.

Both you and your new manager should spend time evaluating other employees for future managerial positions. You don't want to saddle your replacement with the same situation you were in, after all, with too much to do and not enough time to do it in. Ideally, you'll always be cultivating a supervisor or two so you'll have a replacement on hand should one of you take ill.

Keep in mind that not all employees will embrace your choice of manager. Jealousy might rear its head among those who feel they could do a better job. Employees who are really hurt might even leave. Don't second-guess yourself, though. Anyone who gets bent out of shape over your decision isn't ready to be a manager anyway—and might not even be suitable for your staff in the long run.

As you assume the job of overseer and then leave even that aside, it's time to redefine your role as owner or company president. You'll still brew an espresso from time to time, but you want the manager to feel that she can do her job without you constantly watching over her shoulder.

Positioning yourself as the owner or president also lets the staff know they can't rely on you to fill in for them whenever they need a day off. Create a list of your duties—accounting, payroll, hiring, marketing—and share this list with the staff so they understand your new role in the business. (Admittedly, you handled all these duties even when you were involved with the day-to-day operations. In your new role, though, you'll concentrate more on the big picture and less on the brushstrokes.)

Considering Expansion

Every successful business owner gets the question: "So when are you going to open a second location?"

"A second location?" the business owner typically replies. "I'm barely in control of the first, and I still have two years of loan payments, and ...."

Yet the idea sticks with them, and late at night when they should be sleeping, they wonder if expansion might indeed be possible some day.

You're still at the start of your business adventure, but we advise you to always keep expansion and growth opportunities in the back of your mind. Even franchising isn't too outrageous to think about if you have a winning business formula.

However, before launching into any of the following expansion activities, be sure your current business is profitable and runs smoothly. Any problems that exist in your current location will become twice as bad if you spread them to a new shop rather than spend the time needed to solve them first.

Counter *Talk*

Melissa recommends you keep your business's mission in mind as you expand. If your company mission is to support the local community, for example, how can your expansion help with that goal? How can your new locations highlight what makes you unique?

Opening a Second Location

If one coffee shop is successful, then two coffee shops should bring in twice as much money, right? Well, yes and no. All the rules for opening and running a first location apply equally to a second, so if your new shop is in a remote location and never advertises, you have no chance of hitting the ball out of the park a second time.

If, however, you apply all the knowledge learned while opening your current coffee shop to researching and merchandising a new location, you'll likely achieve a better return on the new investment than you did on the first.

After all, consider the benefits. First, your food and supply costs will probably be lower. When you buy in larger volumes, whether coffee beans, bagels, or bags, suppliers tend to offer larger discounts. This means you can either charge lower prices at one or both locations (in case you need to go up against competitors) or net a higher return per item.

Also, you can advertise for two stores almost as cheaply as one. When you first open a new location, your advertising costs will be high because you'll want to spread the word about the new place as quickly as possible. After the initial rush, though, you'll get twice the bang for your advertising buck because you can promote both locations for the same price as one.

You'll have a stronger presence in the market, too. Customers who might have visited infrequently due to distance might be able to shop at your new location more often, perhaps even every day. Having two locations also indicates a general level of success. After all, you wouldn't have opened a second shop if the first wasn't doing well.

You'll also have a stronger staff. Employees at your current shop likely will be able to work a day or two at the new location to help you get started. These seasoned employees can train the new hires quickly, which means fewer mistakes and a higher level of customer satisfaction.

Finally, you can avoid "learning mistakes" on subsequent locations. Just as new hires can learn from the old pros, you can learn from the mistakes you made while opening your first shop and be in better shape at the second location. This isn't to say you won't make mistakes at all; you probably will, but then you'll have an even longer list of mistakes to avoid when you open a third shop in the years ahead.

When you make the move toward building a business empire—that's right, an empire!—you have to readjust your approach to day-to-day operations. You can't be as hands-on as you might have been in the past because you just won't have the time. Sure, you'll serve customers from time to time, but in general, you'll delegate authority to others rather than do the job yourself. You can only be in one place at one time, which means you'll need competent, independent managers at each location who can handle daily operations while you focus on ordering, accounting, and thinking about the big picture.

Once you have two stores, that picture takes on a new look. You've diversified your investment so you're no longer relying on the success of only one store. Slow sales at one location might be balanced by steady or rising sales at the other. The customers at one store might favor literary events, while those at the other turn out in huge numbers for craft workshops. (We talk more about holding special events in Chapter 13.)

Next, you'll start examining surrounding markets to see where a third location might go. Melissa has heard from a number of other coffee shop owners that three coffee shops is the sweet spot when it comes to growing a business that can be financially profitable and sustainable for the long haul. This might be hard to picture now, but someday it could happen to you!

Counter *Talk*　Don't rule out alternative locations for your second shop such as a kiosk inside a library or hospital. These may not be as glamorous as a full-size shop, but they offer guaranteed traffic and can bring in even more profit than a traditional location. (For more about the pros and cons of different types of locations, check out Chapter 7.) No matter what type of shop you open, Melissa recommends you maintain a flagship store that shows what your brand is all about and gets people excited about your mission. For example, Starbucks likely earns more from its drive-thrus than anything else, yet the company also runs Starbucks Reserve shops that elevate the brand.

Expanding Your Current Location

Instead of opening a second location, you might consider expanding your current shop to add a stage, make more room for tables, or enlarge the kitchen so you can make treats in-house.

Think through these plans carefully before launching into them. You'll need to get approval from the town to run a larger business, which might require new permits from the health department and other governmental agencies. You need to work out details of the expansion with the building owner, such as who will bear which costs. Expansion might leave the owner with a more valuable property in the long run, so don't assume you should be the one to bear all the costs.

During the actual construction, you might have to close the business or restrict yourself to delivery sales. Do you have the cash flow to survive this interruption, and can you survive higher loan payments if you're financing the expansion? Do you risk your customers finding a competing coffee shop to visit during this time? Will you pay employees during the renovation or ask them to go for a week or two without pay?

Call in your crew of professionals—your attorney, accountant, and mentor—and ask their opinions on whether this expansion is right for you or if you should take another path. There are many positive reasons for expanding a business, but expanding too soon is one of the top reasons small businesses fail.

Also ask yourself what you expect to get out of this expansion. Are you adding products and services that will bring in more income, or are you expanding nonproductive space like seating? Will the increased income from making your own baked goods compensate for the expense of the new equipment and the downtime during construction?

Compare the cost of expansion with the cost of opening a second location. Expansion allows you to stay more hands-on, since you still have only one shop, but you might receive even more benefits for the same cost by opening a new store.

Finally, keep in mind that expansion and an identical second store aren't your only options for growth. You can start an espresso cart in a mall, a café in a museum, a juice bar in a gym, or a snack shop in the park. By finding—or making—opportunities like these, your business can grow in all sorts of unexpected ways.

Expanding Without Getting Bigger

You also can find growth opportunities by reaching out to new customers. If you roast whole beans in-house, you can approach gas stations, convenience stores, offices, and other businesses about supplying them with fresh ground beans once or twice a week. (And if you *don't* roast beans, you can always consider adding this service.)

If you've developed unique blends and roasts, you can try to market them from coast to coast online. Develop a website that focuses on mail-order sales—while still providing local store hours and addresses—and include the URL on everything you give to customers.

Promote mail-order sales within the shop, and to your email newsletter subscribers, to encourage current customers to give coffee as gifts to faraway relatives. Experiment with sending direct mail to mailing lists you purchase from catalog companies or trade for with local businesses.

Consider adding services like delivery, catering, or even drive-thru service to serve customers in specialized situations. As with wholesale roasting and online sales, these services require you to spend funds on labor and raw materials—expenses you should naturally earn back through sales—but you avoid the huge capital costs of a second building.

Franchising

Besides opening a second (or third) shop of your own, you can consider franchising, or selling the concept of your business to other entrepreneurs.

You do have a concept, right? A unique approach to the coffee business that distinguishes you from the coffee chains, both local and national, that already exist? Sure you do—your concept encompasses the design, color, layout, and other special elements of your existing shop(s).

Whether or not this concept has long-term potential is another question. Your best bet might be to contact a franchise expert to see if your existing concept can be packaged in a way that will appeal to others across the country.

You might think franchising your coffee shop allows you to make money for doing practically nothing, but that's far from the truth. Once you franchise, your customers are no longer the ones buying the coffee; your customers are now the owners of the coffee shops that bear your name. Your focus now is on marketing strategies that benefit the owners of these businesses because you profit when they do better.

Franchising is a big step away from the day-to-day operations of a coffee shop. If interacting with customers and joking around with employees is what excites you the most about business, put aside thoughts of franchising and focus on the business at hand. If, however, you dream of larger things, plan for a franchise from your earliest days.

Due to abuses in the sale of franchises in the 1950s and 1960s, a number of government organizations adopted guidelines franchisers must follow. These guidelines have been revised often over the decades, and the current most widely used document is the Franchise Disclosure Document from the Federal Trade Commission (ftc.gov). Different states may follow different guidelines, however, so be sure to consult with your attorney to find out what rules you have to follow.

Getting Out While the Getting's Good

Some business owners love the daily challenge of bringing in customers or the ongoing battle to raise current sales over last year's sales; others learn that life as an entrepreneur really doesn't suit them. They might have enjoyed the challenge of opening a store, but the daily grind is reducing them to pulp. If you're in the latter category, don't feel that you have to stay in business forever. If your coffee shop is surviving and growing, you likely can find a buyer willing to take it off your hands.

Don't just throw an ad online, though. There's a lot more to selling a business than a simple financial transaction. To begin with, how much is your business even worth? A year's worth of sales? The value of your inventory? Online valuation calculators like CalcXML (calcxml.com/calculators/business-valuation) can give you a rough estimate of how much your business is worth.

This estimate is just a starting point, though. You need to account for the location, your standing in the community, goodwill among customers (measured by the percentage of repeat customers), and many other factors that can boost or depress that price. Whatever number you arrive at, add at least 10 percent to the total to create negotiating space with potential buyers.

In addition to the base price, you have to worry about contracts, mortgages, and every other piece of paper that has your name on it. When you sell the business, you want your name off everything so you can't be held financially responsible for debts that develop after the new boss takes over.

Unless you've sold a business previously, you should probably hire a business broker to manage the sale. The broker negotiates with potential buyers, explains how you can get more for your business, and handles all the legal nitty-gritty such as when exactly you'll hand the keys over.

Selling isn't forever, of course. If you enjoy the thrill of starting a coffee shop more than running one, you can always start another (noncompeting) café with the idea of selling that one as well. Starting a business takes a certain talent that not everyone has. If you've got it, you can use it to finance many new opportunities.

So there you have it—all the basics on how to start and run a successful coffee shop. Of course, you'll learn tons as you go along, too, and eventually you'll become a pro at all things coffee shop related. Check out the appendixes at the end of this book for more helpful resources, including a glossary, business forms and checklists, and coffee-related publications and websites.

Here's to brewing success!

Glossary

acidity   The usually pleasant bitterness of coffee characterized by a feeling of dryness at the back and edges of the mouth; one of several characteristics used to describe a coffee's flavor. *See also* aroma, balance, body, and sweetness.

adjusting collar   The part of the grinder the operator rotates to increase or decrease the fineness of ground coffee.

aftertaste   The flavor, or bouquet, that remains in the mouth after swallowing coffee.

airpot   An insulated thermal coffee pot with a built-in pumping mechanism; also known as a thermal carafe.

Americano   An espresso with water added to dilute the espresso so it's more similar to drip brew.

arabica   One of the two major types of coffee; typically grown at high elevations and known for creating better-tasting coffee than robusta coffee beans. *See also* robusta.

aroma   The smell of freshly brewed coffee; one of several characteristics used to describe a coffee's flavor. *See also* acidity, balance, body, and sweetness.

autofill   A feature on espresso machines that controls and maintains the water level within the machine's boiler.

balance   An evaluation of how a coffee's characteristics all work together. *See also* acidity, aroma, body, and sweetness.

barista   Italian for "bartender"; in English, a professional maker of espresso beverages.

barista art   The art of making patterns in a latte's steamed milk.

bean hopper   The cone-shaped holder on the top of an espresso grinder that's filled with whole coffee beans to be ground.

blend   A batch of coffee beans from different crops, whether from one region or from different parts of the world.

body   The weight or mouthfeel of the coffee, how light and fluid or thick and heavy it feels; one of several characteristics used to describe a coffee's flavor. *See also* acidity, aroma, balance, and sweetness.

boiler pressure gauge   The instrument inside an espresso machine that can determine the steam pressure within the machine's boiler.

breve   A cappuccino made with half-and-half instead of milk.

brew pad   The switches on an espresso machine that correspond to a desired shot (double shot, single ristretto, and so on).

burr   The sharp plate or plates within a grinder that chop and mill coffee beans. Also known as a grinder burr.

café au lait   A coffee made with half coffee and half latte milk.

cappuccino   One or more servings of espresso topped with equal amounts of cappuccino milk and foam. A "dry" cappuccino has more foamed milk and less hot steamed liquid milk.

cappuccino milk   Steamed milk that's lighter and more velvety because it's aerated more. To make cappuccino milk, while steaming, add air until the pitcher is warm to the touch. *See also* latte milk.

chai   A common word for "tea" in many countries; in the United States, a milky spiced tea made with some combination of cardamom, cinnamon, cloves, ginger, black pepper, fennel, and allspice, as well as a sweetener.

coarse picking   A harvest of tea leaves that grabs up to five leaves from the stem of the tea plant; these leaves produce a harsher-tasting tea than those gathered in a fine picking. *See also* fine picking.

cold brew coffee   Coffee brewed with cold or room temperature water for 12 or more hours. It's known for its smooth taste and lower acidity than regular coffee.

condiments   Anything added to hot or cold drinks, such as sugar, honey, nutmeg, cinnamon, cocoa, vanilla, milk, and half-and-half.

crema   The rich, golden-brown foam at the top of a good shot of espresso; the sugars of the coffee are concentrated in this foam. The characteristics of the crema depend on the grind, the length of the extraction time, and other factors. Also known as creama.

CTC   An acronym for "crush, tear, curl," which describes the manufacturing process for teas that end up in tea bags.

cup fault   A general term for an overwhelming problem with the taste or odor of coffee; if it's noticeable but not overwhelming, it's known as cup taint.

cupping   A coffee tasting technique that lets producers and buyers check the quality of the coffee. Also known as cup tasting.

diffusion disc   A component in the group of an espresso machine that diffuses hot water; also known as a diffusion block.

dispenser   A bottle resembling an old-time seltzer bottle that uses nitrous oxide charges to blast liquid cream into a whipped condition and dispense it through a nozzle.

dispersion screen   A mesh screen in the group of an espresso machine that diffuses hot water after it passes the diffusion disc and before it reaches the coffee grounds.

distribution tool   A round, flat tool used to create a uniform brew bed before the espresso is tamped.

dome lid   A rounded coffee cup lid that leaves room for whipped cream on specialty coffee drinks.

doser   The device mounted on a grinder that measures and dispenses ground coffee into a portafilter. (Not all grinders have dosers.)

double (or *doppio*)   Any beverage that contains two shots of espresso, such as double mocha.

dry   An espresso beverage made with less steamed milk and more foam than usual.

earthy   A term often used to describe the flavor of Indonesian coffees, which comes from drying the coffee beans on dirt instead of concrete or another medium.

espresso   Very strong coffee brewed in 1.5-ounce batches at an extremely high temperature and pressure.

espresso con panna   An espresso topped with whipped cream.

espresso macchiato   An espresso topped with a dollop of foamed milk.

espresso puller   An old term for a professional maker of espresso beverages, which is outdated because most espresso machines are now automatic and don't require the user to pull down on a handle.

espresso Romano   A serving of espresso with a twist of lemon on the side.

exotic   A term used to refer to coffees with unusual aroma or flavor; typically applied to coffees from East Asia and Indonesia.

extraction   The passing of hot water through ground coffee.

extraction time   The length of time water stays in contact with coffee grounds during extraction.

Fair Trade   A voluntary program based on dialogue, transparency, and respect that supports disadvantaged coffee producers.

filter insert   The stainless-steel basket that forms a cup inside a portafilter to hold coffee grounds during the brewing process; available in single-, double-, and triple-shot sizes.

fine picking   A harvest of tea leaves in which only the top two leaves and bud are plucked from the plant. *See also* coarse picking.

first wave   The first appearance of instant coffee (like Folgers), which people could make at home by just boiling water. *See also* second wave, third wave, and fourth wave.

flavored syrup   A sweet syrup used to flavor coffee drinks and other beverages.

floral   A flavor characteristic that reminds one of flowers and their aroma.

foam   Steamed milk that has been infused with air to turn it into a light froth. A cappuccino is generally topped with foam.

fourth wave   This newest wave goes beyond coffee as a fine food to focus on the entire coffee production process, from farming to brewing. Barista art is considered fourth wave. *See also* first wave, second wave, and third wave.

French soda   A drink made with flavored syrup, mineral water or club soda, and half-and-half.

fruity   A term used to refer to coffees that carry overtones of fruit flavors in their aroma or taste.

granita   A flavored, slushy drink that originated in Italy and is often served by espresso operators.

grinder   A machine that mills coffee beans into a powdered or granulated form.

group   A brewing port on an espresso machine.

group head   The port on the espresso machine where the portafilter locks in for brewing. Hot water runs through the group head, over the grounds held in the filter insert, and out the spouts on the bottom of the portafilter into a waiting cup.

group portafilter gasket   The bit of rubber that seals out air when the portafilter is placed in the group casting.

insert retaining spring   A wire clip that holds the filter insert in the portafilter.

Italian soda   A drink made with flavored syrup and mineral water or club soda.

knockbox   A container into which coffee grounds are disposed after completing an espresso shot.

latte   Italian for "milk"; one or more servings of espresso, with latte milk filling the rest of the cup.

latte milk   Steamed milk that's heavier and more liquid because it's aerated less. To make latte milk, while steaming, add air for 1 to 3 seconds. *See also* cappuccino milk.

lungo   An espresso made using more water and a longer extraction time, resulting in a weaker drink.

macchiato   An espresso topped with only a bit of foam.

manual fill valve   A device used to manually add water to the boiler of an espresso machine.

milk thermometer   A thermometer, typically measuring from 0°F to 220°F (–18°C to 104°C), used to measure the temperature of milk as it's being steamed.

mocha   One or more servings of espresso mixed with chocolate syrup or powder, with latte milk filling the rest of the cup and optionally topped with whipped cream.

organic   Coffee grown without artificial chemicals such as pesticides or herbicides.

portafilter   A device that looks a bit like a bicycle handlebar grip with a small, round metal cup on one end. The coffee grounds for espresso are dosed into the portafilter basket and tamped, and the portafilter is attached to a group head on the espresso machine for brewing.

puck   The used grounds you dump out of a portafilter. The puck should come out as one piece.

pump pressure gauge   The instrument on an espresso machine that measures the extraction pressure of the water used in brewing.

ristretto   A half-size or restricted shot of espresso, typically only .75 ounces; the first, sweet burst of espresso that comes out of the machine.

robusta   One of the two major types of coffee; grown at low elevations and preferred by producers of canned coffee for its low cost and high yield. *See also* arabica.

second wave   A term referring to the rise of pricey specialty coffee in coffee shops and coffee available for home brewing. Many chain coffee shops today are considered second wave. *See also* first wave, third wave, and fourth wave.

shot   A single serving of brewed espresso, typically 1.5 ounces.

single   Any beverage that contains one shot of espresso, such as a single espresso macchiato.

skinny   Any beverage made with skim milk.

spicy   A term that describes coffees with the flavor or aroma of a particular spice or blend of spices.

steam valve   The part of an espresso machine that controls how much steam flows into milk during the steaming process.

steam wand   A pipelike extension from an espresso machine that emits steam; typically made from stainless steel with a nozzle on the tip.

sweetness   A measure of how smooth, mild, and flavorful a coffee is; one of several characteristics used to describe a coffee's flavor. *See also* acidity, aroma, balance, and body.

tamp   The act of pressing ground coffee into the portafilter insert before brewing.

tamper   A mushroom-shaped wood or aluminum handle with a flat metal base that's used to pack the espresso grounds into the portafilter.

thermal carafe   An insulated thermal coffee pot with a built-in pumping mechanism; also known as an airpot.

third wave   The recent time period in coffee evolution during which coffee is considered a fine food like wine and not a commodity. *See also* first wave, second wave, and third wave.

varietal   The specific coffee grown in each region or country.

wet   An espresso beverage made with less foam than usual.

Forms and Checklists

A lot of business processes and analysis can now be completed online or via apps, but some of us still like to use old-school paper and pencil. The forms and checklists in this appendix help you keep track of your cash, inventory, and more. We also included Brewpoint's written dress code and daily task checklists, which you are free to borrow for your own shop.

Daily Checklists

Each day your coffee shop is open, you'll do some of the same things. In this section, we share Melissa's checklists for the tasks the Brewpoint owners, managers, or staff do every time they open, every midday, and every closing. Feel free to copy these checklists and customize them for your shop.

Opening Checklist

- ❑ Turn on iPad and clock in
- ❑ Unlock cash drawer
- ❑ Check cash
- ❑ Fill and place creamer pitchers
- ❑ Put out planter
- ❑ Check iced coffee and tea
- ❑ Put away dry dishes
- ❑ Empty water/brew coffee (Staff leaves water in the carafe overnight to keep it warm.)
- ❑ Turn on music

Midday Checklist

- ❑ Feel free to help out the evening shift if it's slow; if it's busy, make a note of what you didn't get to
- ❑ Take out garbage
- ❑ Weigh out batches of beans (You'll have a plastic sealed container with preweighed coffee batches for the brewer ready so when you need to brew coffee you can simply pull out a batch, grind it, and brew it.)
- ❑ Check that condiments are stocked and clean
- ❑ Wipe down tables
- ❑ Dust shelving
- ❑ Refill tea containers
- ❑ Do dishes
- ❑ Restock all disposables (cups, lids, sleeves, and so on)
- ❑ Check restrooms
- ❑ Use coffee equipment cleaning tablets on one carafe
- ❑ Spot sweep shop

Closing Checklist

- ❑ Do dishes
- ❑ Clean restrooms
- ❑ Use coffee equipment cleaning tablets on rest of carafes
- ❑ Weigh coffee batches
- ❑ Refill teas
- ❑ Clean espresso machine
- ❑ Sweep
- ❑ Mop
- ❑ Wipe down counters
- ❑ Wipe down tables
- ❑ Bring in planter
- ❑ Lock all doors
- ❑ Count drawer
- ❑ Take out all garbage
- ❑ Ensure all fridges are closed
- ❑ Clock out
- ❑ Turn off all lights
- ❑ Lock front door after you exit

Preopening Shopping List

The number of things you need to purchase for your new coffee shop can be overwhelming, so we've put together this list to help you stay organized. Keep in mind that the equipment you need depends on the food and drinks you sell. So if you won't sell smoothies, for example, you don't need a smoothie machine.

Office Supplies and Equipment

- ❏ Computer (laptop)
- ❏ Printer
- ❏ Point-of-sale (POS) device (such as a tablet)
- ❏ Work phone with voicemail
- ❏ Binders
- ❏ Notepaper
- ❏ Pens and pencils
- ❏ Clipboards
- ❏ File folders
- ❏ Tape (Scotch, masking, duct)
- ❏ Glue
- ❏ Paper clips
- ❏ Hook-and-loop tape
- ❏ Bulletin board and pushpins
- ❏ Stapler
- ❏ Calendar
- ❏ Filing cabinet

Furniture and Design

- ❏ Tables
- ❏ Couches
- ❏ Chairs
- ❏ Bar fixtures
- ❏ In-store shelving
- ❏ Wall hangings
- ❏ Lighting (such as large dome lights, small dome lights, chandeliers, rope lights, track lights, decorative beam lights, industrial lights, recessed lights, and so on)
- ❏ Speaker system
- ❏ Security/camera system
- ❏ Metal food-grade shelving (for stockroom)
- ❏ Employee lockers
- ❏ Safe
- ❏ Floor mats

Coffee Equipment and Supplies

- ❏ Batch brewer
- ❏ Batch brew grinder
- ❏ Scale
- ❏ Espresso machine
- ❏ Espresso grinder
- ❏ Espresso tamper
- ❏ Espresso pad (to tamp the espresso on so you don't do it directly on your counters)
- ❏ Distribution tool
- ❏ Display refrigerator
- ❏ Undercounter refrigerator (unless your shop is tiny, the more refrigeration space, the better)
- ❏ Grab-and-go refrigerator

Coffee Equipment and Supplies (continued)

- ❑ Freezer
- ❑ Ice machine
- ❑ Smoothie machine
- ❑ Blender
- ❑ Water spout
- ❑ Water filtration system
- ❑ Water softener
- ❑ Pitcher rinser
- ❑ Hot water tower
- ❑ Microwave
- ❑ Grill
- ❑ Oven
- ❑ POS device stand
- ❑ Pour-over system (optional)
- ❑ Pour-over grinder (optional

Dishes and Utensils

- ❑ Cutting boards
- ❑ Measuring spoons
- ❑ Display plates
- ❑ Covers for plates
- ❑ Trays for baked goods
- ❑ Ceramic cake plates
- ❑ Cake and pie servers
- ❑ 8-, 12-, and 16-ounce mugs
- ❑ 2- and 4-ounce demitasse cups
- ❑ Espresso cups (to pour espresso into from the machine)
- ❑ Cold drink glasses
- ❑ Demitasse saucers and spoons
- ❑ Tea pots, cups, and saucers
- ❑ Bakery tongs and spatulas
- ❑ Knives, forks, and spoons
- ❑ Long-handled spoons (with small head for mixing)
- ❑ Straws and straw holder
- ❑ Napkins and napkin dispensers
- ❑ Condiment dispensers
- ❑ Milk thermometers
- ❑ Milk frothing pitchers

Cleaning Supplies

- ❑ Espresso machine cleaner (We like Cafiza brand.)
- ❑ Coffee equipment cleaning tablets (We like Tabz brand.)
- ❑ Short- and long-handled brooms
- ❑ Dustpan
- ❑ Mop
- ❑ Buckets
- ❑ Sponges
- ❑ Cleaning cloths
- ❑ Paper towels
- ❑ Dusting brush
- ❑ Scrub brush
- ❑ Squeegee
- ❑ Short ladder or step-stool (for cleaning lights and vents)
- ❑ Garbage cans (large and small)
- ❑ Trash bags
- ❑ Dish soap
- ❑ Sanitizing solution
- ❑ Restroom hand towels
- ❑ Restroom hand soap
- ❑ Towel and soap dispensers
- ❑ Toilet paper
- ❑ Toilet brush

Daily Cash Sheet

Use this sheet to reconcile the money in the cash drawer with the sales tracked by the cash register, computer, or POS. Create enough of these to last a month at a time; you'll use the numbers in your weekly write-ups and monthly recaps, as described in Chapter 20.

Daily Cash Sheet

Date: _____ Day of week: _____
Store location: _____
Completed by: _____
Hours worked: _____
Comments and weather: _____
_____
_____

Evening Count

Rolled coins	_____	Cash	_____
Quarters	_____	Checks	_____
Dimes	_____	Credit cards	_____
Nickels	_____		
Pennies	_____	Total receipts	_____
$1s	_____	Minus float	− _____
$5s	_____		
$10s	_____	Net cash	_____
$20s	_____	Tape reading	_____
$50s and up	_____		
Cash total	_____	Amount over/under	_____

Sales Reports

	Total Sales	Customer Count		
10 A.M.	_____	_____		
1 P.M.	_____	_____		
Close	_____	_____		
Average check (sales/ customer count):	_____			
Amount over/under	_____	**Payouts**	**Cost**	
Overrings	− _____	_____	_____	
Payouts	− _____	_____	_____	
Final over/under	_____	_____	_____	
		_____	_____	
Total	_____	_____		

Weekly Summary

This form helps you look for sales trends, such as whether certain days of the week tend to have more sales and if you have the right number of employees in the shop depending on the number of transactions. Chapter 20 offers more detail on how to get the most out of your weekly summary sheet.

Weekly Summary

Date: _____   Week ending: _____

Completed by: _____   Store location: _____

Sales Forecast

	Forecast	Actual	Comments/Weather
Monday	_____	_____	_____
Tuesday	_____	_____	_____
Wednesday	_____	_____	_____
Thursday	_____	_____	_____
Friday	_____	_____	_____
Saturday	_____	_____	_____
Sunday	_____	_____	_____
Total	_____	_____	_____
Customer count	_____	_____	_____

Average Check (Sales/Customer Count)

Forecast	Actual	Comments
_____	_____	_____

Labor Hours

	Forecast	Actual	Comments
Monday	_____	_____	_____
Tuesday	_____	_____	_____
Wednesday	_____	_____	_____
Thursday	_____	_____	_____
Friday	_____	_____	_____
Saturday	_____	_____	_____
Sunday	_____	_____	_____
Total	_____	_____	_____

Sales per Person Hour (SPPH)

	Forecast	Actual	Comments
Monday	_____	_____	_____
Tuesday	_____	_____	_____
Wednesday	_____	_____	_____
Thursday	_____	_____	_____
Friday	_____	_____	_____
Saturday	_____	_____	_____
Sunday	_____	_____	_____
Total	_____	_____	_____

Monthly Income and Expense Summary

This form helps you review the financial health of your entire business by comparing income and expenses from month to month. Use a month's worth of daily cash sheets to fill in this summary, as we discuss in Chapter 20.

Monthly Income and Expense Summary	
Month: _____	Year: _____

Income	Expense as a % of Income
Sales _____	(a) _____
Cost of goods – _____	(b) _____ (b ÷ a)
Gross income _____	(c) _____

Expenses	
Labor _____	_____
Rent _____	_____
Phone _____	_____
Electricity _____	_____
Gas _____	_____
Office expenses _____	_____
Professional fees _____	_____
Insurance _____	_____
Advertising _____	_____
Promotion _____	_____
Total expenses _____ (d)	

Income prior to
the cost of money _____ (c – d) = (e)

Loan payments _____ (f)

Total income _____ (e – f) = (g)

Total income as
a % of sales _____ (g ÷ a)

Inventory Sheet

Use this sheet every 6 to 12 months to get an overview of what's turning over, what's sitting on the shelves not moving, and how much capital you have tied up in inventory. You'll need this info for your taxes, too, and you can use this sheet for your weekly inventory to help with ordering. If you have a box that's only partially full, estimate the portion of the box that's full. For example, you might write down that you have 2¾ boxes of cup lids.

Inventory Sheet			
Date: _____		Count taken by: _____	
Item	**Number on Hand (a)**	**Unit Cost (b)**	**Extended Cost (a × b)**
_____	_____	_____	_____
_____	_____	_____	_____
_____	_____	_____	_____
_____	_____	_____	_____
_____	_____	_____	_____
_____	_____	_____	_____
_____	_____	_____	_____
_____	_____	_____	_____
_____	_____	_____	_____
_____	_____	_____	_____
_____	_____	_____	_____
_____	_____	_____	_____
_____	_____	_____	_____
_____	_____	_____	_____
_____	_____	_____	_____
_____	_____	_____	_____
_____	_____	_____	_____
_____	_____	_____	_____
_____	_____	_____	_____
_____	_____	_____	_____
_____	_____	_____	_____
_____	_____	_____	_____
_____	_____	_____	_____
_____	_____	_____	_____
_____	_____	_____	_____
		Total cost	_____

Brewpoint's Written Dress Code for Employees

To better help you put together your own dress code for employees working in your coffee shop, Melissa has agreed to share Brewpoint's employee dress code:

An employee's personal appearance and hygiene is a reflection on the company's character. Employees are expected to dress appropriately for their individual work responsibilities and position.

We believe in the freedom of personal expression, while maintaining a clean, unified, professional front for our staff. Below are our strict policies for dress code, but from there you are allowed to express your differences and creativity! With that said, employees are expected to dress and groom themselves in a manner that prioritizes professionalism and safety.

Employees must …

* *Dress and groom themselves in a way that prioritizes cleanliness and safety.*

* *Wear an apron when working behind the bar.*

* *Keep hair clear of the eyes and face.*

* *Tie back, braid, or otherwise control longer than shoulder-length hair.*

* *Wear closed-toed shoes.*

* *Comb or otherwise groom facial hair.*

Employees must not …

* *Wear sweatpants, workout leggings, or other activewear.*

* *Wear shoes with more than a half-inch heel or shoes that do not cover the entire foot.*

* *Wear soiled clothing and/or aprons.*

* *Wear clothing that might snag, hook, or trip you or other employees (e.g., very loose shirts, untied shoes, and so on).*

* *Wear clothing that would expose you to direct cuts or burns (e.g., clothing with tears, short shorts, and so on).*

* *Have fake fingernails.*

* *Wear jewelry (with the exception of a plain wedding band).*

* *Wear dresses/skirts unless an additional garment is worn beneath.*

* *Wear wristwatches.*

Employees who do not adhere to this dress code policy may be sent home.

APPENDIX

C

Resources

Ready to start planning for and creating your coffee shop? You'll need lots and lots of products, from equipment and accessories to the actual coffee beans. In this appendix, we gathered some resources to help you with that, plus some marketing resources and helpful publications and websites.

Keep in mind that this is not an exhaustive list. Many, many more roasters, equipment suppliers, and so on are out there, so if you don't find what you need in the following pages, search online for something that will work for you.

Coffee Roasters

California

Caribbean Coffee Company
caribbeancoffee.com

Equator Coffees and Teas
equatorcoffees.com

Florida

Joffrey's Coffee and Tea Company
joffreys.com

Panther Coffee
panthercoffee.com

Illinois

Brewpoint Coffee Roasters
brewpointcoffee.com

Louisiana

Rêve Coffee Roasters
revecoffeeroasters.com

Maryland

Quartermaine Coffee Roasters
quartermaine.com

Michigan

Leelanau Coffee Roasting Co.
leelanaucoffee.com

New York

Dallis Bros. Coffee
dallisbroscoffee.com

North Carolina

Counter Culture Coffee
counterculturecoffee.com

Ohio

City Roast Coffee
cityroastcoffee.com

Oregon

Kobos Coffee
koboscoffee.com

Rhode Island

Downeast Coffee Roasters
downeastcoffee.com

Utah

Millcreek Coffee Roasters
millcreekcoffee.com

Washington

Espresso Vivace
espressovivace.com

Wisconsin

Steep and Brew Coffee
steepandbrewcoffee.com

Wyoming

JH Roasters
jacksonholeroasters.com

Green Bean Importers

Cafe Imports
cafeimports.com

Coffee Courses (database of green coffee importers)
coffeecourses.com/green-coffee-importers

Organic Products Trading Company
optco.com

Royal Coffee
royalcoffee.com

Sustainable Harvest
sustainableharvest.com

Organic Coffee

Equal Exchange
equalexchange.com

Sustainable Harvest
sustainableharvest.com

Flavored Syrups

Kerry Foodservice
kerryfoodservice.com

Monin
monin.com

Torani
torani.com

WebstaurantStore
webstaurantstore.com

Espresso Machines and Accessories

Espresso Zone
espressozone.com

Faema Source
faemasource.com

Rosito Bisani
rosito-bisani.com

Seattle Coffee Gear
seattlecoffeegear.com

WebstaurantStore
webstaurantstore.com

Whole Latte Love
wholelattelove.com

Coffee Retailer Associations

Coffee Association of Canada
coffeeassoc.com

International Coffee Organization
ico.org

National Coffee Association
ncausa.org

Organic Crop Improvement Association
ocia.org

Specialty Coffee Association
sca.coffee

Coffee Industry Publications, Podcasts, and Websites

Barista Magazine
baristamagazine.com

Cat and Cloud Coffee Podcast
catandcloud.com/pages/podcast

Coffee Review
coffeereview.com

CoffeeTalk **magazine**
coffeetalk.com

Daily Coffee News
dailycoffeenews.com

Fresh Cup **magazine**
freshcup.com

Keys to the Shop **podcast**
keystotheshop.com

Perfect Daily Grind
perfectdailygrind.com

Roast Magazine
roastmagazine.com

Sprudge
sprudge.com

STiR Tea and Coffee **magazine**
stir-tea-coffee.com

Tea and Coffee Trade Journal
teaandcoffee.net

Marketing Resources

Hootsuite free social media calendar templates
blog.hootsuite.com/how-to-create-a-social-media-content-calendar/#templates

HubSpot free social media calendar template
offers.hubspot.com/social-media-content-calendar

For Further Reference

Throughout the book we cited some sources you might want to check out for further reference. Here they are by chapter.

Chapter 1

Commodity.com: "What Are the USA's Most Popular Commodity Imports and Exports?"
commodity.com/usa/#USAs_Top_5_Commodity_Imports

World's Top Exports: "Coffee Imports by Country"
worldstopexports.com/coffee-imports-by-country

Chapter 6

Statista: "Coca-Cola's Brand Value from 2006 to 2018"
statista.com/statistics/326065/coca-cola-brand-value

Chapter 7

Total Food Service: "How to Create a Restaurant Floor Plan"
totalfood.com/how-to-create-a-restaurant-floor-plan

Total Food Service: "How Much Rent Is Too Much for Your Restaurant?"
totalfood.com/how-much-rent-is-too-much-for-your-restaurant

Chapter 8

Specialty Food Association: "Growth of U.S. Coffee Shops to Slow to Just Over 2 Percent in 2017"
specialtyfood.com/news/article/growth-us-coffee-shops-slow-just-over-2-percent-2017

Chapter 12

PeopleKeep: "2 Common Mistakes When Asking 'Am I an Applicable Large Employer (ALE)?'"
peoplekeep.com/blog/2-common-mistakes-when-asking-am-i-an-applicable-large-employer-ale

PeopleKeep: "What Are My Employer Health Insurance Requirements as a Small Business in 2019?"
peoplekeep.com/blog/what-are-my-employer-health-insurance-requirements-as-a-small-business-in-2019

Chapter 16

GlobeNewswire: "Global Tea Market Will Reach USD 49,456.52 Million by 2024"
globenewswire.com/news-release/2018/08/08/1549020/0/en/Global-Tea-Market-Will-Reach-USD-49-456-52-Million-by-2024-Zion-Market-Research.html

Chapter 20

CNBC: "This Crime in the Workplace Is Costing US Businesses $50 billion a Year"
cnbc.com/2017/09/12/workplace-crime-costs-us-businesses-50-billion-a-year.html

Hootsuite: "All the Facebook Demographics That Matter to Social Media Marketers"
blog.hootsuite.com/facebook-demographics

Hootsuite: "28 Twitter Statistics All Marketers Need to Know in 2019"
blog.hootsuite.com/twitter-statistics

Hootsuite: "Top Twitter Demographics That Matter to Social Media Marketers"
https://blog.hootsuite.com/twitter-demographics

Hootsuite: "Top Instagram Demographics That Matter to Social Media Marketers"
blog.hootsuite.com/instagram–demographics

Hootsuite: "23 Pinterest Statistics That Matter to Marketers in 2019"
blog.hootsuite.com/pinterest-statistics-for-business

Hootsuite: "Top LinkedIn Demographics That Matter to Social Media Marketers"
blog.hootsuite.com/linkedin-demographics-for-business

Discount Deals for Coffee Shops

In this section, Melissa shares a few links that provide discounts on some of her favorite coffee-business products. Please note that these offers may not last indefinitely. Alpha Books, DK, and Penguin Random House LLC are not monitoring these discounts, nor their expiration dates, and are not responsible for discounts after the offers expire.

Brewpoint Coffee Roasters
Get $100 in credit after placing your first order with Brewpoint.
wholesale@brewpointcoffee (email for more information)

Deputy
Take $100 off the scheduling and HR app Deputy.
deputy.com/r/melissav108

PrintWithMe
Mention Brewpoint Coffee in your inquiry email to get free shipping of in-house café printers.
printwithme.com

Square POS
Get $1,000 of free processing on Square POS.
squareup.com/i/brewpoints

Index

F

About the Authors

Linda Formichelli has created content for more than 200 premium magazines and businesses, such as WebMD, *Family Circle,* OnStar, Cleveland Clinic, CVS, and TripAdvisor. Linda's other books include *The Renegade Writer: A Totally Unconventional Guide to Freelance Writing Success* and *Commit: How to Blast Through Problems and Reach Your Goals Through Massive Action.* She lives in the Raleigh, North Carolina, area with her writer husband, W. Eric Martin; her ballet-dancing, YouTube-animating son, Traver Martin; and three cats.

Melissa Villanueva is the CEO and owner of Brewpoint Coffee in Elmhurst, Illinois. Brewpoint Coffee has been featured in *Forbes,* Fast Company, Sprudge, and a number of other publications for its inspiring small business journey.

Have you ever looked for an espresso machine on craigslist only to buy a coffee shop instead? That's the story of Brewpoint Coffee. Melissa and her husband, Angelo, had recently started dating, were both unemployed, and had little coffee experience, but when they saw a coffee shop for sale on craigslist, they knew it was too perfect to pass up. Now, Brewpoint Coffee has grown to three coffee shops, a coffee roastery, an event space, and wholesale operations focusing on helping other business owners build creative coffee shops in their own communities.